Labouring Children

Labouring Children

British Immigrant Apprentices
to Canada, 1869-1924

Joy Parr

CROOM HELM   LONDON

McGILL-QUEEN'S UNIVERSITY PRESS
MONTREAL

© 1980 Joy Parr
Croom Helm Ltd, 2-10 St John's Road, London SW11

British Library Cataloguing in Publication Data

Parr, Joy
    Labouring children.
    1. Indentured servants – Canada – History
    2. Children – Employment – Canada – History
    3. Alien labor, British – Canada – History
    I. Title
    331.3'1   HD4875.C3

    ISBN 0-85664-898-1

McGill-Queen's University Press
1020 Pine Avenue West, Montreal H3A 1A2

ISBN 0-7735-0517-2

Legal deposit 2nd quarter 1980
Bibliothèque Nationale du Québec

Printed and bound in Great Britain by
REDWOOD BURN LIMITED
Trowbridge & Esher

CONTENTS

List of Tables, Figures and Illustrations

Introduction   11

1. British Working Children   14

2. Salvation and the Safety-valve   27

3. The Promised Land   45

4. Family Strategy and Philanthropic Abduction   62

5. Apprenticed or Adopted   82

6. Household and School   99

7. Adulthood   123

8. Twentieth-century Policy   142

Appendix: Analysis of Case Records   158

Select Bibliography   162

Index   177

TABLES, FIGURES AND ILLUSTRATIONS

Tables

5.1   Agricultural Productivity of Ontario and Rural   89
      Placement Locations for Barnardo Boys and Girls,
      1882-1908

6.1   Physical and Mental Health in Britain and in Canada,   112
      Barnardo Sample, 1882-1908

7.1   Proportion of Child Immigrants in Contact with the   126
      Homes, Barnardo Sample

7.2   Occupations, Barnardo Men   131

7.3   Adult Occupations, All Barnardo Men Reporting,   138
      Canadian-, British-, and European-born Men

Figures

2.1   Annual Immigration of British Juveniles to Canada,   40
      1868-1924

3.1   Location of Distributing Homes in Canada, 1869-1924   49

5.1   Southern Ontario, Agricultural Productivity as Measured   90
      by Proportion of County Land in Canada Land Inventory
      Soil Capability Classes 1 to 3

Illustrations

Photographs courtesy of Barnardo Photo Library

1.   Hope Place, London, 1911
2.   Petticoat Lane, London, 1900
3.   Boys with Meal Tickets
4.   Boarded out Children at Cavan School, Durham County, Ontario, 1912
5.   Girl in Service in Ontario, 1898 (Marchmont 23, p. 82)
6.   Boy, aged 13, Sawing Wood, 1894 (Marchmont 18, p. 15)
7.   Feeding Chickens, Hamilton, Ontario, 1912
8.   Hoeing Corn, 1912

for
Gordon Minto Parr
and
Isobel Mitchell Parr

INTRODUCTION

Between 1868 and 1925 eighty thousand British boys and girls were sent to Canada to work under indentures as agricultural labourers and domestic servants. All were unaccompanied by parents, although only one-third of them were orphans. Most were not yet fourteen and still too young to leave school for full-time employment in the United Kingdom, although their educational opportunities would be limited in Canada and their work heavy. It seems strange to find such a policy flourishing in the late nineteenth and early twentieth centuries.

The movement seems out of step with its time. The British child-savers who apprenticed youngsters in rural Canada in the 1880s described themselves as followers of Lord Shaftesbury, the English reformer who had restricted child labour in British factories half a century before. The programme of placing youngsters in Canadian districts where farm help was scarce expanded even though governments were defining children as students rather than workers through compulsory schooling regulations. More British boys and girls were taken away from their native country before the age of knowledgeable consent during the decade before the First World War, when the foundations of the national welfare state were being laid, than at any other time.

The leading figures connected with the programme appear out of character. Revivalist evangelicals who became known for their close family ties and family-modelled institutions used emigration firmly to separate children from parents. Although renowned for innovations in careful casework methods, these pioneer social workers broadcast youngsters into the back concessions in Canada and left them with less supervision than even the English poor law provided at home. Concerned parents and confused children from labouring families, an environment widely believed at the time to be the domain of economic imperative rather than of sustained affection, often found ways to frustrate the rescue workers' intentions and maintain contact across imposing distances. On the other hand the men and women with whom they were placed, living amid the supposed abundance of the Canadian countryside, proved demanding masters and mistresses, stinting in praise, payment and the provision of clothing. Nor did rural neighbours welcome youngsters whose backgrounds they suspected.

Women and men who came to Canada through the child emigration homes later insisted that theirs was not a 'pitiful tale'. And it was not.

And yet their history does reveal a darker side of evangelicalism, of turn-of-the-century childhood, and of Canadian rural life than the record has so far been allowed to express.

Of the bright side of evangelical social work in Britain we know much — the courageous efforts of middle-class mission workers to provide relief to the poor, their exuberant optimism in the face of repeated reversals, the institutional innovations that made their rescue homes more humane and healthful environments in which to spend a childhood. We know less about the ways in which class differences between rescuer and rescued affected the quality of help evangelicals offered the working-class families in whose lives they intervened. If the revivalists' energy sustained effective policies, it also prolonged such programmes as child emigration despite ample evidence of their limitations. Institutions aimed at simulating family life instead split families apart behind high walls.

In the half century after 1870, legal initiatives to redefine the rights and roles of children and the responsibilities of parents abounded on both sides of the Atlantic. Reformers argued that all young people ought to be allowed fourteen years' exemption from intensive contribution to the household economy, schooling at the cost of society to prepare them for adulthood, and humane treatment from their kin during this lengthened period of dependence. The child immigrants' history suggests that childhood was quite different between classes and between rural and urban areas. Perhaps immigrant slum children in new or marginal farm districts were atypically removed by rank and region from the mainstream of a substantial reform impetus. They certainly were overworked, harshly treated and little more influenced by common school and child protection movements in 1924 than in 1870.

Descriptions of nineteenth-century rural life are so imbued with agricultural idealism, portraits of urban life so emphatic about the squalor and hopelessness of the slums, that it is almost difficult to understand why so many people left the Canadian countryside for the cities at the turn of the century. Everyone reads about the intermittent community gatherings which brought people together from a distance, but not about the loneliness of isolated farms; the absence of mechanical work discipline in agriculture is always noted, but not the ruthless tyranny of the seasons. Yet frostbite and gangrene are as much industrial hazards as lint and smoke-filled lungs. Limbs were lost to binders as well as to drill presses. And in Canada the child immigrants did not join a hardy yeomanry; they encountered rigid rural hierarchy.

What follows is a study of the life and work of child immigrants in Britain and Canada. I have included brief notes in Chapters 2, 3 and 8 on the history of evangelical social work and on the development of social welfare and immigration policy. But this story is intended to be more about what children experienced than about how adults organised themselves. Notwithstanding, my debts to adults are large.

Mary Joynson of Dr Barnardo's and James Minto of the Quarrier Homes of Scotland allowed me to examine their large collections of child emigrant case records. The staff at Homelea, Bridge of Weir and Roy Ainsworth, Roy Clough, Alfred Tobatt, Thomas Tucker and Anne Wingate of Barnado's, Barkingside found space for me to work and time to answer my questions. I learned from their generosity, curiosity and broad-mindedness as well as from the records in their care. I hope they will not feel I have betrayed their trust.

Some of the best information on child emigrants lurks in unlikely places. I have come upon these references more through dependence upon others than native diligence and in this respect I am especially grateful to Anna Davin, Jean L'Esperance, Beth Light, Stephen Roberts, Graeme Patterson, Peter Bower, Catharine Ross, Russell Hann, Suzann Buckley, Mary McGeer and June Gow. Marilyn Barber, Deborah Gorham, Sam Shortt and Diane Brydon offered timely help while I was preparing the manuscript for press. Margaret Somerville drew the maps.

In its various drafts this study has already passed through many hands. William Parker, Frank Turner, Susan Trofimenkoff, Peter Ward, Veronica Strong-Boag, Sharon Cook, Alison Prentice, Jane Abray, Ian Davey, John Norris, Ed Wickberg and Jim Winter have pointed out errors, imprecisions and infelicities and thus made the manuscript better than I could have made it on my own. The students in my graduate family history seminar at the University of British Columbia between 1977 and 1979 pressed me to clarify my thinking on these and related themes. My largest debts are to Robin Winks who supervised my studies at Yale with astuteness and good cheer, Gillian Wagner whose scholarly enthusiasm I have found happily contagious and Neil Sutherland who knows more about Canadian childhood than I ever shall and has been to me the most generous and perceptive of guides. Larry MacDonald edited the manuscript with skill and wry humour. I am grateful for both. This book is dedicated to my parents, children of rural Ontario, who taught me to view the villages and back concessions with a gentle blend of scepticism and love.

Kingston, Ontario

1   BRITISH WORKING CHILDREN

England does not know what childhood is. [1]

There were visitors who came away from Salford, East London and East Glasgow eighty years ago claiming that in those crowded streets and lanes there were no children. School Board inspectors declared that there was no childhood among the poor, that there was only labour. European travellers reported that the labouring boys and girls of England were treated like men. Mission workers protested that their youngest clients were always pondering over things, apparently unable to play, unaware what play was. The pioneering social investigator Charles Booth described the elementary school pupils he met in East London as 'anxious-eyed, with faces old beyond their years' and 'never no time to play'. [2]

Plainly tens of thousands of young people who had not yet reached their fourteenth birthday grew up among the labouring poor of Britain in the late nineteenth and early twentieth centuries. Their names appear on the school board and workhouse registers. Their numbers appear in the census. Their faces appear in photographs of the markets and wharves where they worked and of the crowded courts where they lived. It is true that they did not usually play in distinct places called children's playgrounds or sleep in separate children's rooms. They did not read children's books or wear specially designed children's clothes. Their inexperience was probably not praised as child-like; their mistakes were probably not excused on the ground that boys would be boys. But if outsiders said they were not children, their parents knew, and they knew, that they were not adults.

Eighty thousand of these girls and boys born among the urban labouring poor of Britain, children in the lights of their own class if not to others, while still very young were sent to Canada through the efforts of philanthropic rescue homes and parish workhouse schools. They came from that 30 per cent of the British population which lived in poverty. They had been born in those parts of British cities in which, in the 1890s, children at birth might expect to live only thirty-six years and one in four would not reach his or her first birthday. Boys and girls from the slums were shorter and thinner, weaker and less active than the average British child. The conditions that killed so many also severely impaired the later lives of those who did not die. And children faced the same implacable economic constraints that so sternly governed the lives of their elders. [3]

Men from among the British labouring poor in the late nineteenth and early twentieth centuries did not earn a living wage. Women and children worked to provide basic necessities. When the labouring power of any part of the family failed, all suffered. In such crises parents were forced to place their children with parish and philanthropic institutions, some of which later sent on to Canada the distressed children first presented to them. [4]

The crisis points in a family's life were not entirely unpredictable. Manufacturer and sociologist Benjamin Seebohm Rowntree found 'five alternating periods of want and comparative prosperity' among the labouring people he studied in York, a pattern he called the poverty cycle. He found that during the years when children lived at home their economic relationships with their parents underwent several radical changes. At first they lived in scarcity because they and their young siblings kept their mothers from full-time paid work. As they grew older and more economically useful family circumstances improved. Boys and girls in their teens and young people in their early twenties found themselves with spare pennies jingling in their pockets at the end of the week. These relatively pleasant times continued up to marriage and afterwards until the first child arrived. With more children the parents' child-poverty deepened, to be relieved again only as their own children became productive. Men and women with adolescent children at home once again lived relatively well. As sons and daughters left to marry and live on their own, the last phase of a cycle began, the drift back into the poverty of the elderly person alone. This pattern was ubiquitous among labouring people, a stark and inevitable cycle. Its effects appeared even in the physical strength and stamina of siblings, older children being less robust because they 'starve more', whereas 'by the time the younger ones come along, the older ones are starting to work, and there is more money coming in, and more food to go round'. [5]

The poverty cycle, induced principally by the changing needs and productive capacities of children, had profound effects upon the relationships between parents and their sons and daughters, delineating the stages in a child's life and the differences between childhood and adulthood. Working people whose lives were governed by the poverty cycle relied regularly upon their kin for help in times of crisis because they were less likely to refuse the request; in turn, relatives were aided because they were more likely to return the favour. But circumstances made everyone aware of the degree to which family associations made them better or worse off. Economic calculation forced itself upon family relations; kin lived together when sharing a household made them better off. Single persons considered leaving the common dwelling-place when it appeared that they might improve their lot by being on their own. With a subsistence crisis always looming, family members had to take account of the burdens and the benefits of family ties. [6]

But there was trust and affection too. Kin shared what little they had, confident that their generosity would neither be abused nor go unrepaid. The family performed vital psychological functions, and calculative considerations were not always paramount. [7] Nevertheless, the poverty cycle did force economic considerations to the fore in nineteenth-century British families living on the margin of subsistence.

The child immigrants' families were plainly part of this group and were certain to be aware that family links implied clear economic gains and losses. This knowledge shaped parents' demands of their children and children's attitudes toward their parents.

Almost all these families would have been counted among Rowntree's four poverty classes in York or among Booth's labouring poor of London. But the child immigrants came from urban centres throughout Great Britain. And although with rare exceptions they came from families bound to the poverty cycle, the range of deprivation among the poor was large. An attempt to portray the childhood experience of the immigrants could thus render only those parts that would likely have been widely shared through the poverty cycle until some graver crisis intervened to force them into an institution. What follows is therefore an optimistic portrait, a description of childhood in the most stable and adequately provisioned sections of the labouring poor, presented to place the child immigrants' Canadian apprenticeships in perspective.

In any time or any culture a child begins life as a frail and dependent being. Among the child immigrants' families this dependency usually continued through the first six years of life. Infants and toddlers drew on family resources for food, clothing and shelter — though of course their demands in any of these respects were small. What the youngest children did need, what heavily burdened their kin, was physical care and supervision. Baby-minding required the time and attention of more mature family members, time that might otherwise have been spent in the paid labour market, attention that might otherwise have increased the efficiency of the small craft manufactures pursued in the home, energies that in terms of the immediate economic interests of the family would have been better invested in the adults and older children who were making material contributions to the well-being of the household.

The care of young children sorely taxed the family's resources. Sometimes women withdrew from the labour market to tend their first-born, and the family made do without their wages for the duration of the youngster's dependency. In other cases parents paid cash to a neighbour for the care of toddlers and infants while they were both away at work. Women who found themselves raising several preschool children alone often paid a substantial portion of their income to the nearby nurse or the local crèche, especially in urban centres outside London where factories had replaced domestic industry and removed the possibility of supporting the family on handicraft work in the home. The records of the child emigration agencies are full of cases in which widows' youngest children were surrendered to the homes because adequate day-care became beyond the laundry worker's or charwoman's means. Schooling was an inexpensive alternative to paid nurses, crèches or mothers tarrying unpaid as baby-minders at home. The expense of child-minding made working mothers particularly eager to send their youngsters to school as soon as possible. [8] In 1912 it was contended that in the poorer districts of London there were more children in the elementary schools at the non-compulsory age of 3 to 5 than in the succeeding years of 5 to 7. [9]

By age 6, boys and girls were no longer as dependent upon the family. Each now had recognised responsibilities toward their kin and useful roles within the household economy. For the next five or six years, although their cash contributions to the family income would not be large, they performed important services in the interest of the group. Bartering their board, shelter and clothing for their labour, they typically became, from age 6 to 12, the care-takers of the working-class household.

Among the families from which the young immigrants to Canada were drawn, child care was principally children's work. Once one sibling entered the care-taker phase, particularly if the eldest child was a girl, paid nurses or crèches were less often required. More of the mother's attentions might be freed for other household tasks or paid labour. Dependent infants and toddlers were now the care-taker's charges; the household had become self-sufficient in baby-minding.

While their mothers retained household responsibilities for cooking and laundry, baby-care was entrusted to girls from 6 to 12 and to boys — chiefly those under 10 — who could be cajoled into such unmanly work. Girls packed their young siblings into perambulators and go-carts and went about on family errands or escaped the family's crowded rooms into the neighbouring streets to play.   The Fabian journalist Magdalene Pember Reeves, writing in 1913, reported seeing infants, unwitting participants in their older sisters' fantasies, careering down streets in prams transformed by youthful imagination into ambulances and toboggans, or hidden together in a corner under one nursemaid's eye so that friends might by turns have hands free for skipping. By and large girls' play was more subdued and less adventurous than boys because girls were constrained by toddlers tugging at their skirts. [10]

In the households of widows or widowers, children aged 6 to 12 were likely to have heavier responsibilities. To them fell the cooking, cleaning and laundry which their mother had done before she died or before their father's death forced her to work longer hours away from home to keep the household together. One man remembers that his widowed mother worked by day waitressing and then by night at catering jobs in Manchester. He kept the home fires burning, collecting his sister from school and fetching their dinner from a neighbour or from a cooked food shop. At bedtime they settled themselves upstairs, the boy with a string tied around his leg and dangled out of the window. His mother, returning late from work, thus wakened him to descend and let her in. In most families in which the mother worked away from home, girls in the care-taker stage 'kept house', tidying the rooms and preparing the evening meal in their mothers' absence. Mission workers who wanted girls of this age admitted to their homes could expect especially strong parental resistance. Without the care-taker's unpaid services, many a household delicately balanced on the edge of subsistence would have been lost. [11]

In London, where the old patterns of domestic industry were still common in the late nineteenth century, many children 6 to 12, both boys and girls, worked at home with their parents making lucifer matches, paper bags, flowers and clothing. Young children were valued in this work for their agility and quickness, which towards the end of the care-taker stage made girls more useful in home manufactures than boys. [12]

The slum workshops of the late nineteenth century were not so well serviced as the rural cottage industries, their counterparts of a century before. No agent arrived at the door with raw materials in hand or, after disputing the quality of the work, carried the finished articles away. Instead, children before going to school ran to fetch their mother's and sisters' materials and each evening returned what had been completed during the day.

Fetching and carrying was an important part of the responsibilities of each child in the care-taker stage. Many daughters of widows worked with their mothers in the wash-house, sorting and packaging bundles, turning the wringer, helping to carry laundry to their mothers' customers and to collect work for the next day. Much of this running about was to save the family money or to preserve a parent's limited energy for more demanding tasks. Sometimes the child's role was more strictly to save face — to take goods to the pawnshop, to ask a shop-keeper for a small loan, to coax from him extraordinarily small quantities or luxury goods ('fancies') on credit when the family bill was already long. [13]

There were also children in the care-taker stage who worked outside their home before they reached school-leaving age. They loitered about railway stations to make a few pennies carrying bags, scoured vacant lots and rubbish heaps for odd bits to sell as scrap, ran with bread and tea for men in the lock-up or with nursing infants to their mothers employed at the mills. They shone shoes, or sold rush-pipes and matches or firewood on the streets. Some earned money running messages. At times even the vestiges of early industrial child labour practices cropped up in later nineteenth-century case records for care-taker age children. One lad came into an emigration home from Kilmarnock in Scotland when he was 11 in February 1872; an orphan, he had been working in the coal pits with a man who gave him food and lodging in return for work. [14]

Parents urged their sons and daughters into such employment in the family interest. Youngsters surrendered to their mothers the proceeds of bottle collecting, dragging barrows and carts in the market or mixing lather at the barber's, and hoped for a small bit back for their own fun. Both Alexander Paterson and Reginald Bray who lived among the working people of London in the early twentieth century claim this pattern was a general one even among the artisan class. Boys and girls worked under parental suggestion or compulsion principally to augment the family income but perhaps also, Paterson suggests, because their mothers thought it 'better for a boy to wander round the streets for the purpose of delivering newspapers than to wander round for no purpose at all'. [15] In 1898 almost 150,000 school-age British children were working for wages. Seven years later employed boys and girls comprised 20 per cent of all school children in the poorer districts of London, the districts from which child emigrants came. [16]

Some school board visitors railed against this paid work, arguing that it kept children from school or made them too weary to benefit from their attendance in class. More thoughtful observers understood that wage work was but a small part of the labour the poor were forced to exact from their children. In the poorest sections of London Charles Booth found only 52 per cent of children attending school regularly. Younger children among the labouring poor were sent off to class each day to get them out of the way, but older children attended only when their home responsibilities were not pressing.[17]

Before the First World War school board officials shared with working-class parents a 'strong sense of the domestic responsibilities' of children 6 to 12 and were unwilling to tamper unduly with their care-taker role at home. Charles Booth called home work 'fairly reasonable grounds' for keeping children from school. Even reformers who were unbending about the state's obligations to protect the health of such children were reluctant to be 'too stringent' in the regulation of care-takers' vital family work, which was often important in lifting the household to or above the poverty line. School attendance officers had to be flexible and lenient in their work among the poor, accepting explanations about absences and compromising about fines. They found their recently created notion of the school-age child in direct conflict with a longer-standing definition of the role of children 6 to 12 within the household economy, a role still too essential to be challenged.[18]

At some time between 12 and 14, depending upon their progress and record of attendance, youngsters were relieved of the burden of being present at school. They were free then to take full-time work, and their role within the family economy changed once more. They were no longer care-takers, bartering their services for a share of the family's goods. They became contributors to the family income whose individual fortunes in the job market affected, sometimes substantially, the well-being of their parents and siblings.[19]

Older children were often the mainstays of the child emigrants' families. The crisis that led parents to surrender a dependent or care-taker-aged child to an institution would have made them particularly reliant upon the help of older boys and girls who were beginning to bring home wages.[20] Thomas W., who homesteaded in 1910 near Swift Current, Saskatchewan, had lived until he was 9 in Bethnal Green, East London, one of a family of seven who subsisted on parish relief and the earnings of his elder sister. When their relief was cut off, Thomas came to a London home because his sister's pay as a matchbox maker was not by itself enough to support them all. Lydia S. was a Lancashire weaver of 16 when in February 1901 she decided to leave home, probably in exasperation with her mother's drinking. Mother and brother were left destitute by her departure, thrown from their lodgings and found sleeping in waterclosets. The National Society for the Prevention of Cruelty to Children was called in, and the boy was placed by magistrate's order in an emigration home. Henry E. and his brother Robert were admitted when they were 8 and 9 so that their widowed mother could find a situation in service. There was one other brother in the family, an errand boy who had been their sole support. His dependants being cared for elsewhere, this 13-year-old continued on his own at his job. [21]

But commonly among the labouring poor, school-leavers were expected to be contributors to the family income. They surrendered their wages to their parents as a matter of course, not as an exceptional response to a particular family crisis. Their role as contributors was shaped by patterns of earning capacities generally understood and traditions about family responsibility generally respected among British working people in the late nineteenth and early twentieth centuries. [22]

Young men and women taking up their first jobs often turned over the whole of their earnings to their parents. Alexander Paterson, observing South London in 1911, described 'each boy and girl' being impelled by 'some unwritten law' to 'bring back their wages to the mother'. Robert Roberts remembers from his boyhood in Salford that 'most Edwardian elders in the lower working class' demanded their children's earnings 'as a natural right — a prerogative unchanged from the previous century'. This pattern changed, as did so much else, among working people during the First World War, but in Manchester in the 1920s, although 'the old custom was slowly dying', boys felt obliged to follow it still, to 'tip up the wages' to their parents and count as their due only the sixpence or shilling they received back in 'spends'. [23]

Boys and girls who turned over their pay packets unbroken were accepting a traditional working-class description of the life-cycle that characterised children as debtors. Contributors were acknowledging the obligations they had accumulated as care-takers and dependants, making restitution to the family economy for the burden they had been in their earlier years. After leaving school, children were expected 'to compensate parents for all the "kept" years of childhood', and sons and daughters of working-class families commonly accepted the responsibilities this parental expectation implied. Joseph Kett describes a 'jarring mixture of complete freedom and total subordination' in nineteenth-century American youngsters. The same dilemma characterised the last stage of a British labouring childhood. [24]

Not only did parents control their children's earnings, but they often chose the school-leaver's first job as well. Unskilled and semiskilled labourers with thirteen- and fourteen-year-old children were beginning to notice their own physical strength fading, to anticipate declines in their own earnings at manual work. As parents they wanted the best for the family income, which sometimes meant manoeuvring teenagers into dreary but steady jobs they heartily detested. Parents counted low-paying apprenticeships the prerogative of skilled labourers' children and a luxury the families of poorer workers could not afford. Walter Greenwood wanted to work with his hands. His mother insisted that in Manchester, with short-time, strikes and lock-outs, a white-collar job was preferable. A neighbour girl, Hetty Boarder, wanted to work in a theatre. Her mother insisted she had a responsibility to take a more regular job. Greenwood at 14 took the work his mother found him as a pawnbroker's clerk; Hetty went not into the theatre but into a steam laundry. [25]

In London, the interests of parents and school-leavers were more generally in harmony. The best-paid work for a boy of 14 in a commercial city — street work as a van-boy, a newsboy, a runner for the post office, or a beer-boy at a work-site — offered exactly the variety, the freedom, the movement, that 'element of adventure' the school-leaver coveted, while also providing that immediate boost to family income parents urgently required. The conflict in London emerged later when the position both school-leaver and parent agreed upon was filled by a younger lad leaving the sixteen-year-old in a 'blind-alley', unskilled, wanting 'a man's wage and. . . only fit for a boy's job'. [26]

Although contributors' first wages went entirely to their mothers, after a time some fixed weekly sum was usually agreed upon, and young men and women kept the rest for clothing, entertainments or their 'future'. Boys were usually expected to pay more to their parents than girls. Helen Bosanquet, a London social worker, thought this was because they ate more. It may also have been because they had done less for the family in the preceding care-taker stage. [27]   Charles Booth thought that contributors and their mothers set a fixed weekly sum for board and lodging when mothers might 'otherwise "make a profit" ' from the whole of their sons' and daughters' earnings. Aware that his readers might misconstrue this as a mercenary or callously calculative arrangement, Booth added by way of caution that 'though it may savour more of business than the family tie', this approach to family finances was 'natural enough' and had 'become customary' among the labouring poor. [28]

In their later years at home older children in York commonly contributed 'a sum for board and lodging equivalent to that paid by ordinary lodgers', in the 1890s from five to ten shillings a week. But sons and daughters were less expensive to keep than lodgers because they demanded less furniture and space of their own and were less likely to default in their payments to the household exchequer. An earning child added only from 2s 10d to 3s 8d to the expenses of the household. [29] Young men and women paid no more to live at home than they would have paid to live elsewhere, often a bit less. Yet their families were better off for their presence and their payments because their contributions exceeded the cost of their keep.

For these young people childhood was drawing to a close. Their debts were almost extinguished. They had very nearly earned the autonomy of adults. They no longer took direction from their parents about the kind of work they did and paid less heed than they had when younger to direction about the kind of company and hours they kept. Older boys came to expect the extra rations to keep up their strength which male breadwinners were allowed. Domestic quarrels and the discomfort of the dwelling might drive young men and women in their late teens from home into lodgings. Alternatively, they left to marry, according to the family order of things, in their early twenties when their 'kept' years of childhood had been fully repaid. [30]

Through the duration of the juvenile immigration movement, childhood among the British labouring poor changed. On one hand working-class childhood became a concern of public policy. State regulations affecting children's employment, school attendance and health became more stringent. The state came to be described as the parents' partner in the important national work of child-rearing. On the other hand working people came to want more schooling for their sons and daughters and to think of children 6 to 12 less as workers and more as helpers than they had previously. By Edwardian times more children were cared for by adults as dependants than during Victoria's reign; care-takers more often helped at home in addition to, rather than instead of, going to school; more contributors began to work full-time at 14 rather than 12. Nevertheless working people continued to describe the debts children must repay parents before they might become autonomous adults as a matter of 'custom', 'natural right' and 'unwritten law'. [31] The influence of the poverty cycle upon the seasons of a labouring childhood had not disappeared.

Notes

1. Paul de Rousiers, *The Labour Question in Britain* (Macmillan, London, 1896), p. 35.
2. David Rubinstein, *School Attendance in London, 1870-1904* (University of Hull, Hull, 1969), pp. 59, 73; Charles Booth, *Life and Labour of the People of London* (Macmillan, London, 1902-4), I, vol. 3, p. 219; Public Archives of Canada (PAC), Charlotte Alexander Papers, vol. 2, case of Ellen Smith; Alexander Paterson, *Across the Bridges* (Edward Arnold, London, 1912), p. 38.
3. Booth, *Life and Labour*, I, vol. 2, pp. 20-1; L.G. Chiozza Money, *Riches and Poverty*, 3rd ed. (Methuen, London, 1905), pp. 42-3, 125, 159, 195; Arthur Newsholme, *The Elements of Vital Statistics*, 3rd ed. (Swan Sonnenschein, London, 1899), pp. 127-8, 131, 134-5; Margaret Alden, *Child Life and Labour* (Headley Bros., London, 1908), p. 19; Paterson, *Across the Bridges*, p. 35; Reginald Bray, *Town Child* (T.F. Unwin, London, 1907), p. 94.
4. Helen Bosanquet, *Rich and Poor* (Macmillan, London, 1896), p. 79; A.L. Bowley and A.R. Burnett-Hurst, *Livelihood and Poverty* (G. Bell and Sons, London, 1915), pp. 29, 31; Neil McKendrick, 'Home Demand and Economic Growth: a new view of the role of women and children in the industrial revolution', in N. McKendrick (ed.), *Historical Perspectives* (Europa, London, 1974), pp. 158, 201; Bray, *Town Child*, p. 90; Booth, *Life and Labour*, I, vol. 1, pp. 140-6.
5. Benjamin S. Rowntree, *Poverty. A Study of Town Life* (Macmillan, London, 1901), pp. 52-85, 136-7; Frances Collier, *The family economy of the working classes in the cotton industry 1784-1833* (Chetham Society, Manchester, 1965), pp. 50-2; Economics Club, *Family Budgets* (P.S. King and Son, London, 1896), pp. 59, 61; Florence Bell, *At the Works* (Edward Arnold, London, 1907), pp. 49-50; Bosanquet, *Rich and Poor*, pp. 78-9; John Foster, *Class Struggle and the Industrial Revolution* (Weidenfeld and Nicolson, London, 1974), p. 97; Michael Anderson, *Family Structure in nineteenth century Lancashire* (Cambridge University Press, Cambridge, 1971), pp. 166-7; Jack London, *The People of the Abyss* (Macmillan, London, 1904), p. 290.
6. Anderson, *Family Structure*, pp. 66, 75, 131, 160; Michael Anderson, 'Family and Class in Nineteenth-Century Cities', *Journal of Family History*, vol. 2, no. 2 (1977), p. 148.
7. Anderson, *Family Structure*, pp. 11-12, 76-8; Michael Katz, *The People of Hamilton, Canada West* (Harvard University Press, Cambridge, Mass., 1975), p. 302; Anderson, 'Family and Class', pp. 147-8; Michael Katz, 'Essay Review', *Journal of Social History*, vol. 7, no. 1 (1973), pp. 90-2; Standish Meacham, *A Life Apart* (Thames and Hudson, London, 1977), pp. 158-9.
8. Margaret Hewitt, *Wives and Mothers in Victorian Industry* (Rockliff, London, 1958), p. 63; Anderson, *Family Structure*, p. 74; Barnado 228 B 3.94, 573 B 3.05, 994 G 10.08, 934 G 8.05, 903 G 9.03, 882 G 9.98.
9. Paterson, *Across the Bridges* p. 35.
10. Bray, *Town Child*, pp. 86, 100-1; Helen Denby, 'Children of Working London', in Bernard Bosanquet (ed.), *Aspects of the Social Problem* (Macmillan, London, 1895), p. 37; Paterson, *Across the Bridges*, p. 36; Bosanquet, *Rich and Poor*, p. 101; Bell, *At the Works*, pp. 49-50; Magdalene Pember Reeves, *Round About a Pound a Week* (G. Bell and Sons, London, 1914), p. 191; Liverpool 4, pp. 121-2.
11. Bosanquet, *Rich and Poor*, pp. 108-9; Walter Greenwood *There was a time* (Jonathan Cape, London, 1969), p. 70; George Sims, *How the Poor Live* (Chatto and Windus, London, 1889) p. 22; Booth, *Life and Labour* I, vol. 3, p. 219; Barnado 949 G 5.06, 680 B 7.07, 637 B 8.06, 835 G 6.00. For a

comparable rural example see Jennie Kitteringham, 'Country work girls in nineteenth-century England', in Raphael Samuel (ed.), *Village Life and Labour* (Routledge and Kegan Paul, London, 1975), p. 84.

12. Rubinstein, *School Attendance*, pp. 59-60; Hewitt, *Wives and Mothers*, p. 158; Gareth Stedman Jones, *Outcast London* (Clarendon Press, Oxford, 1971), pp. 22-3; Barnardo 221 B 10.93.

13. Kathleen Woodward, *Jipping Street* (Harper and Brothers, New York, 1928), p. 12; Booth, *Life and Labour*, I, vol. 3, p. 230; Robert Roberts, *The Classic Slum* (Pelican, Harmondsworth, 1973), pp. 27, 113; P.G.F. Le Play, *Les ouvriers européens* (L'imprimerie impériale, Paris, 1879), vol. 1, pp. 275-6; Reginald Bray, 'The Boy and the Family', in E.J. Urwick (ed.), *Studies of Boy Life in Our Cities* (J.M. Dent, London, 1904), pp. 70-9; Margaret Davies, *Life as we have known it* (Hogarth, London, 1931), p. 4.

14. Meacham, *Life Apart*, p. 175; Greenwood, *There was a time*, pp. 38, 66; Quarrier History 9, p. 165; Quarrier Emigration 6, pp. 302, 389; Barbardo 24 B 1.85, 132 B 3.91, 204 B 6.93.

15. Paterson, *Across the Bridges*, pp. 69-70; Bray, 'The Boy and the Family', pp. 86-7.

16. Rubinstein, *School Attendance*, pp. 71, 73-4; Bowley and Burnett-Hurst, *Livelihood and Poverty*, p. 107; O. Jocelyn Dunlop, *English Apprenticeship and Child Labour* (T. Fisher Unwin, London, 1912), pp. 314-16.

17. Sims, *How the Poor Live*, p. 18; A. Watt Smythe, *Physical Deterioration* (John Murray, London, 1904), pp. 133-4; Booth, *Life and Labour*, I, vol. 3, p. 235; Rubinstein, *School Attendance*, p. 61; Meacham, *Life Apart*, pp. 169-72.

18. George Sims, *Living London* (Cassell and Company, London, 1902), p. 90; Sims, *How the Poor Live*, pp. 19-23; Rubinstein, *School Attendance*, p. 61; S.J. Gibb, *The Problem of Boy Work* (Wells, Gardner and Co., London, 1906), pp. 11-12; Bosanquet, *Rich and Poor*, pp. 155-6; Booth, *Life and Labour*, I, vol. 3, p. 230.

19. Nettie Alder, 'Children as Wage-earners', *Fortnightly Review*, vol. 73 (May 1903), p. 927; Gillian Sutherland, *Elementary Education in the nineteenth century* (Historical Association, London, 1971), pp. 34-5; Bowley and Burnett-Hurst, *Livelihood and Poverty*, p. 107; Meacham, *Life Apart*, pp. 172-4; de Rousiers, *Labour Question*, pp. 166-7, 320-1; Woodward, *Jipping Street*, p. 93.

20. Barnardo 960 G 10.06, 885 G 4.03, 844 G 7.00, 64 B 8.87, 85 B 6.88, 244 B 6.94, 291 B 4.96, 331 B 9.97, 427 B 7.01, 435 B 9.01, 465 B 7.02, 611 B 9.05, 616 B 3.06, 681 B 7.07.

21. Barnardo 332 B 9.97, 205 B 6.93, 440 B 9.01.

22. Joan W. Scott and Louise A. Tilly, 'Women's Work and the Family in Nineteenth-Century Europe', *Comparative Studies in Society and History*, vol. 17, no. 1 (1975), pp. 50-5; Louise A. Tilly, Joan W. Scott and Miriam Cohen, 'Women's Work and European Fertility Patterns', *Journal of Interdisciplinary History*, vol. 6 (1976); Le Play, *Les ouvriers européens* (1855), p. 28, (1879) I, pp. 275-6.

23. Paterson, *Across the Bridges*, p. 22; Roberts, *Classic Slum*, p. 52; Greenwood, *There was a time*, p. 184.

24. Roberts, *Classic Slum*, p. 52; Kett, *Rites of Passage*, p. 29. The emphasis here on a longer-term cycle of reciprocation at the core of attitudes towards the family in the stable working class clearly differs from Anderson's theories concerning short-run calculative orientation. *Family Structure*.

25. Greenwood, *There was a time*, pp. 102-3, 110-11.

26. Rowntree, *Poverty*, pp. 59-60; Arthur Greenwood, *Juvenile Labour Exchanges and After-care* (P.S. King and Son, London, 1911), pp. 7-8; Paterson, *Across the Bridges*, p. 80; Gibb, *Boy Work*, pp. 3-5; Booth, *Life and Labour*, II,

vol. 5, p. 319; Children's Home, *Report* 1890-1, p. 4.

27. Bowley and Burnett-Hurst, *Livelihood and Poverty*, p. 66; Rowntree, *Poverty*, p. 30; de Rousiers, *Labour Question*, pp. 166, 311; Bosanquet, *Rich and Poor*, p. 88; Charles E.B. Russell, *Manchester Boys* (University Press, Manchester, 1905), p. 15; Walter Greenwood, *Love on the Dole* (Jonathan Cape, London, 1935), p. 57; Peter N. Stearns, 'Working-class women in Britain, 1890-1914', in Martha Vicinus (ed.), *Suffer and Be Still* (Indiana University Press, Bloomington, 1972), p. 110; Booth, *Life and Labour*, II, vol. 5, p. 319; Bray 'The Boy and the Family', pp. 88-9.

28. Michael Katz has responded in this way to a similar analysis in Michael Anderson, *Family Structure*, without, I would argue, due regard for the particular context of family life among the labouring poor. Katz, *People of Hamilton*, pp. 300-2; Katz, 'Essay Review', pp. 90-2; Anderson, 'Family and Class', pp. 146-8; Booth, *Life and Labour*, II, vol. 5, p. 320.

29. Rowntree, *Poverty*, pp. 86, 110; Anderson is in error in fixing the upper limit of the earning child's cost to the household at 3s 8d, Anderson, *Family Structure*, p. 128; Booth, *Life and Labour*, II, vol. 5, p. 323.

30. Paterson, *Across the Bridges*, p. 15; Greenwood, *There was a time*; Anderson, *Family Structure*, pp. 128-9; Booth, *Life and Labour*, IV, vol. 17, pp. 43-6; Bray, 'The Boy and the Family', p. 89; Roberts, *Classic Slum*, p. 52; Rowntree, *Poverty*, p. 113; Bosanquet, *Rich and Poor*, p. 78; Laura Oren, 'The Welfare of Women in Labouring Families: England, 1860-1950', *Feminist Studies*, vol. 1 (Winter-Spring 1973), p. 110.

31. Anna Davin is studying this important transformation among the working-class girls and women of London. I am grateful to her for sharing her unpublished work with me; see Anna Davin, 'Imperialism and Motherhood', *History Workshop Journal*, no. 5 (1978), pp. 9-65; Bray, *Town Child*, pp. 104-6, 116; Paterson, *Across the Bridges*, p. 37; Rubinstein, *School Attendance*, p. 73; Gareth Stedman Jones, 'Working class culture and working class politics in London, 1870-1900; notes on the remaking of a working class', *Journal of Social History*, vol. 7, no. 4 (1974), pp. 486-7. These policy changes are discussed in greater detail in Chapter 8.

2 SALVATION AND THE SAFETY-VALVE

God setteth the solitary in families. [1]

Every boy rescued from the gutter is one
dangerous man the less. [2]

In many respects the British child emigrants were not typical of their
time. Most people who left Britain in the nineteenth century paid their
own passage; the child emigrants were assisted to leave Britain by
philanthropic institutions, English parish authorities and Canadian
immigration departments. Most nineteenth-century emigrants left
voluntarily; the child emigrants were off to Canada before they had
even reached the legal age of consent. Few British emigrants were any
longer indentured in their overseas destinations; almost all child
emigrants were apprenticed soon after they arrived in Canada. These
characteristics made child migration more like British transportation
and indentured service policies of the seventeenth and eighteenth
centuries than the private and voluntary population movements of the
nineteenth and twentieth. [3]

But the foundations of the programme were nonetheless firmly
Victorian. More than 20 million people left Great Britain for destinations beyond Europe in the century between the end of the
Napoleonic Wars and the beginning of the First World War. Thirteen
million of these emigrants went initially to the United States, 4 million
to Canada and 1.5 million to Australasia. The movement outward was
particularly large compared with the size of the British population
remaining behind in the years 1846-55, 1866-75 and 1881-90, periods
of economic uncertainty and social tension. These are the three Victorian intervals during which, at least in London, philanthropists and
policy-makers were most fearful that distress among the working class
would lead to civil disorder. These are also periods during which
interest in child emigration was most keen. [4]

Two recurring preoccupations drew propertied Britons to assisted
juvenile emigration and apprenticeship: the political concern for public
safety and the religious concern for the salvation of individual working-
class children. Child emigration was to be both a safety-valve for
internal disorder and a path to salvation. Often both cases were argued
at once, because for Victorians public policy and the Christian mission
were seldom easily separated.

In the seventeenth and eighteenth centuries orphaned and deserted
children were apprenticed to local householders or sent out from the
cities to distant villages where factory hands were required. But by

the 1830s changes in factory legislation and technology restricted the scope of children's work outside the family. 'London has got too full of children' Police Magistrate Robert Joseph Chambers claimed before the Select Committee on Emigration of 1826, and idle young hands were turning to crime. After 1838 Boards of Guardians discontinued apprenticeship and placed parish youngsters in workhouses. The workhouses too became overfull with children: from 1834 to 1908 one in three paupers in any given year was under 16.

The Children's Friend Society for the Prevention of Juvenile Vagrancy offered to relieve this congestion in parish facilities and the streets through emigration to less regulated labour markets abroad. Although the 1834 Poor Law did not permit the emigration of children without families, between 1830 and 1841 several hundred young people, some from charitable institutions, some from workhouses, were taken to New Brunswick, the Canadas, Swan River, South Australia and the Cape of Good Hope. Exploitative placements in the Cape and the Rebellions of 1837 in the Canadas quickly discredited the society, and in the early 1840s only the graduates of reformatories continued to be sent overseas. [5]

But by 1848 the revolutions in Europe, Chartism and the crowding of distressed Irish migrants in English and Scottish cities created the uncertainty and fear which made drastic social remedies acceptable, among them the emigration of labouring children. Teachers in the growing numbers of 'Ragged Schools' founded to tame 'wild street arabs' through moral and practical teachings began to argue that without an 'outlet for the product' their lessons inculcating honesty and habits of industry were in vain, that as their schools had become 'the approved substitute for the Prison...the Government should substitute the colony for the Penal Settlement'. [6]   Boards of Guardians from Kensington, Marylebone and St Pancras and officials from the Central London and North Surrey District Schools convinced the Poor Law Board that 'the Mother Country could only benefit from the absence of young paupers, the future inmates of our workhouses, our tramp-sheds and our jails'. [7]

In the dark days of 1849 Parliament granted £1,500 to support Ragged School emigrants. The Poor Law Act was amended in 1850 so that Guardians could send orphaned and deserted children abroad. Several parties from poor law unions and the Ragged Schools did go to the colonies. Over four thousand Irish girls were sent to New South Wales and South Australia. Then in the early 1850s prosperity returned. The President of the Poor Law Board discouraged child emigration, emphasising that young paupers' labour became yearly more valuable and that Guardians could best exercise their 'duties of protection' when their young charges were close to hand. The Ragged School migrations dwindled. But a highly visible precedent for philanthropic child emigration and the legal sanction to send work-house children abroad had been established. [8]

In 1866 the last epidemic of cholera struck London, its effects compounded by scarlet fever and smallpox. The harvests of the late 1860s were poor. Bread prices were high. The winter of 1867 was exceptionally severe, and a financial crisis lay upon Britain. In the preceding decade pauperism appeared to have been increasing. Certainly in London, where poor law policy was formulated, the number of paupers was rising dramatically. Unemployment increased as distress in the city's industrial and workshop production intensified. The Thames shipbuilding industry collapsed in 1867. The small work-shops of the metropolis which produced textiles, leather goods and small metals lost their customers to factories in the north of England and the continent. Working-class housing stock shrank as broad thoroughfares and railway lines to serve central London were cut through poor districts where land prices were cheapest. More working people were known to be suffering. More working people were sus-pected of republicanism. The Second Reform Bill was passed. But the sense of disquiet remained. [9]

New charities stepped into the breach, such as Octavia Hill's pro-grammes to provide more and better working-class housing, and a host of new shelters for children to supplement and improve upon the workhouse schools. And once more, in crisis, philanthropists and public authorities began to send working people abroad. The National Emigration League and several philanthropic societies from east and south London sponsored parties to Canada in 1868. The Poplar Poor Law Union despatched one group of pauper men and families to the St Lawrence in 1867 by borrowing money using future tax revenues as security under the terms of the 1834 Poor Law Act. Other Boards of Guardians made similar plans. [10]

William Dixon, the senior Canadian emigration agent in England, reported with alarm an 'almost universal' feeling 'that the only remedy to overcrowded workhouses was mass evacuation of their inmates'. [11] The Poplar paupers had been flamboyantly unsuccessful in their first months in Canada. In this they followed long precedent. Most assisted urban immigrants had had difficulty establishing themselves in the small and predominantly agricultural labour market of British North

America. In self-defence the Dominion cabinet passed an order in council in June 1868 barring entry to immigrants who did not have means to provide for themselves. British charitable motives were particularly suspected. One London lady who regularly publicised her emigration projects through *The Times* was described by Dixon as no more than 'a passenger agent of the sharpest description'. [12]

This woman, Maria Susan Rye, daughter of a noted London solicitor, had begun emigration work among gentlewomen in 1860 after she became disillusioned with the prolonged struggle for a married woman's property bill and apprehensive that her work training ladies for work in commerce and trades would compromise their particular value as moral guardians in the home. [13] Rather than pursuing suffrage agitation, Rye offered the satisfactions of marriage and motherhood in the colonies as an alternative to political and social changes in the status of women in Britain. Some 'governesses and educated ladies' did accept her assistance. More often her parties consisted of working girls without funds, compelled to be flexible in search of a livelihood abroad. By 1868 Miss Rye and her emigrant women were no longer welcome in Australia. [14]

Rye turned her attentions next to Canada. A passage to Canada cost less than half the Australian fare, and she had reason to believe the Canadian government would support her work. [15] Her first two Canadian parties, the ones that attracted Dixon's attention, were a mixed lot, the majority of them women whose fares were paid by the parishes seeking to be rid of them, the others charity cases of varied backgrounds financed by appeals through *The Times*. All were described as intending domestics. [16]

Her next project fared much better. On 28 October 1869 Miss Rye embarked from Liverpool with a party of pauper children, seventy-six girls, most under 11, wards of Boards of Guardians in Liverpool, Wolverhampton, London and Bath. The children were well received by Canadians, who expected young paupers to adapt more easily than their elders. Lord Shaftesbury and the Social Science Association advised a large programme of emigration for girls 7 to 12 from London workhouse schools. The President of the Poor Law Board agreed and urged all Guardians to consider emigration for numbers of their parish children. [17]

Guardians favoured emigration because it relieved pressure in crowded workhouse and industrial schools. The policy was also economical. Emigration cost the equivalent of one year's maintenance in a parish facility. A child of 7 sent to Canada seven years before he could begin work in England saved the parish six years' keep. The central Poor Law Board approved child emigration in 1870 because it placed children in households, away from a world inhabited only by paupers in which young people became frail and passive and acquired habits of public dependence. Guardians had recently experimented in boarding out children in England following the model widely used in Scotland and Ireland.[18] Canada seemed to promise a supply of temperate moral and pious rural homes far in excess of the numbers available in England.

Not all initial reactions were positive. George Cruikshank, illustrator of Dickens and Harriet Beecher Stowe, thought 'such transportation of innocent...children a disgrace to the Christian world' and drew a savage caricature of Miss Rye shovelling little girls the size of mice up from the gutters into a giant mud cart, 'like so much guano, or like so many cattle for a foreign market'.[19] But Canadian governments and the Canadian public supported the programme, providing transportation subsidies, grants-in-aid and an inexhaustible supply of applicants for the children's services. Quickly parishes acted upon the urging of the Poor Law Board. Through the six years until the movement was halted again in 1875 Rye took 902 pauper children to Ontario, and Annie Macpherson, who began similar work in 1870, took a further 350.[20]

The boarding-out places of pauper children in Britain were closely supervised. In 1873 as economic conditions improved and the sense of urgency in dealing with distress and potential turbulence among the working class abated, Boards of Guardians became more cautious and reflective about their responsibilities and began to make enquiries through the Colonial Office into the prospects and circumstances of their young wards in Canada.[21] A Dominion Privy Council report assured them that all the children were placed in respectable families and so 'put in positions to succeed in life', but other reports from Canada were more ambiguous.[22] A New York woman informed the poor law authorities through prominent British friends that her own observations in the Niagara district where many pauper youngsters were placed suggested that 'Miss Rye's treatment of the children' called 'loudly for enquiry'.[23] The husband of a former assistant at Rye's Niagara Home appeared before the Islington Board of Guardians with a long list of specific criticisms with which to buttress his contention that if parish girls were 'too young to be placed out' in Britain they were 'certainly too young for a new country where more would be required from them and where there was no supervision or apprentice law'.[24]

Andrew Doyle, the senior Local Government Board Inspector despatched to Canada in 1874, returned after three months of visiting children in Ontario with similar conclusions:

> to send them as emigrants can be regarded not as a way of improving their position, but simply of getting rid of them at a cheap rate ... If they be reasonably well prepared for service, it is difficult to understand why they would be sent out of a country in which one hears from every household complaints of the dearth of domestic servants, and of the want of young hands in various branches of industry.

He reported that the well-intentioned informality with which Miss Macpherson and Miss Rye administered their Canadian work led to poor placements and inadequate supervision and that pauper children were frequently overworked and abused. He recommended that the programme continue only for very young children who might be genuinely adopted and only if they could be as well protected in Canada as in Britain through regular independent inspections. [25]

In March 1875 the English Local Government Board, successor to the Poor Law Board, withdrew its sanction of 'mere philanthropic machinery and organisations' for the care of English pauper children overseas. The decision was a popular one in London at the time, consistent with the high standards being demanded of comparable English boarding-out experiments and with the needs of a buoyant economy for servants and labourers in Britain. Miss Rye protested that Doyle was mistaken. The Canadian government claimed to have proved he was mistaken. But the Local Government Board continued to regard the emigration of pauper children as a reckless and unnecessary policy. When in 1878 the Dominion Department of Agriculture offered to send immigration agents out yearly to visit newly arrived youngsters, the Board rejected the proposal as an exercise in 'make-believe' — at least until changing English conditions gave them grounds for pause in 1883. [26]

While the emigration of pauper children was suspended Miss Macpherson continued to take youngsters to Canada from her Home of Industry in Spitalfields, East London, and from similar evangelically sponsored institutions throughout Great Britain. Miss Rye opened a home at Peckham, South London, and expanded the small philanthropic phase of her work. The two pioneers in the movement were joined by Louisa Birt, Macpherson's sister, who had founded the Liverpool Sheltering Home in 1872, J.T. Middlemore, who ran two refuges in Birmingham, Rev. Bowman Stephenson of the Wesleyan Methodist National Children's Homes and men and women from several Roman Catholic dioceses in England. About five hundred children went to Canada annually through the late 1870s. This number more than trebled between 1879 and 1883.[27]

Through the mid 1880s the prosperity of the preceding decade disappeared. In London unemployment rose. The housing shortage remained. The structural decline in workshop manufactures continued. A severe cyclical depression deepened.[28] Descriptions of the state of the nation became more desperate. The managers of refuges grew more fearful of the large numbers, estranged spirits and bleak prospects of city children.

Samuel Smith, a member of Parliament who helped Louisa Birt found the Liverpool Sheltering Home, wrote in 1883 of England as lingering on the edge of a volcano, and of the poor as 'foul sewage' stagnating beneath 'our social fabric', certain if untreated to cause 'terrible disasters'.[29] The small journals published by rescue homes for children deployed similar rhetoric. 'The machinery of national life' was 'out of order'.[30] 'The miserable and helpless' metropolitan poor would not long remain immune to the 'poisonous doctrines of Nihilism and Socialism'.[31] They were becoming 'a positive danger to the State'. The children of the streets were the raw materials from which the 'dangerous classes' were formed.[32]

The foremost argument for child emigration in these years was its value as a 'safety-valve to tide over the troubles at home'.[33] The policy was commonly described as 'not a matter of humanity alone, but of public safety',[34] a way to make 'starving and desperate men into contented and loyal subjects', 'neglected female children' into 'happy, honest mothers of a stalwart' colonial race.[35] Concern about the children's safety abroad was overwhelmed by concern for public safety at home. In the mid-1880s only measures as thorough as removal overseas were considered sufficient to the task of 'destroying the memories of pauperism in children' and saving them from becoming 'as corrupted as their parents were before them'.[36]

Philanthropically sponsored child emigration rose from 540 in 1880 to 1,297 in 1883 and 2,104 in 1888 as more children's homes adopted the policy and successively larger parties of young people were sent to Canada. Pressure on the Local Government Boards to allow children from parish workhouses and industrial schools to be placed abroad again grew more intense. Miss Rye arranged for the Princess Louise and the Canadian High Commissioner in London, Sir Alexander Galt, to ask that the question be reopened. The Charity Organisation Society, the Howard Association, the Metropolitan Poor Law Guardians' Association and a number of members of Parliament lobbied the Board. [37] The Dominion government renewed its offer to inspect pauper children in Canada. [38]

In spring 1883 the offer was accepted on comparatively lenient terms. The Guardians' child emigrants were to be inmates of workhouse schools for at least six months, generally to be no older than 10 if female and to be certified by a medical officer as well as two justices of the peace. Catholic children were to be placed only with Catholic families, Protestant children only with Protestants. The Guardians were to secure a satisfactory Canadian agent, usually a British philanthropic children's home with an emigration branch, which would find suitable placements in the Dominion and regularly inform the English and Canadian governments of the young people's whereabouts to facilitate the promised inspection. [39]

Thereafter children were regularly sent to Canada from many English and Welsh parishes. But youngsters were so widely distributed, often to isolated farms, and the staff of Dominion immigration agents was so small and overworked that the irregular and cryptic reports sent back to Boards of Guardians were never very satisfactory. [40] In 1886 the Local Government Board did suspend the programme for workhouse children again for a few months, hoping to secure better supervision. The action had no enduring effect. The financial and political reasons for continuing to send pauper boys and girls to Canada were too compelling. When the economic distress of the 1880s receded, the advocates of child emigration as a safety valve for social unrest were replaced by proponents of an imperial mission to populate Greater Britain. Over eleven thousand pauper children were sent to Canada between 1870 and 1914. [41] Not until socialists secured influence with Boards of Guardians in the twentieth century did concern for the welfare of the state's children placed abroad gain force again. [42]

Many of the men and women connected with philanthropic child emigration work were, like Maria Rye and Samuel Smith, social conservatives searching for policies that would relieve distress among the poor but not require change in Britain. In some instances they defended this position on practical grounds. Thomas John Barnardo, director of the home that sent more children to Canada than any other, argued that because he could count on monied men and women to feed the boys and girls in his institutions but received no such help from the socialists it was logical for him to choose homes for his graduates with

Canadian farmers, who were seldom socialists, communists or anarchists and slow to lend themselves 'to any of the crazy fads and theories for reorganisation of society'. [43]   Certainly the middle-class backgrounds of child emigration workers, sons and daughters of businessmen and professionals, disinclined them to seek change. [44]   But whereas emigration for workhouse and industrial-school children was most often advocated on political grounds as a conservative policy to preserve public order at minimum cost, the managers of charitable children's homes explained their decision to place children in Canada in terms of theology and religious practice.

Over 20 per cent of the British child immigrants came to Canada under the auspices of evangelical, revivalist, non-denominational institutions whose numbers grew rapidly in Britain during the late 1860s. The evangelical pioneer in child emigration was Annie Macpherson, a Scots-born Quaker who began to take parties of youngsters to eastern Ontario in 1870. Her sisters, Louisa Birt and Rachel Macpherson Merry, expanded the work in succeeding years to include a children's shelter in Liverpool and distributing homes in southwestern Ontario and the eastern townships of Quebec. Through personal contacts and her writings in the widely circulated evangelical weekly the *Christian*, Macpherson persuaded the founders of Britain's largest non-denominational children's homes, Dr Thomas John Barnardo, William Quarrier, Leonard Shaw and J.W.C. Fegan to experiment with juvenile emigration by sending some of their youngsters with her parties. [45]   All these men in time established their own emigration branches and like Macpherson took a large proportion of the children admitted to their homes to Canada.

Evangelical child-savers used emigration more widely than any of the Protestant denominations or the Roman Catholic church. Two theological arguments predisposed them to do so. Evangelical child-savers were premillennarians. They believed that Christ would return to earth before the millennium dawned and before a godly human society came into being on earth. They saw contemporary social distress in Britain as part of divine preparation for the Apocalypse foretold in scripture, the progressive deterioration of the 'wrecked vessel' earth which would occur before the Messiah established His Kingdom. Such evangelicals believed that social reform challenged the divine plan and that because the future was in God's hands, not man's, the most appropriate form of Christian social work was interim relief. Evangelical rescue workers were pained and angered by the suffering they saw around them. But this sense of the divine ordering and ultimate transitoriness of human troubles made Macpherson, for example, while acknowledging the growing presence of the 'dangerous classes', implore only that 'more timely help' be 'given in this season of sore want', salving her anger with the expectation of divine retribution. 'God is watching the grasping capitalists and the oppressors of the poor, the grinding task-masters who cannot wring another farthing out of the toilers.' While awaiting the millennium, child emigration allowed evangelical child-savers to help individual boys and girls in a practical way and place them upon the path to conversion. [46]

Macpherson, William Quarrier of Glasgow and J.W.C. Fegan of Deptford and Southwark were also strict dispensationalists. They saw God's hands at work directing the most minute of daily events and his will being progressively revealed through signs. The conviction that it was necessary to wait upon God's initiative before commencing any work 'in His Name' placed evangelical children's homes in a peculiar financial predicament for which emigration offered particular relief. Macpherson, Quarrier and Fegan placed their needs regularly before the Lord in prayer but would not solicit the general public for financial support.

> Feeling we had no direction in Scripture to state our wants to the world by newspaper appeals, and trembling lest in our desire to aid thousands in our great cities going fast down to darkness, we might lose Our Father's blessing by any step of ours in getting the public gaze upon our feeble efforts and the virtue go therefrom. [47]

Barnardo was condemned by members of his Board for tending to 'act instead of waiting God's initiative' and to 'lean more on man' for help than God. In consequence evangelical institutions were rarely financially secure. By reducing the length of stay of each child, emigration decreased the cost of rescuing each youngster and increased the turnover through the homes. For evangelicals dependent upon prayer and the support of the faithful for the continuation of their work and eager to retrieve as many children as possible from the lapsed masses, emigration therefore had particular appeal. [48]

Child-saving drew upon a broader Christian constituency. All children were, through their innocence, identified with Jesus. Helping children was an honour akin to sheltering the Christ-child himself. To turn away from a child in distress was to deny the Lord, who too had entered this world in lowly circumstances.

> An archway their only shelter
> The pavement their nightly bed
> Thou, too, when on earth dear Saviour,
> Hadst nowhere to lay *thy* head.
>
> So we know thou art here, dear Master,
> Thy form we can almost see;
> Do we hear thy sad voice saying,
> 'Ye did it not to me?' [49]

By 1876 there were probably thirty thousand neglected children on the streets of London. [50] Lord Shaftesbury described them as street arabs, 'bold and pert and dirty as London sparrows but pale and feeble and sadly inferior to them in plumpness of outline'. The child-savers gave youngsters the clothing, food and medical care they urgently required and then turned to more serious spiritual matters. The popular image of the street arab emphasised his discernment, forethought, love of liberty and cunning business sense. The strain and anxiety shown by working and wandering younsters and their precocity and sharpness in pursuit of a living worried Christian child-savers more than their physical deprivations. It was this very acuity and independence that made their childhoods seem unnatural. [51]

The Victorians endowed the family with great spiritual as well as moral and social importance. In the family circle children 'learned the civilising obligations of moral duty and responsibility' and 'observed Christian love at work'. Childhood was properly a 'season of dependence and of preparation for better things in the future' characterised by playfulness, cheerfulness and innocent prattle, that is, by openness and receptiveness to the lessons of moral parents. Children without families were outside the primary civilising institution in society. Christian child-savers feared that youngsters raised without family affection would 'dread and hate those who ought to be nearest them', and that children without pious parents would 'grow in evil' until they prized 'the fruits of evil' as 'the best things in the world'. [52]

Thus all Christian children's institutions wanted family settings for their young wards. They rejected barrack-style orphanages as too like the workhouse schools, imposing order through rigorous discipline, developing in children a mental numbness rather than pliancy before enlightened example. Increasingly through the 1870s and 1880s British children's homes were built upon the German Rauhe Haus model as villages in which boys and girls lived in cottages with a house mother and father. Well-chosen Canadian households promised to be a still more accurate approximation of a natural family. [53]

The search for family settings led two Protestant denominations to establish small emigration programmes. Thomas Bowman Stephenson, head of the Wesleyan Methodist National Children's Homes, began to send boys to Canada in 1872. The Church of England Waifs and Strays Society, established in 1881 by Edward and Robert de Montjoie Rudolf, who were concerned about the quality of religious instruction Anglican children were receiving in non-denominational evangelical homes, began its emigration work through Sherbrooke, Quebec, in 1884. Neither the Methodist nor the Anglican programme was as large as those of the evangelical, non-denominational homes, but both were long-lived. [54]

In 1869 Canadians were willing to accept Miss Rye's parties of children because they believed boys and girls were still malleable, teachable, not yet committed to evil ways. A similar belief in the innocent impressionability of childhood was the broadest common denominator among Christian children's workers. Cardinal Manning and Benjamin Waugh, a Congregational minister and secretary of the Society for the Prevention of Cruelty to Children, in an article entitled 'The Child of the English Savage' for the *Contemporary Review* described boys and girls as most like God of all creatures in 'early purity, beauty, brightness and innocence' and the most capable 'of eternal union with God in beatific vision'. [55] Protestants who favoured child emigration worried that this malleability made children vulnerable before 'depraving influences' in Britain and hoped that the same qualities would draw them into 'straight paths of usefulness in loving Christian families' in Canada. [56] Catholic societies began to send children to Catholic districts in Canada because they thought the children of their flock the most likely to lose their faith in England to the 'great widening sea of indifference, unbelief' and Protestantism. [57]

The first Catholic child emigration programmes began while Cardinal Manning was Archbishop of Westminster. Not at all a social conserva-tive, Manning believed that God forbade his clergy to 'be looked upon by the people as Tories, or of the Party that obstructs the amelioration of their condition, or as the servants of the plutocracy instead of the guides and guardians of the poor'. [58] His relations with his poorer parishioners were always better than those with the old-established Catholic families of England, and unlike the evangelical rescue workers with whom he shared the child emigration policy he favoured social reform. [59]

Catholic dioceses adopted child emigration because they feared the effects of public or Protestant institutions upon the children of Catholic parents, but they could not afford to build enough separate facilities to care for their own youngsters in England. When the Roman Catholic hierarchy was re-established in England in 1850, the church began from nothing. By the 1870s and 1880s construction of Catholic orphanages, reformatories and industrial schools had not yet caught up with demand, and although the law guaranteed that Catholic children would upon application be transferred from workhouse schools and Protestant homes to Catholic facilities, Protestant child-savers complained with some justification that Catholic youngsters surrendered for transfer were often promptly released into the streets. [60]

Roman Catholic child emigration began under the auspices of Father Nugent of Liverpool in 1870, expanded after 1874 to include the Westminster Diocese, and through the 1880s and 1890s grew to cover Salford and Southwark as well. Catholic children were placed in the Irish communities of eastern Ontario and western Quebec and in the French-Canadian communities of Quebec and Manitoba. The agents of the rescue societies claimed to find 'thoroughly Catholic homes' where children 'who would lose their faith if obliged to stay in England' could be 'kept for the church'. [61]

The fees paid by Boards of Guardians for young paupers entrusted to Catholic care were too small to finance building plans in Britain but large enough to fund children's emigration to Canada. Thus the straitened Catholic diocesan children's committees began to concentrate upon the emigration of workhouse children. Their Canadian parties contained a larger proportion of youngsters financed by the Boards of Guardians than those sent by Protestant agencies, and their numbers over-represented the incidence of Roman Catholics in workhouses and in the English population. [62]

As a social policy child emigration was not radical. Altogether perhaps eighty thousand young people were sent to Canada. Their leave-taking may have reduced overcrowding in workhouse schools and philanthropic children's homes, but the absence of one or two thousand children removed from Britain yearly between 1868 and 1925 would not have changed the congested urban housing and labour markets noticeably. Probably few outside their immediate families knew they had gone. However, for the family whose child was taken so far away while still very young, and of course for the boy or girl involved, the change brought about by emigration was radical indeed. The family split was total and the policy irreversible.

A programme at once severe, irrevocable and mildly palliative appealed to Victorian social conservatives and revivalist Christians for working-class children in innocent danger of drifting into the lapsed masses and the dangerous classes.

Fig. 2.1: Annual Immigration of British Juveniles to Canada, 1869-1924

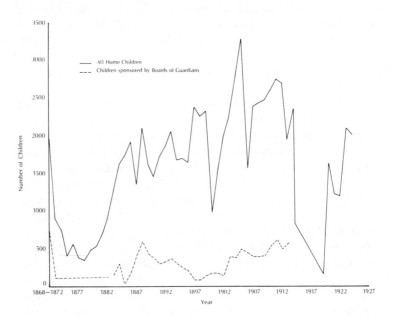

Source: PAC, RG 76 66/3115/7, Manpower survey 22 Dec. 1917; PAC, MG 28 I 10 Canadian Council on Social Development vol. 6; Annual Poor Law and Local Government Board Reports, *British Parliamentary Papers.*

Notes

1. Thomas Barnardo, 'The Dangerous Classes', *Night and Day*, vol. 3 (1879), p. 66.

2. Psalm 68, verse 6.

3. Charlotte Erickson, *Emigration from Europe, 1815-1914* (A. and C. Black, London, 1976), pp. 9, 10, 17; Imre Ferenczi and Walter Willcox, *International Migrations* (NBER, New York, 1929), vol. 1, pp. 81-5.

4. N.H. Carrier and J.R. Jeffery *External Migration, 1815-1950* (HMSO London, 1953), p. 33; C.E. Snow, 'Emigration from Great Britain', in Walter Willcox (ed.), *International Migrations* (NBER, New York, 1931), vol. 2, p. 244; Gareth Stedman Jones, 'Working class culture and working class politics in

London, 1870-1900; notes on the remaking of a working class', *Journal of Social History*, vol. 7, no. 4 (1974), p. 467.

5. This phase of the juvenile emigration movement is described in detail elsewhere. See Ivy Pinchbeck and Margaret Hewitt, *Children in English Society* II (Routledge and Kegan Paul, London 1973);' Alexander G. Scholes *Education for Empire Settlement, A Study of Juvenile Migration* (Longmans, London, 1932); G.J. Parr, 'The Home Children: British Juvenile Immigrants to Canada, 1868-1924', unpublished PhD thesis, Yale University, 1977; Stanley C. Johnson, *A History of Emigration from the United Kingdom to North America, 1763-1912* (Frank Cass, London, 1966); W.S. Shepperson, *British Emigration to North America* (University of Minnesota Press, Minneapolis, 1957); W.A. Carrothers, *Emigration from the British Isles* (P.S. King, London, 1929); Sidney and Beatrice Webb, *English Poor Law History* (Longmans, London, 1906), vol. 1, pt. 2, p. 246; 'Report from the Select Committee on Emigration from the United Kingdom', *Br.P.P.* 1826 IV; Children's Friend Society, *Report* (1837).

6. 'Emigration from the Ragged Schools', *Ragged School Union Magazine* (*RSUM*), March 1850, p. 62; 'The Impulse of Emigration needed to carry on the Ragged School Movement', *RSUM*, January 1850, pp. 37-9; 'Emigration from the Ragged Schools', *RSUM*, December 1850, pp. 289-90; 'A Batch of Emigrants' Letters', *RSUM* 1851, p. 110; 'Shall the needy and helpless be emigrants or convicts?' *RSUM* 1852, p. 148; George Bell, 'Emigration in connection with Ragged and Industrial Schools', *RSUM* 1852, pp. 182-6.

7. Public Records Office (PRO), Ministry of Health 19 (MH 19), vol. 22, 5197/50, 2688/52.

8. Pinchbeck and Hewitt, *Children*, II, p. 558; Great Britain, *Statutes*, 13 and 14 Vic. c. 101, 4; 'Report of the Colonial Land and Emigration Commissioners' (1849), p. 3; PRO, MH 19, vol. 22, 2688/52, 7657/53.

9. Jones, 'Working class culture', p. 467; Gareth Stedman Jones, *Outcast London* (Clarendon Press, Oxford, 1971), pp. 15, 24-5, 50-1; H.J. Dyos, 'The Slums of Victorian London', *Victorian Studies*, vol. 9 (1967), p. 37; David Owen, *English Philanthropy* (Belknap Press, Cambridge, Mass., 1964), p. 217.

10. *Times*, 29 Oct. 1869; *Leader* (Toronto), 4 Nov. 1868; Norman Macdonald, *Canada, Immigration and Colonisation 1841-1903* (Macmillan, Toronto, 1966), pp. 93-4.

11. Public Archives of Canada (PAC), Agriculture (RG 17) 26/2311, William Dixon to L. Stafford, 26 Dec. 1868.

12. PAC, RG 17, 25/2252, William Dixon to L. Stafford, 12 December 1968; Macdonald, *Canada*, p. 96.

13. 'Miss Maria Rye', *Our Waifs and Strays*, vol. 9, no. 237 (Jan. 1904), p. 215; *Dictionary of National Biography*, Supplement, 1901-11, pp. 245-6; *Times*, 17 Nov. 1903; Lee Holcombe, *Victorian Ladies at Work* (David and Charles, Newton Abbott, 1973), pp. 6-9, 16; M.S. Rye, *Emigration of Educated Women* (1861), p. 4, also reprinted as 'The Colonies and their Requirements', *English Woman's Journal*, vol. 8, no. 44 (Jan. 1861), pp. 165-71; Miss Rye's work is described in greater detail in Parr, 'Home Children', ch. 1 and 2, and in two articles by Wesley Turner, '80 stout and healthy girls', *Canada, an historical magazine*, vol. 3, no. 2 (1975), pp. 36-49, and 'Miss Rye's children', *Ontario History*, vol. 68, no. 3 (1976), pp. 169-203.

14. Maria Rye, 'On assisted emigration', *English Woman's Journal* (*EWJ*), vol. 5, no. 28, p. 238; Rye, 'Female Middle Class Emigration', *EWJ*, vol. 10, no. 26 (Sept. 1862); Rye 'On Female Emigration', *Transactions of the National Association for the Promotion of Social Science* (1862), p. 811; PAC, RG 17, 25/2252, William Dixon to L. Stafford, 12 Nov. 1868; 21/1884, Dixon to J.C. Taché, 28 May 1868.

15. PAC, RG 17, 21/1884, clipping from *Wolverhampton Chronicle*, 13 April 1868; 21/1826, Rye to Dept. of Agriculture, 15 April 1868; *Times*, 3 April 1868, 10 April 1868.

16. PAC, RG 17, 21/1844, W. Dixon to J.C. Taché, 28 May 1868, Dixon to Secretary, Poor Law Board, 19 May 1868; *Leader*, 4 June 1868, 16 July 1868, 28 July 1868, 21 August 1868, 19 October 1868; *Times*, 31 July 1868; *Montreal Witness*, 25 June 1868; *Ottawa Times*, 13 June 1868; *Montreal Gazette*, 11 July 1868.

17. *Times*, 29 Oct. 1869; PRO, MH 19, vol. 86, Memo to the President, 'Emigration of Children under the care of Miss Rye', 14 May 1874.

18. Pinchbeck and Hewitt, *Children*, II, pp. 522-3; Webbs, *Poor Law History* I, pp. 271-7; Florence Davenport Hill, *Children of the State* (Ayr, London, 1868).

19. Victoria and Albert Museum, Print Room. George Cruikshank, 'Our Gutter Children' (Wm. Tweedie, London, 1969).

20. 'Report of the Immigration and Colonisation Committee', Canada, *Journals of the House of Commons*, 1875, vol. 9, App. 4, pp. 20, 23.

21. PRO, MH 19, vol. 86, Memo of 14 May 1874; MH 19, vol. 5, 1026D/73, John Hibbert to E.H. Katchball-Hugessen, 4 April 1874.

22. PRO and PAC, Colonial Office 42/718, Gov. No. 166A, 'Report of the Privy Council', 26 June 1873; PAC, RG 7 Gl, vol. 191 (2), Kimberley to Dufferin, 24 April 1873; PRO, MH 19, vol. 5, 48527/73, A.S. Holland to Local Government Board, 26 July 1873.

23. PRO, MH 19, vol. 86, Memo of 14 May 1874.

24. PRO, MH 19, vol. 86, Memo of 14 May 1874; Allerdale Grainger, *Charges against Miss Rye before the Poor Law Board at Islington and her reply thereto* (p.p., n.d. 1874).

25. 'Report to President of Local Government Board by Andrew Doyle, Local Government Board Inspector, as to the emigration of pauper children to Canada', *Br.P.P.*, 1875, LXIII (Doyle, 'Report' 1875), pp. 23, 30-5.

26. *Times*, 10 March 1875, 17 March 1875, 19 March 1875, 22 April 1875, 23 April 1875, 6 June 1875; 'Copy of a letter by Miss Rye to the President of the Local Government Board', *Br.P.P.*, 1877, LXXI; 'Copy of the reply of Mr. Doyle to Miss Rye's report', *Br.P.P.*, 1877, LXXI; PAC, RG 17, 129/13598, Edward Jenkins to Minister of Agriculture, 11 March 1875, RG 17, 1628, Alexander Mackenzie to Edward Jenkins, 23 March 1875; PAC, RG 76, 65/3115, 'Report of the Privy Council', 5 July 1875; PRO CO 42 753 (b-590), 'Report of the Privy Council', 4 January 1878; PRO, MH 19 vol. 6, 7425/78, W.R. Matheson, C.O. to Secretary LGB, 28 January 1878; A. Doyle to W. Salt, 11 February 1878; Hugh Avery to W.A. Matheson, 5 March 1878; vol. 6 64704/78, Lord Dufferin to M.E. Hicks-Beach, 15 August 1878; PAC, RG, 7 vol. 213 (II), M.E. Hicks-Beach to Lord Dufferin, 10 July 1878; PAC, RG 17, 229/23541, Report of the Privy Council, 8 August 1878; PRO, MH 19, vol. 6, 51572/78, W. Salt comments, n.d.; 64708/78, W. Salt's comments, 23 Sept. 1878; J. Lambert's comments, 1 Dec. 1878; Doyle's findings and Canadian reactions to his report are discussed in more detail in Chapter 3.

27. PAC, Immigration (RG 76) 66/3115, 22 December 1917.

28. Jones, *Outcast London*, pp. 280-1; Jones, 'Working class culture', pp. 467-8; Owen, *English Philanthropy*, p. 212.

29. Samuel Smith, 'Social Reform', *Nineteenth Century*, vol. 13 (May 1883), pp. 911-12; Smith, 'The industrial training of destitute children', *Contemporary Review*, vol. 47 (Jan. 1885), pp. 107-19.

30. *Night and Day* (Dec. 1884), p. 179.

31. *Our Waifs and Strays* (July 1883), p. 8.

32. Liverpool Sheltering Homes, *Annual Report* (1882), p.6; 'The Dangerous Classes', *Night and Day* (1879), p. 66.

33. Samuel Smith before the annual meeting of the National Children's Home, *Children's Advocate* (Sept. 1884), pp. 165-6.

34. *Christian*, 9 January 1891, p.4.

35. *Night and Day* (Dec. 1884), p. 180; (1887), pp. 59-60; Smith, 'Social Reform', p. 911.

36. 'Report of a Conference convened by the Central Emigration Society 20 March 1885', in PAC, RG 17, 443/48308, p. 12.

37. *Times*, 10 April 1883, 18 April 1883; Helen Bosanquet, *Social Work in London 1869-1912* (John Murray, London, 1914), pp. 319-20; Howard Association, *Report* (1883), p. 5; PRO, MH 19, vol. 20, 30243/83.

38. CO 384/145, Emigration-Canada No. 4525, Privy Council Report (Canada), 22 February 1883; PRO MH 19, vol. 7, 29889/83.

39. 13th Local Government Board Report, *Br. P.P.*, 1883-4; PAC, RG 17, 370/39748, A. Galt to Minister of Agriculture, 7 May 1883.

40. Some of these reports are printed in 15th L.G.B. Report, *Br.P.P.*, 1886; 16th L.G.B. Report, *Br.P.P.*, 1887; 18th L.G.B. Report, *Br.P.P.*, 1889. Others may be found in PRO, MH 19, vol. 11, Sections for 1889, 1892; and PAC, RG 76, 133/32405 (1896), 164/45794 (1897), 190/69918 (1898), 226/222479 (1902), 324/318481 (1904).

41. Emigration policy for pauper children is discussed in Parr, 'Home Children', ch. 2. Statistics on pauper emigration come from the Poor Law and Local Government Board Reports and PAC, RG 76, 66/3115.

42. See Chapter 8.

43. *Night and Day*, vol. 11 (1887), pp. 59-60; *Ups and Downs*, Sept. 1899, p. 4.

44. See Parr, 'Home Children', ch. 3.

45. Lillian M. Birt, *The Children's Homefinder* (James Nisbet, London, 1913); Clara Lowe, *God's Answers* (James Nisbet, London, 1882); George E. Morgan, *A Veteran in Revival* (Morgan and Scott, London, 1909), p. 150; *Christian*, 1 Dec. 1904, 29 Oct. 1874, 3 Feb. 1876, 9 Nov. 1876, 21 Dec. 1876, 25 April 1878, 2 Oct. 1879, 27 Sept. 1883, 22 Oct. 1885, 14 Oct. 1887, 24 Feb. 1888, 9 Jan. 1891.

46. *Christian*, 18 Feb. 1886; *Occasional Emigration Papers*, No. 12, Nov. 1872; Ernest T. Sandeen, *The Roots of Fundamentalism: British and American Fundamentalism 1880-1930* (University of Chicago Press, Chicago, 1970); Gillian Wagner, *Barnardo* (Weidenfeld and Nicolson, London, 1978), pp. 11-12, 39-40.

47. PAC, Lowe Papers (MG 29 B13, vol. 1), Dixon, General Correspondence, Annie Macpherson to William Dixon, 1 March 1872.

48. Lord Radstock to Barnardo, 20 August 1893, in S. Barnardo and J. Marchant, *Memoirs of Dr. Barnardo* (Hodder and Stoughton, London, 1907), P. 230; *Christian*, 16 May 1872, p. 5; 18 January 1883, p. 31; Doyle, 'Report' 1875, p. 23.

49. George Needham, *Street Arabs and Gutter Snipes* (Hubbard, Philadelphia, 1888), p. 288: Benjamin Waugh and H.E. Manning, 'The Child of the English Savage', *Contemporary Review*, vol. 49 (1886), p. 688; *Children's Advocate*, February 1883, pp. 28-9; John Herridge Batt, *Dr. Barnardo* (Partridge, London, 1904), p. 4; Southwark Rescue Society, *Boys and Girls*, July 1896, p. 2; Alan Trachtenberg, 'The Camera and Dr. Barnardo', *Aperture*, vol. 19, no. 4, p. 72.

50. J.J. Tobias, *Urban Crime in Victorian England* (Schocken, New York, 1967), pp. 85-7; Kathleen Heasman, *Evangelicals in Action* (Bles, London, 1962), p. 69; W.Y. Fullerton, *J.W.C. Fegan* (Marshall, London, 1930), p. 46.

51. *Times*, 31 March 1869; Needham, *Street Arabs*, p. 22; *Rescue*, January 1893, p. 1; Annie Macpherson, *The Little London Arabs* (p.p. London, 1870); T.J. Barnardo, *A City Waif, how I fished for and caught her* (J.F. Shaw, London, 1885); Barnardo, *The True Story of a Young Thief* (J.F. Shaw, London, 1885); *Night and Day*, vol. 1 (1878), pp. 21, 75.

52. PAC, RG 17, 81/7857, J.T. Middlemore to Wm. Dixon, 20 Feb. 1873; *Night and Day*, vol. 2 (1878), pp. 21, 75, 78, vol. 5 (1881), p. 120; *Our Waifs and Strays*, January 1883, pp. 4-5.

53. Heasman, *Evangelicals*, pp. 97-8; Pinchbeck and Hewitt, *Children*, II, pp. 523-38.

54. *Children's Advocate*, August 1871, p. 1; August 1872, pp. 2, 7; April 1872, p. 6; March 1883, pp. 73-5; *Christian*, 11 November 1887, pp. 1-2; William Bradfield, *Life of Thomas Bowman Stephenson* (Kelly, London, 1913), pp. 133-9; Church of England Waifs and Strays Society, *The First Forty Years* (p.p. London, 1922), pp. 2, 40; *Our Waifs and Strays*, vol. 2 (March 1885), p. 3; Church of England, *Handbook for Workers* (p.p., London, 1895), vol. 2, pp. 18-19.

55. Waugh and Manning, 'Child of the English Savage', p. 688.

56. Smith, 'Social Reform', p. 901; Liverpool Sheltering Homes, *Report* (1882), p. 9; *Christian*, 25 July 1878, p. 8.

57. K.S. Inglis, *The Churches and the Working Class in Victorian England* (Routledge and Kegan Paul, London, 1963), pp. 122, 139; J.G. Snead-Cox, *The Life of Cardinal Vaughan* (Herbert and Daniel, London, 1910), vol. 1, pp. 407, 412; vol. 2, p. 270.

58. From Manning's autobiographical notes, 1890, reprinted in Vincent Alan McClelland, *Cardinal Manning, His Public Life and Influence* (Oxford University Press, London, 1962), p. 10.

59. McClelland, pp. 10, 13, 22; Inglis, pp. 308-14; G.P. McEntee, *The Social Catholic Movement in Great Britain* (Macmillan, New York, 1927), p. 152.

60. McClelland, pp. 33, 38, 46; E. Bans and A.C. Thomas, *Catholic Child Emigration to Canada* (pp., Liverpool, 1904); John Bennett, 'The care of the poor', in *The English Catholics, 1850-1920* (Burns Oates, London, 1950), pp. 536-68; Edward St John, *Manning's Work for Children* (Sheed and Ward, London, 1929), pp. 27-31, 77, 106-9; *Christian*, 30 Dec. 1886, 22 Mar. 1889, 24 May 1889, 15 Nov. 1889, 20 Dec. 1889, 3 Jan. 1890, 10 Jan. 1890, 17 Jan. 1890; 23 May 1890.

61. Bennett, 'The care of the poor', pp. 561, 575; Snead-Cox, *Vaughan*, II, pp. 246-7; PAC RG 17, 376/40513, Thos. Seddon to Minister, 12 June 1883; 379/40886, R. Yates to J. Lowe, 14 August 1883; 373/40118, E. Hudson to Dept., 18 June 1883; RG 76, 119/22857, response to 1895 Branch circular.

62. St John, *Manning's Work*, p. 136; 'Report of the departmental committee appointed to consider Mr Rider Haggard's report on agricultural settlements in British colonies', *British Parliamentary Papers*, 1906, LXXVI, vol. 2 pp. 222, 262; PAC, RG 17, 516/56920, Thomas Seddon to John Ennis, 17 Nov. 1886; Table III-2, 'Proportion of Roman Catholics among Poor Law sponsored children and among all juvenile immigrants, 1898-1911', in Parr, 'Home Children', p. 97.

3 THE PROMISED LAND

Behold the Lord thy God hath set the land before thee: go up
and possess it...Moreover, your little ones shall go thither and
upon them will I give it, and they shall possess it. [1]

The majority of these children are the offal of the most
depraved characters in the cities of the Old Country...I say
this country young as it is should put its foot upon the impor-
tation into this country of that class of people. [2]

The belief that agricultural work is pure and purifying, that rural life is
innocent and peculiarly blessed by the gods, is very old. In the nineteenth century this ancient idealisation of agriculture, the association
of rural life with morality and city life with corruption, of agriculture
with nature's bounty and commerce with man's capacity to destroy,
gained new force in Britain. Industry replaced trade as the mainstay of
urban growth. The landscape and the physical health of workers were
blighted in industrial districts. The more ugly and congested cities
became, the more the countryside seemed the reservoir from which
civic, moral and spiritual virtue sprang; the more those seeking to solve
the problems of the cities turned to the countryside for solutions; the
more rural communities saw expanding cities as a threat to their way
of life. [3]

The two most publicised contemporary back-to-the-land proposals,
William Booth's farm colonies and Rider Haggard's agricultural settlements in the Dominions, were designed to rescue urban working-class
men and their families. From mid-century on, agricultural training
became a particularly important part of child-saving as well. The
origins of the practice were continental. In the wake of the revolutions
of 1848 two German Protestants, Pastor Fliedner of Kaiserwerth and
Johann-Heinrich Wichern of Hamburg, had begun to place destitute
and criminal youngsters in the countryside to separate them from the
city breeding grounds of atheism and radical politics. Many British
evangelicals engaged in city missions with children visited Kaiserwerth
and Wichern's Rauhe Haus. Annie Macpherson wrote often about the
lessons she had learned from them. Following the German model many
later Victorian institutions for children were built outside cities, often
with farms attached to provide fresh food and outdoor work to strengthen the characters and constitutions of urban children. Several rescue
homes which sponsored child emigrants also ran agricultural training
programmes in Britain. Quarrier's village at Bridge of Weir, the

National Children's Home at Bolton, Lancashire, and Fegan's institutions at Stony Stratford and Goudhurst are examples. [4]

A like-minded American, Charles Loring Brace, met Wichern in Germany in 1851, returned to found the New York Children's Aid Society in 1852, and began placing city youngsters in the midwestern states in 1854. Brace argued that 'the best of all asylums for the outcast child' was 'the farmer's home', that the family life of the countryside was 'God's reformatory'. His faith in rural virtue was so unquestioning that from 1854 until 1891 he sent 86,000 New York children west to places found for them through newspaper advertisements. Macpherson visited Brace's circle in New York in 1866. Rye inspected the midwestern part of the work in 1868. By 1870 both were placing British city children in Canadian country homes and echoing Brace's insistence that the 'cultivators of the soil' were the best parents for the children of the urban poor. [5]

British evangelical child-savers' notions about agricultural Canada, like Brace's descriptions of the rural midwest, were highly idealised, romantic, naturalist and thus easily integrated with popular contemporary analogies between children and young plants. Barnardo called Canada a 'fair garden-like country, yielding abundantly'. Macpherson and Birt liked to refer to emigration as 'spring transplanting'. Their colleague Samuel Smith saw children 'planted in a quiet farm' and saved from the towns by an enlivened interest in animals, flowers and gardens. [6] The sponsors of child emigration claimed that plentiful food and the 'grand Canadian air' made 'slender sickly saplings' thrive and transformed pallid city boys into 'brawny sun-burnt' lads as different from their former selves as 'chalk from cheese', that agricultural work 'depauperised', 'unworkhoused' and gave young people pride in 'honest industry'. [7]

The child emigrants' institutional guardians saw Canada as a frontier society unburdened by class distinctions where their youngsters would have free schooling and opportunities, despite their working-class parentage, to rise to the 'highest levels' of Canadian society. In 'a new country recently recovered from the forest' where everything was 'rough and ready', children were expected to learn a 'spirit of independence'. Barnardo, Stephenson and Macpherson emphasised particularly the equality within Canadian households, arguing that because servants shared table and sitting room with colonial employers their young wards would be treated as family, sharing 'with the farmers' own family work and food, school and play'. [8]

Most important, British advocates of child emigration described

Canadians as more pious, moral and temperate than Britons. Barnardo claimed never to have seen beer or wine in any Canadian home. Family worship was said to be more common in the Dominion than in the Mother Country, family life 'more wholesome, practical, kindly and humanising', more loving and more often a path to 'personal godliness'. More Canadians than Britons were said to practise their faith and be willing to shelter needy children in order to lead them to Christ. [9] Thus Canada seemed the ideal welcoming place for the outcast child.

Documentation on individual masters and mistresses is difficult to find. Applicants for boys and girls sent descriptions of their own families and the child they needed, together with a reference from their clergymen and a small fee to the home's representative. The homes did not interview prospective employers. Master and child typically encountered each other first on a railway station platform. Youngsters whose placements were unsuccessful were sometimes returned to the home, more often sent on direct by train to their next place. Employer's applications and references have rarely been preserved; the case records identify them only by name and postal address.

The British agencies admitted that most masters and mistresses wanted youngsters for the work they could do, but the financial terms upon which children were indentured varied considerably. Most rescue home children were placed on farms, although some girls worked in small towns and a small number of teenagers were found domestic situations in cities. We do know that the societies were not fastidious in their selection of situations, fundamentally because they believed rural homes were intrinsically good places for children, additionally because numbers of the young emigrants had physical limitations or difficulties in adjusting to Canada which restricted their options and their British guardians' latitude for choice.

The first distribution homes for young emigrants, Rye's Our Western Home at Niagara-on-the-Lake and Macpherson's Marchmont at Belleville, were established in two of Ontario's oldest agricultural districts, regions settled by British Loyalists after the American Revolution. This central Canadian focus remained a feature of the juvenile immigration movement throughout its history.

There were homes in other parts of the Dominion. Macpherson's sister, Louisa Birt, placed her parties in Nova Scotia before she acquired her home at Knowlton, Quebec, in 1877. J.T. Middlemore, after experimenting with a farm home near London, Ontario, moved his Canadian headquarters to Fairfax Station near Halifax. Several other smaller organisations also established homes in the Maritimes, probably because these locations minimised their transportation costs. On the other hand their proximity to homestead lands made western locations seem attractive. Barnardo ran two Manitoba branches, a city home in Winnipeg and a farm school at Russell. The London Children's Aid Society also placed youngsters from Winnipeg. The Roman Catholic dioceses found situations for some children through Manitoba and Saskatchewan orphanages.

But the largest emigration agencies placed most of their boys and girls in southern Ontario, western Quebec and Quebec's Eastern Townships, south of Montreal. Barnardo's main home for boys was in Toronto, that for girls in Peterborough. J.W.C. Fegan's Canadian branch was also in Toronto. Macpherson placed her youngsters from headquarters at Galt and then Stratford, leaving Marchmont to the care of Ellen Bilbrough and her husband Robert Wallace for Glasgow and Manchester children. The Methodist National Children's Home worked out of Hamilton. Quarrier built his Canadian branch, Fairknowe, at Brockville. The Church of England Waifs and Strays Society joined Birt in the Eastern Townships with homes for both girls and boys at Sherbrooke. Most Catholic children were placed out from institutions in Ottawa and Montreal.

Within central Canada some placement patterns can be seen. Catholics settled their wards in areas of western Quebec and eastern Ontario where the Catholic church was strong, priests were numerous and 'a more Catholic atmosphere' prevailed. Some youngsters were sent to French-Canadian families, a difficult predicament for English-speaking girls and boys, justified on the grounds that rural Quebeckers were particularly 'faithful and loyal to their religion, and steady and persevering in their work'. After 1904 the separate English diocesan committees consolidated their Canadian work through Ottawa, and placed most of their children with Irish-Canadian families in the mixed agricultural and lumbering districts of the Ottawa Valley.[10]   The Waifs and Strays Society preferred Anglican households for their children and found many Church of England parishioners among the gentry settlers of the Eastern Townships. Quarrier of Glasgow chose Brockville because the surrounding countryside had been settled by Scottish pioneers, and Scots cultural and religious influences remained strong in the region. The other Protestant homes would not place their wards with Catholic families but otherwise did not discriminate in their choice on the basis of denomination. Barnardo's, whose work was larger than any other, sent children throughout Ontario. Fegan, Rye, Macpherson and the National Children's Home served the

Figure 3.1: Location of Distributing Homes in Canada, 1869-1924

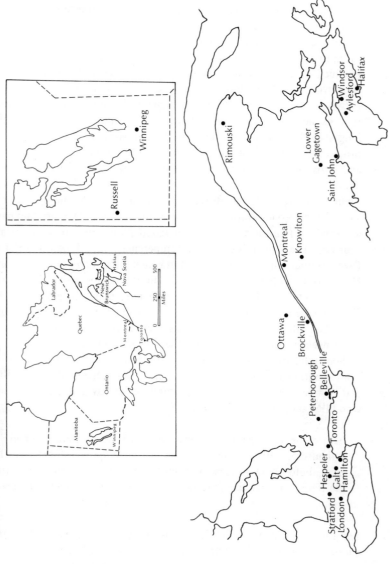

more immediate districts surrounding their distribution centres. [11]

Farmers in southern Ontario and western Quebec were at that time more strongly affected by rural-urban migrations and the declining size of farm families [12] than the Maritimes or the west and hence more troubled by agricultural labour shortages. Whereas Nova Scotia, New Brunswick and Prince Edward Island retained a surplus of rural workers between 1880 and 1920 [13] and immigrants intending to enter agriculture swelled the farm labour force of the prairie provinces, in the longest-settled rural districts of English-speaking central Canada proprietors claimed they had increasing difficulties finding hired boys and girls and in consequence especially welcomed the immigrant children. [14]

In many respects the British evangelicals' view of the agricultural society their young wards entered was correct. Rural Ontario did have a strong puritanical streak. Farm families did tend to be pious abstainers. The Woman's Christian Temperance Union began in 1874 in Owen Sound, Ontario, in a district in which many Barnardo, Fegan and Macpherson children were placed. In the 1890s more than forty thousand Ontario residents belonged to temperance organisations. [15] The churches were the most important institutions in rural communities. And although they were not as likely as the British child-savers to be evangelicals, Ontarians did take their religion seriously.

Social historians have since described rural central Canada after Confederation as a place not unlike that Macpherson, Barnardo, Birt and Samuel Smith portrayed, a world of 'sturdy independent men' who tilled their own hundred acres

before the opening of the West had introduced pure commercial agriculture, before modern power had been applied directly to the farm, before the process of suburbanisation had begun, but after the hardships and the crudities of the pioneer age had been overcome. [16]

Yet the arcadian image of the Canadian countryside was called into question soon after the child emigration movement began. The child-savers' own agricultural idealism caught them out. More clear-eyed British observers protested that the British homes substituted simple faith for the scrupulous supervision their young wards required. In Canada, what is more, critics who shared the evangelicals' belief that the city was evil and the countryside innocent concluded that youngsters raised in the worst British slums were a medical and moral threat to rural Canada.

The first extended debate over child emigration began after Andrew Doyle, the senior inspector deputed by the Local Government Board to investigate charges against Miss Rye, filed his report in February 1875. Doyle was sixty-five years old and had worked for twenty-six years to strengthen the workhouse system in districts under his charge. He opposed boarding-out in British households for pauper children and wanted even the children of widows admitted to workhouse schools on the ground that youngsters received better training and better supervision in institutions. He was a man who idealised order and suspected informality. [17]

And he found much to suspect in Canada. While acknowledging the good intentions of the British child-savers and their Canadian friends, Doyle noted that Miss Rye and Miss Macpherson were placing children in homes about which they knew little and then supervising them imperfectly or not at all. In visits to four hundred British boys and girls in Ontario and Quebec he claimed to have found an intolerable incidence of ill-treatment, overwork and physical abuse. He thought the programme worth continuing, especially for young children, but only if a well-regulated system replaced the well-meaning voluntarism which placed young people at risk.

He recommended for Canada the same kind of programme he would have established in a British parish: enlarged distributing homes in which children would stay for long periods after they arrived, with infirmaries and industrial training courses, institutions certified like industrial schools and periodically scrutinised like workhouses. He wanted each prospective situation vetted by an official familiar with the community, preferably a member of the local county council. He wanted youngsters once placed to be regularly visited by expert independent observers such as provincial district school inspectors. [18]

In England in 1875 these suggestions were not contentious. [19] Boarded-out children received that kind of training and protection in Britain. However, Doyle's report was condemned as not 'suitable to the social conditions or agreeable to the feelings and habits of thought of the people of Canada'. [20] Rural members of Parliament interpreted the recommendations as a plan to extend the English workhouse system into Canada. [21] The press described it as a plot by 'British Bumbledom' to leave the countryside 'pock-pitted with Beadles' and strewn with red tape. [22]

No workhouse system existed in the parts of Canada where the child immigrants were placed. Rural beliefs in voluntarism were strong.

Doyle implied that neighbourly concern would not sufficiently protect young strangers in the back concessions, and that class distinctions in the countryside led the community to treat pauper children differently from the children of proprietors. Both implications rankled.[23] Canadians believed, as the British child-savers did, that the neighbourly and democratic traditions of their agriculturalists were beyond reproach. The government offered to send members of the existing immigration field staff once to visit children sponsored by English parishes, but declined to do more, claiming that further regulation would trespass upon the integrity of Canadian families and be antithetical to Canadian 'social habits'.[24]

With the exception of the controversy surrounding Doyle's report, during the first three decades of its history there was no forceful or sustained opposition to the juvenile immigration movement in Canada. References to the failings of the philanthropists' policies frequently appeared in the press and before Parliament, but they were most often observations offered in passing as examples of weaknesses in broader immigration and child welfare policy or instances drawn briefly from the periphery of the commentator's concern. The pattern was an unfortunate one for the young people involved. Individual children bore the burden of heightened public censure, but the group as a whole did not benefit from the badly needed reforms that systematic well-articulated criticism might have brought.

In central Canadian rural areas two groups spoke out publicly against child immigration: county sheriffs and gaolers, and country doctors who were Dominion members of Parliament. They argued from a defensive position, sharing their constituents' fears that the rapid growth of the cities and the declining pre-eminence of agriculture threatened their political influence, their economic security, the vitality of their community institutions and their distinctive way of life. They suspected the urban pasts of children from British slums and feared for their effect on the healthy, peaceful countryside.

Physicians and the local constabulary raised similar concerns. Urban life, and slum life in particular, was described by both doctors and sheriffs as an insidiously degenerative physical condition. Peter McDonald, the Liberal member for Huron, argued in 1888 that children selected from 'districts where immorality, crime and syphilitic disease prevailed' would 'be tainted with the same poisons when brought' to Canada. William Thomas Trunks Williams, chief of police of London, Ontario, thought child immigrants from the slums went 'wrong through hereditary taint' which made them both physically weak and unable morally to resist temptation. [25]

The southwestern Ontario doctors arguing before the Commons Agriculture and Colonisation Committee in 1888 for strict medical screening of child immigrants condemned children most for carrying the 'virus of syphilis' or 'syphilitic tendencies' into the countryside. This emphasis is curious because social diseases were not at all common among the child immigrants, certainly by comparison with eye, skin and lung infections. But the accusation of syphilis allowed descriptions of the personally degenerative effects of a disease to be linked with condemnations of the promiscuity presumed to be characteristic of slums. The sense of contagion so vague and powerful made certain children who were presumed to be syphilitic the embodiment of everything rural people feared about the growing cities. The home children became harbingers of the physical degeneration, moral decay and family breakdown associated by threatened farmers with urban life and industrial work. [26]

For so apocalyptic a view of child immigration the members of Parliament recommended a very mild remedy: medical screening of prospective emigrants. Pre-sailing physicals were instituted in 1888, and attestations to the children's 'good health' were required at the port of landing. However, the health of rescue home children sent to Canada did not markedly improve. [27]

County sheriffs linked disease and criminality through a conception of class as conveniently loose as the physicians' notions of syphilis. Children came from a bad class, a criminal class, a lunatic class, a class 'imbued with crime since infancy'. The 'criminal nature' of the child immigrants was formed by their class, so that like syphilis criminality was partly the result of defective rearing by depraved parents and partly an inescapable genetic burden, a 'hereditary taint'. Thus the rural police who dealt with child immigrants expected little more in the way of moral reformation than country doctors expected of physical rehabilitation. Appearing before the Ontario Prison Reform Commission in 1891, nine years after large-scale child immigration began, the sheriffs of Wellington, Huron, Bruce, Middlesex and Peel counties were already convinced that a good deal of the drunkenness and prostitution in their districts was a result of the child immigrants' presence and predicted that the province's prisons and asylums would soon be overflowing with the refuse of the rescue homes. [28] These grim forecasts were set down in the public record and circulated widely through the provincial press, but the Prison Reform Commission, concerned largely with urban ills, recommended no specific remedies for this country disorder, and none was forthcoming for another seven years.

Few children were placed in urban areas, but the predicament of those who were so clearly revealed public policy weaknesses that they often figured prominently in city controversies, most frequently in discussions of abuses in the Dominion immigration system or provincial programmes to care for neglected and dependent young persons.

The most sustained urban opposition to juvenile immigration came from labour. During the 1880s through the newly formed Dominion Trades and Labor Congress skilled workingmen's organisations protested against the harmful effects of indigent immigration upon settled wage-earning families. Child immigration was upheld as a particularly damaging aspect of a generally unacceptable practice. The Dominion government encouraged immigration through subsidised trans-Atlantic fares, free railway transport inland and, in the case of the child immigrants and many similar organised parties, per capita payments to the recruiting agencies. To craftsmen plagued by intermittent unemployment, the bonus system seemed as redundant as the labourers it brought to Canadian cities. The rescue home children were cited as examples of how 'troublesome and destructive' such immigrants could be, and the homes' staffs held up as models of the deceitful and self-serving behaviour to be expected of such foreign agents. Representatives of organised labour alleged that British philanthropists brought out children who 'sported a fair growth of whiskers' and farm apprentices who showed a marked inclination for urban wage labour, and that their emigration programmes were motivated not by 'European benevolence' but by the shrewd calculation that such an imposition 'upon Canada's generosity' would relieve their own governments of unregenerate paupers.

Thus the categories of unwelcome immigrants coalesced. Each year between 1885 and 1890 the Dominion Trades and Labor Congress demanded that 'paupers, indigents and orphans from abroad' be denied government assistance and refused admission if imperial authorities should attempt 'to unload' them on Canadian shores. These protests had some effect. The assistance to child immigrants was not stopped, but as part of general reductions in immigration spending the Ontario system of railway passes was suspended in 1884 and Dominion passage assistance withdrawn in 1888.[29]

The labour movement was most concerned with child immigrants as competitors in the labour market. But in their opposition was a mingling of empathy. The rural apprentices' working conditions did reflect those of the factory system at its worst. Labour representatives grouped Ontario farmers with all capitalists and described the child immigrants as 'mere drudges', 'no better than slaves' until their indentures were completed. And as reports of ill-treatment multiplied, the plight of the children was used to condemn imperialism: 'the Great British nation so lost of all morals and Christianity[as to]lose the soul of a child for a few dollars'; the homes were claimed to be mere pawns of the great landowners of Britain who would rather 'get rid of their undesirable population than offer them justice at home'. [30] However, labour accounts of the child immigrants' experience strengthened other labour causes; they did not further the children's own cause.

Until 1896 Dominion officials were extremely reluctant to put any further barriers in the way of a work they judged 'the most valuable and least costly of all immigrations'. From 1893 agencies were required to demonstrate that they had an appropriate distribution home in Canada, but no stipulations concerning the quality of after-care were made. The most conspicuous cases of abuse were stopped. For example, W.J. Pady, who from 1889 to 1894 dumped poorly clothed young immigrants in Montreal and Winnipeg claiming as his reception home his son's small board shanty at Emerson, Manitoba, was prohibited from bringing more children to Canada. The required inspections of workhouse children in the first year after placement were duly made, but by temporary staff rather than seasoned immigration officials or by men unfamiliar with the areas through which they travelled. Visits were usually undertaken in winter when personnel could be spared and sleighing was easy, but when farm work too was slack and the conditions of children's employment could not accurately be judged. Reports on these inspections reached the Canadian branch agencies indirectly through the English Local Government Board and the English Boards of Guardians, so that pauper children were often left in unsuitable homes for a year or more after their removal was recommended. [31]

During the 1890s national attention focused increasingly upon settling the west. Wholesale condemnation of the immigration system was no longer a tenable position for responsible labour leaders. As an alternative in 1891 the Knights of Labor put forward a policy which conceded the need to assist western homesteaders while condemning aid that would increase competition between agricultural or industrial wage labourers. The deepening depression in the next four years made urban labour councils resist this suggestion. But by 1896 D.J. O'Donoghue and Alfred Jury of the Toronto Trades and Labor Council, seeking more labour influence in the rising Liberal Party, engineered a strategic compromise. The Dominion Trades and Labor Congress programme for 1896 was consistent with the priorities of the new Liberal administration under Wilfrid Laurier, recommending that 'a very liberal system of colonisation...be inaugurated' while condemning the 'character of immigrants encouraged and assisted' in the past. [32]

If skilled labouring men gained a useful ally in the new government, the child immigrants did not. Laurier's appointee to the Interior portfolio and the Immigration Branch, Clifford Sifton, formerly attorney general of Manitoba, found reasons in good business principles and sound accounting practice to share labour's criticism of assisted urban immigrants. He regarded the English city-dweller as wanting in skill and tenacity in the only role which would not displace working Canadians, that of agricultural proprietor, and hence sympathised with labour's characterisations of juvenile immigration as 'one of the most objectionable features of the system pursued by the late Government'. [33] Sifton appointed a labour representative, Alfred Jury, as Canadian immigration agent at Liverpool and commissioned a report from him on the workings of the British emigration homes. In 1900 a separate division of the Immigration Branch was established, responsible specifically for the annual inspection of English Local Government Board wards and generally for the oversight of the child immigration agencies. [34]

The fourth and most persuasive group of Canadian critics of child immigration consisted of urban middle-class reformers. Their arguments were not substantially different from those put forward by rural sheriffs and physicians and urban labour leaders. But the directors of city children's aid societies and houses of industry, their board members, businessmen such as the distiller William Gooderham, professors such as Goldwin Smith and the wealthy ladies of the National Council of Women, lodged their complaints on different grounds. Like labour leaders they viewed the child immigrants as unwelcome competitors, not so much for jobs as for good rural foster homes in which to place the growing numbers of neglected and dependent Canadian youngsters. As a matter of professional or social responsibility they questioned the quality of care British apprentices received, both from their masters and mistresses and from their institutional guardians, comparing British practice unfavourably with contemporary North American standards in child-saving. For propertied urban Canadians whose wealth was grounded in secondary manufacturing protected by the tariff, the children were illustrations of the grime, poverty and class conflict bred by free trade in Britain. As much as their rural contemporaries, urban observers saw the child immigrants as 'evil influences', the bearers of 'evil habits' acquired by birth or early nurture in a degenerate society and unlikely after emigration to be unlearned. [35]

The urban reformers had more influence than rural officials, however, and from 1896 onward they convinced successive provincial governments, which had jurisdiction over the welfare of immigrants once they arrived in Canada, to pass protective legislation for the British children. The model Act was passed in Ontario in 1897. It required that agencies settling children in the province maintain complete case records, visit youngsters yearly, screen children for 'vicious tendencies' and physical and mental infirmities, accept responsibility for wards who became public charges within three years of landing in the province and promptly investigate reports of ill treatment. Employers who found children unsuitable were obliged to return them to the agency rather than evicting them to fend for themselves, and school boards which had previously balked at admitting rescue home children into their classrooms were obliged to receive them. Manitoba and Quebec passed this legislation soon afterwards and similar protection was offered to British children in Nova Scotia and New Brunswick in 1905. [36]

To critics of the child migration movement these Acts seemed a step 'long needed and in the right direction', but they proved ineffective. No staff was hired specifically to enforce them. Provincial departments concerned with child welfare gave priority to the problems of native-born young people. The moribund Ontario legislation was in fact unobtrusively removed from the statute books during a revision two decades later. It passed away unlamented, indeed unnoticed.

The British rescue home children became symbols of everything Canadians feared most about newcomers to the Dominion. Although as individuals they gradually learned how to wear down their unwelcome differences and trade on their employers' need for labour, as a group they were never quite able to allay the rural suspicion of the cities and the class from which they came or the distrust of those mysterious absent parents who begot them and then assigned their care to others. Urban men and women who knew individual home children only at a distance reinterpreted rural reports in light of their own concerns. They gave those suspicions and particular complaints general policy significance, and urban elaborations in turn fed back into country fears. In the last three decades of the nineteenth century, as the child migration programme expanded, few of these criticisms helped the immigrant child. Rather, they made increasingly dubious the advantages of being a Briton and a child as an immigrant to Canada. They heightened the tensions of the apprenticeship years and left home children with a heavier burden to carry.

Notes

1. Deut. I, 21, 39.
2. Canada, House of Commons, *Journals* (1888), 'Report of the Agriculture and Colonisation Committee', pp. 10, 12-14.
3. Paul F. Johnston, 'In Praise of Husbandry', *Agricultural History*, vol. 11, (1937), pp. 80-95; Paul F. Johnston, 'Turnips and Romanticism', *Agricultural History*, vol. 12 (1938), pp. 233-4; Walter E. Houghton, *The Victorian Frame of Mind* (Yale, New Haven, 1957), pp. 77-81; Charlotte Erickson, 'Agricultural Myths of English Immigrants', in O.F. Ander (ed.), *In the Trek of the Immigrants* (Augustana College Library, Rock Island, 1964), pp. 60-70.
4. William Quarrier, 'The Cottage Principle', *Occasional Paper*, no. 1, (1870); Annie Macpherson, 'Winter Labour for Spring Transplanting', *Occasional Emigration Papers*, no. 12 (Nov. 1872), p. 1; Ivy Pinchbeck and Margaret Hewitt, *Children in English Society*, II (Routledge and Kegan Paul, London, 1973), pp. 525-6; Kathleen Heasman, *Evangelicals in Action* (Bles, London, 1962), pp. 96-9; 'Institution of deaconesses at Kaiserwerth', *English Woman's Journal*, vol. 3, no. 14 (1859), pp. 95-104; Alexander G. Scholes, *Education for Empire Settlement* (Longmans, London, 1932), p. 16.
5. R. Richard Wohl, 'The "Country Boy" myth and its place in American urban culture: the nineteenth-century contribution', *Perspectives in American History*, vol. 3 (1969), pp. 107-21; Charles Loring Brace, *The Dangerous Classes of New York and Twenty Years Work Among Them* (Wynkoop and Hallenbeck, New York, 1872), pp. 223-5; Miriam Z. Langsam, *Children West: A History of the Placing-Out System of the New York Children's Aid Society, 1852-1890* (State Historical Society of Wisconsin, Madison, 1964); *Times*, 29 March 1869; *Christian*, 4 August 1870; Canada, House of Commons, *Journals*, 'Immigration and Colonisation Committee Report', IX (1875), App. 4, p. 22; Pinchbeck and Hewitt, *Children*, II, p. 562; Lillian Birt, *The Children's Homefinder* (Nisbet, London, 1913), p. 18.
6. George Needham, *Street Arabs and Gutter Snipes* (Hubbard, Philadelphia, 1888), p. 285; 'The Colonies and our Waifs', *Night and Day*, vol. 9 (1885), p. 30; Liverpool Sheltering Homes, *Report* (1882), p. 9; Annie Macpherson, 'Winter Labour for Spring Transplanting'; 'Report of the Departmental Committee appointed by the Local Government Board to inquire into the existing systems for the maintenance and education of children under the charge of managers of district schools and Boards of Guardians in the Metropolis', *Br. P.P.* 1896, XLIII (Mundella Committee), vol. 2, p. 674.
7. Needham, *Street Arabs*, pp. 305, 345; Annie Macpherson, *Summer in Canada* (p.p., London, 1872), pp. 25, 27; *Christian*, 27 Oct. 1870, p. 11; 'Mundella Committee', p. 692; *Our Waifs and Strays*, Aug. 1887, p. 3; Annie Macpherson, *Canadian Homes for London Wanderers* (p.p., London, 1870), p. 7.
8. Macpherson, *Canadian Homes*, p. 34; 'Climbing the Ladder', National Children's Homes, *Report* (1888-9), p. 7; 'Emigration', *Children's Advocate*,

no. 22 (Oct. 1881), p. 148; 'The Canadian Mail', *Children's Advocate* (Nov. 1884), pp. 204-6; William Bradfield, *Life of Thomas Bowman Stephenson* (C.H. Kelly, London, 1913), p. 136.

9. S.L. Barnardo and James Marchant, *Memoirs of the late Dr. Barnardo* (Hodder and Stoughton, London, 1907) pp. 164-5; E. Bans and Arthur Chilton Thomas, *Catholic Child Emigration to Canada* (privately printed, Liverpool, 1904); Norman Hamilton Papers (private possession of Professor Graeme Patterson, Department of History, University of Toronto), E. Crisp to N. Hamilton, n.d., approx. April 1870; Bradfield, *Stephenson*, p. 135; *Christian*, 30 July 1874, 25 July 1878; 'Mundella Committee', vol. 2, pp. 668-70; PAC RG 17 527/58308, Samuel Smith before Henry Matthews, Home Secretary, 11 Feb. 1887; 'English Orphans in Canadian Homes' (1894), in PAC RG 76 119/22857.

10. Bans and Thomas, *Catholic Child*; PAC RG 76 285/252093, 112/22578; *Our Boys and Girls*, vol. 1, no. 1 (1896), p. 6; 'Report by the Departmental Committee appointed to consider Mr. Rider Haggard's report on agricultural settlements in British colonies', *Br. P.P.* 1906, LXXVI, vol. 2, p. 262; Edward St John, *Manning's Work for Children* (Sheed and Ward, London, 1929), p. 79.

11. These patterns are apparent in the agencies' choices of placements for the pauper children they undertook to settle in Canada for British Boards of Guardians. See PAC RG 76 133/32405 (1896), 164/45794 (1897), 190/69918 (1898), 266/222479 (1902), 324/318481 (1904), 434/652682 (1907).

12. Jacob Spelt, *Urban Development in South-Central Ontario* (McClelland and Stewart, Toronto, 1972), p. 154.

13. Douglas C.A. Curtis, 'Out-migration from New Brunswick, 1871-1921', unpublished paper; Kenneth Buckley, 'Historical estimates of internal migration in Canada', in E.F. Beach and J.C. Weldon (eds), *Conference on Statistics, 1960* (University of Toronto, Toronto, 1962).

14. The demand for child immigrant labour is discussed in more detail in Chapter 5.

15. Graeme Decarie, 'Something Old, Something New : Aspects of Prohibitionism in Ontario in the 1890s', in Donald Swainson (ed.), *Oliver Mowat's Ontario* (Macmillan, Toronto, 1972), p. 154; G.P. de T. Glazebrook, *Life in Ontario* (University of Toronto Press, Toronto, 1971), pp. 204-7.

16. A.R.M. Lower, *Canadians in the Making* (Longmans, Don Mills, 1958), pp. 327-8; see similarly, Glazebrook, *Life*, p. 173.

17. *Times*, 25 Dec. 1888; Thomas Mackay, *A History of the English Poor Law* (P.S. King, London, 1904), p. 382; PRO, MH 32, vol 20, 'Doyle Correspondence'.

18. 'Report to President of Local Government Board by Andrew Doyle, Local Government Board Inspector, as to the emigration of pauper children to Canada', *Br. P.P.* 1875, LXIII, pp. 18, 20, 23, 30, 32.

19. *Times*, 10 Mar. 1875; *Saturday Review*, reprinted in *Leader* (Toronto), 12 Apr. 1875.

20. PAC RG 76 65/3115, Privy Council Report, 5 July 1875; *Globe*, 4 May 1875.

21. Canada, House of Commons, *Journals*, 'Immigration and Colonisation Committee Report', vol. 9, app. 4, p. 10.

22. 'Immigration Report', 1875, pp. 10, 13-14, 16, 40; *Mail*, 9 July 1875; *Globe*, 19 Mar. 1875; 6 Apr. 1875, 4 May 1875; *Daily Leader*, 5 April 1875, 25 May 1875; PAC RG 76 65/3115, Privy Council Report, 5 July 1875.

23. 'Immigration Report', 1875, pp. 16, 40-3; Privy Council Report, 5 July 1875; E.A. Bilbrough, *British Children in Canadian Homes* (p.p.), Bellville, 1879), p. 19.

24. PAC RG 76 65/3115, Privy Council Report, 5 July 1875.

25. 'Prison Reform Commission', *Ontario Sessional Papers* (*OSP*) 1891, no. 18, p. 540; Canada, House of Commons, *Journals*, 1888, app. 5, 'Report of Agriculture and Colonisation Committee', p. 15.

26. Neil Sutherland, *Children in English Canadian Society* (University of Toronto Press, Toronto, 1976), pp. 28-33; 'Agriculture and Colonisation Committee', 1888, pp. 10-15; PAC RG 25 A-7 v. 498, John Colmer to the Undersecretary of State, Colonial Office, 28 June 1888; RG 17 395/42680, Maria Rye to John Lowe, 12 February 1884; *Night and Day*, 1887, p. 92; 'Special Report on the Immigration of British Children', *OSP*, 1898 (69), pp. 10-11; 'First Conference on Child-Saving', *OSP*, 1895 (29), p. 32.

27. PAC RG 17, v. 1566, John Carling to Charles Tupper, 9 July 1888; RG 76 51/2209, John Lowe to J.R. Hall, 14 May 1892; 65/3114, T.M. Daly to A.M. Burgess, 13 March 1895; 'Report on Agricultural Settlements in British Colonies', *Br. P.P.* 1906, LXXVI, p. 310.

28. 'Prison Reform Commission', *OSP* 1891 (18), pp. 498, 515, 540-1, 633, 637, 701.

29. PAC, Canadian Trades and Labor Congress, *Report of the Proceedings of the Annual Meeting*, 1883; 1886; 1887, pp. 28-9; 1888, pp. 19,23; PAC, Toronto Trades and Labor Council, Minutebooks, MG 28 I 44, v. 1, 21 October 1887, 6 January 1888, 2 March 1888, 16 March 1888, 20 April 1888, 1 June 1888, 20 July 1888; PAC RG 17 443/48382, Charles Tupper to John Pope, 4 June 1885; 593/67020, clippings from the *Toronto Mail*, 6 October 1888, including detailed report of the proceedings of the Trades and Labor Council meeting of 5 June 1888; 602/68070, G.W. Dower to the Secretary of State, 12 January 1889; 629/71381, Dower to Minister of Agriculture, 2 December 1889; 'Prison Reform Commission', *OSP* 1891 (18), p. 744; PAC RG 17, v. 1658, John Lowe to G.W. Dower, 25 February 1889.

30. PAC, Toronto Trade and Labor Council Minutebooks, 2 September 1887, 19 October 1888, 17 November 1893, 1 January 1894, 19 October 1894, 4 December 1891, 6 October 1893; Leslie E. Wismar (ed.), *Proceedings of the Canadian Labor Union Congresses: 1873-1877* (privately published, Montreal, 1951), report of the immigration committee for 1875; PAC, Dominion Trades and Labor Congress, *Report of the Proceedings of the Annual Meeting*, August 1890; 'Prison Reform Commission', *OSP*, 1891 (18), p. 744; 'First Conference on Child-saving', *OSP*, 1895 (29), p. 34.

31. PAC RG 76 81/7017, John Lowe to J.R. Hall, 4 July 1892; 65/3115, L. Periera to each immigration agent, 27 July 1893; 81/7017, Periera to John Colmer, 7 December 1893, and same to same, 24 January 1894; 64/2932, W.J. Pady file; 65/3115, Periera to Sergeant, General Manager of Grand Trunk Railroad, Manitoba, 12 January 1895; 96/12557, W. Boardman to L. Fortier, 19 April 1894 and Periera to Hoolahan and Doyle, 24 April 1896; 65/3115, A. Burgess to W. Scott, 30 July 1896; 30/674 L. Periera to Robert Wallace, 13 October 1893.

32. PAC, Dominion Trades and Labor Congress, *Report of the Proceedings of the Annual Meeting*, 1890-96; PAC, Toronto Trades and Labor Council Minutebooks, 17 April 1891, 5 February 1892, 6 October 1893, 19 October 1894; PAC RG 17 121/23624, 'Trades and Labor Council opposition to juvenile immigration'.

33. David John Hall, 'The Political Career of Clifford Sifton, 1896-1905', unpublished PhD dissertation, University of Toronto, 1973, pp. 187, 189, 608, 610, 619, 904-6; Note Sifton's comments on D.J. O'Donoghue to Clifford Sifton, 26 March 1897, PAC RG 76 121/23624.

34. PAC, Toronto Trades and Labor Council Minutebooks, 11 March 1897; PAC RG 76 119/22857, L. Periera to John Colmer, 31 January 1899; 28 L.G.B.,

Br. P.P., p. 10; PAC RG 76 65/3115, Joseph Chamberlain to Lord Aberdeen, 12 June 1896; A.M. Burgess to R.W. Scott, 30 July 1896; A.M. Burgess to Clifford Sifton, 29 January 1897.

35. Michael Bliss, *A Living Profit* (McClelland and Stewart, Toronto, 1974), pp. 107-8; Toronto Trades and Labor Council Minutebooks, 6 July 1894; 'Prison Reform Commission, 1891', 744, 687, 616, 41, 44, 729, 687, 215; 'First Conference on Child-saving, 1895', 33-4, 39-40; PAC RG 76 129/28735, Lady Aberdeen to A.M. Burgess, 18 April 1896, Burgess to Aberdeen, 2 May 1896, and Aberdeen to Burgess, 30 May 1896; PAC, Aberdeen Papers, Lady Aberdeen's Journals, v. 10, resolutions of the third annual meeting of the National Council of Women, 14 May 1896; v. 11, President's Memorandum on the business transacted at the Halifax meetings of the National Council of Women, 1897.

36. Ontario, *Statutes*, 1897, c. 53; Manitoba, 60 Victoria 1897, c. 1; Quebec, 62 Victoria 1899, c. 47; PAC RG 76 63/2869, Middlemore Home, *Report* (1905), pp. 18-20; Nova Scotia, *Revised Statutes*, 1900, c. 118; *Statutes*, 5 Edw. VII, 1905, c. 40; New Brunswick, *Statutes*, 5 Edw. VII, 1905, c. 13.

4 FAMILY STRATEGY AND PHILANTHROPIC ABDUCTION

C hrist
A lways
N ear
A lthough
D ear ones
A bsent [1]

The parents are my chief difficulty everywhere; so are the relatives generally. No doubt this is because I take from a very low class. [2]

The lights burned all night in the admission rooms behind Dr Barnardo's 'Ever-Open Doors'. Mr Quarrier's great scroll diaries stood open to record the troubles of the next petitioner. Dedicated mission workers waited in similar rescue homes throughout Great Britain to welcome children in need. But distressed families regarded those warm lights with fear. The open gates were attached to high walls. Family or friends rarely led their children there without anxiety.

Admission to a home separated children from the circle of family affection, placed them beyond the scrutiny and discipline of kin and demonstrated publicly that the family had failed where it ought least to fail — in maintaining the network of mutual help among relatives. When the institution raised the threat of emigration and separation from country as well as from kin and community, as it did in all the cases we shall consider here, even foster parents, step-parents and neighbours tried every alternative before they let the child go.

Thus more than half of the children who emigrated from Dr Barnardo's homes between 1882 and 1908 were admitted solely on economic grounds. In a further third of the cases, while a subsistence crisis brought the child to the home, the investigating worker found moral reasons for counselling the child's admission as well. Only 11 per cent of Barnardo's young immigrants were admitted on moral grounds alone. [3] In other emigration homes the proportion of admissions for economic reasons seems to have been higher, Barnardo having been unusually zealous in his pursuit of the child in 'moral peril'.

The homes' confidential case records contrast sharply with evangelicals' public rhetoric about the young emigrants' early lives. The men and women who took British children to Canada saw their young clients as solitary street arabs, deserted waifs. They described their work in urgent terms as child-saving, preventive and moral rescue or philanthropic abduction and presented a compelling and awesome portrait of neglect, abuse and decay. On the other hand the admission documents show strong family affection and family cohesion among the labouring poor, reveal parents more respectable than suspect and record more admissions on economic than on moral grounds. Why was there this tension between the families' descriptions of their own needs and the child-savers' accounts of the children's needs? The contradiction in views between savers and saved persists doggedly from before admission through emigration and apprenticeship – in fact through the rest of the young emigrants' lives.

Many of the models the evangelicals adduced were drawn from life, from the one admission in ten citing solely moral grounds. There were, for instance, Cinderellas among the child emigrants, ill-used, overworked or abandoned. Even in communities where high adult mortality rates made the stepchild/step-parent relationship common, disputes in second marriages tended to focus upon children from the first, and stepchildren were urged to precocious independence by step-parents' scolding or their own parent's death. Youngsters fled stepfathers who abused them and turned them out of the house, or they were dumped on the doorsteps of rescue homes by stepmothers enjoying a 'good rigg out' purchased with burial club benefits and bound for new fields. [4]

Some parents led such desperate lives that their offspring had terrible burdens to bear. Battered children of prostitutes were sent to the homes when they got 'to know a bit too much' or when their truancy or thievery or profanity were threatening to disturb the anonymity of the family profession. There were sons of mothers whose effigies had been burned at their doors by neighbours offended by the habits of the house. There were daughters who had fled with their mothers from town to town on the spur of community outrage. [5]

But as Reginald Bray, who lived and studied among the poor of London observed, deliberate cruelty to children was rare. 'Good folk' in their denunciations of improvidence and immorality often starkly misrepresented the families upon whom they heaped blame and worried needlessly about circumstances they viewed only hazily across the troublesome distance of rearing and income. [6]

Class variations in marriage practices are a striking case in point. Of the Barnardo child emigrants 29 per cent were born out of wedlock. Unmarried parents were not well regarded in any of the homes. Annie Macpherson turned all illegitimate children away lest admission be construed as assent to immorality. The evangelicals feared that a man and a woman who had avoided church and state injunctions to marry would evade their responsibilities to their dependent children as well. But as George Sims, a broad-minded London journalist, asserted in 1883, in many districts marriage was merely not 'fashionable', though 'so long as neither the hospital, the prison, nor the church yard effects a separation, the couples are fairly faithful, and look upon themselves as man and wife, with the usual marital obligations'. In other circumstances marriage was clearly not practical. A deserted spouse could not obtain divorce on those grounds alone. The cost of a dissolution, about £100, was in any event beyond the means of wage-earners. Even smaller sums might seem unwisely spent on ritual alone. Thus a clergyman's wife urging a sober, steady young couple with two children to give up a day's work to be 'churched' was reminded, 'You know, mum, I couldn't lose five bob just for the sake o' gettin' married.'[7]

Sims's cultural relativism was uncommon in reform circles. One 'deserving, hard-working and temperate' woman sent her children to an emigration home to avoid a Board of Guardians who chose to regard them as the illicit offspring of an immoral life even though father and mother had lived together for ten years and been separated only by death. A Southampton widow supporting ten plump healthy children through prostitution became entangled with the National Society for the Prevention of Cruelty to Children when she declared 'that she should continue her evil life' rather than 'enter the workhouse or part with her children'. Without parish support her circumstances worsened, and she later was obliged to surrender three of her children to Barnardo's.[8]

Children usually arrived at the homes not as the result of one crisis in their immediate family but only after a series of deaths, illnesses, quarrels and lost jobs left them finally with nowhere else to go. Thus, their admissions were typically prompted not by family neglect but by a breakdown in the kin tradition of mutual help under prolonged duress.[9] Grandparents' assistance grew more feeble as grandchildren grew older, more active and more in need of control. As their own families grew larger, aunts and uncles found themselves no longer able to shelter young cousins.[10]

One Barnardo girl was 6 when both her parents died. She went first to an aunt and later, through a season when work was hard to find, to the workhouse. There she caught the usual parish eye infections; the family worried, and a second aunt went to fetch her back. After six months this aunt herself became ill. No other relation could then take the child. It was only at this point, two years after her parents' deaths, that she went to Barnardo's and four months later she was sent to Canada, though her aunts requested that she stay in England and through the following year applied twice to have her back. [11]

Maggie McLennan lost her mother when she was an infant and later, in 1884, lost her father, a wood-sawyer. She stayed on with her step-mother in Glasgow for two years; then the stepmother died, and her stepmother's sister took Maggie and her brother, 'hoping to be able to carry them through'. This arrangement lasted a year. Then quarrels between the young people became so ferocious that for peace in the household and the children's own sake the brother went to lodgings while Maggie went to Quarrier's and thence in 1888 to work in eastern Ontario. [12]

Half of the Barnardo emigrants were the children of widows or widowers; one in six had lost both parents. [13] Day care was difficult for both men and women left to raise children alone. But widowers generally earned more and were thus better able to pay for help. They also were more likely to remarry. The widow's predicament was considerably heavier, and more widows than widowers were forced to turn to Barnardo, Birt, Quarrier and Macpherson for help.

The patrons and correspondents of the rescue homes thought domestic service the widow's only respectable refuge, but it was not an employment which provided much houseroom. What to do with the children? She might try boarding her youngsters with kin or with neighbours, but the wages of a domestic did not easily cover such costs. Gertrude K. went into Kenilworth workhouse with her mother and siblings in 1893. Two children died behind parish walls. In fear of losing more her mother secured an outside situation and boarded the surviving youngsters with her two sisters for a pound a month. Two years later at age 8 Gertrude entered Barnardo's because 'these disbursements left the mother very poor and her mistress complained of her shabby appearance and insisted that she must dress better or give up her situation'. 'The mother begged that Gertrude might not be sent out of the country as the two children she had left were her only comforts for all the troubles she had gone through.' Her plea went unheeded. Gertrude went to Canada in 1902 but was reunited with her mother in New York soon afterwards. [14]

Relief policies for widows were fickle at best. Mothers might lose outdoor relief if they left their husband's parish to take shelter with

kin, if friends helped with the babies while they looked for work, if
they found work, if their children were truant or if they were seen
regularly in the company of gentlemen friends. [15]   Some Boards of
Guardians argued that moral women could support two children. But
even by departing from moral work they usually could not. As the
Women's Industrial Council recognised in 1909, 'the bitter anomaly of
the widow's position [is that] as the head of the family she ought to be
able to earn a family wage: as a woman she can only gain the customary
price of individual subsistence'. The wage system and the relief system
forced widowed families to the emigration homes and left widowed
mothers behind alone. [16]

Instances of brutality and grievous neglect do appear in the case
records, but the families of the children who emigrated to Canada were
characterised more often by cohesion than by fragmentation. When
confronted with a crisis – bereavement, desertion, the loss of work or
health, the birth of an illegitimate child – parents usually found
relatives and friends to help them forestall the loss and shame of ceding
their youngsters to an institution.

The child-savers were not on the whole displeased with the role cast
for them by their clients as helper of last resort. Their scrupulous pre-
admission investigations of the family and employment circumstances
of grandparents, aunts, uncles and cousins and their highly selective
admission criteria were calculated to keep children with their own
families as long as a bare subsistence was available for them there.
Mission workers were convinced that by insisting upon responsible
parenthood they restrained self-indulgence and kept the poor from
'drifting deeper and deeper into the slough of dependence'. [17]   This
same line of reasoning led Boards of Guardians to post spurious emigration lists to frighten parents into reclaiming their young. [18]

The rescue homes often separated siblings, returning some to their
friends while admitting others for training and emigration. A widowed
father, a shoemaker in Belfast whose intemperance regularly kept him
from work, was refused admission for four of his seven boys and girls.
'The managers felt it unwise to relieve [him] of more than three of his
children, especially as the baby [was] not likely to live.' Quarrier's
agency split families, using offers of visits with admitted children as
inducements for good treatment of those left with kin. [19]

Most often, then, family members brought their children reluctantly
and shamefully to the homes, fearing the loss of separation; the homes
accepted children reluctantly too, fearing the parents would quickly

turn vicious without the responsibility of caring for children. There were, however, exceptions to this cautious pattern, exceptions that were dramatic, tragic and heroic. They were tales which Barnardo and his colleagues loved to tell, the stuff of good sermons, guarantees of full collection boxes, romantic transformations of dreary and discouraging tasks to inspire disheartened workers back into the fray. By dint of repetition they came to occupy a central place in the canon of child-saving. These were the tales of philanthropic abduction.

Among the Barnardo emigrants between 1882 and 1908, 6 per cent of boys and more than 8 per cent of girls were shipped to Canada illegally, without their parents' consent. A further 3 per cent of boys and 6 per cent of girls were sent under court order with the permission of the Home Secretary rather than that of their parents. [20] Such extreme measures were rare, though given the moral concern of the child-savers, predictably less rare for young girls than young boys. The pre-admission circumstances which filled the flamboyant rescue tales were also uncommon. Three per cent of boys and 13 per cent of girls were admitted on moral grounds from unstable family situations, [21] while 4 per cent of boys and 28 per cent of girls were admitted on moral grounds from the care of a guardian the admitting officer thought not respectable. [22] In these cases the emigration workers feared the child would be in jeopardy remaining with the family. When such parents refused to surrender the child some institutions resorted to forcible removal or philanthropic abduction; 15 per cent of Barnardo's girls and 9 per cent of his boys were sent to Canada under these uneasy terms. Philanthropic abduction posed a thorny legal problem and excited lively public debate.

Samuel Smith of the Liverpool Sheltering Homes argued that an 'overstrained regard for parental rights' could damage a youngster who might be saved by preventive emigration, preferably under court order at the parents' expense. Thomas Bowman Stephenson of the Wesleyan Methodist National Children's Homes advised emigration for youngsters whose parents showed only 'a sort of unintelligent and almost animal affection which thinks nothing and is prepared to sacrifice nothing for the permanent welfare of the child'. [23] But the most frank exponent of pre-emptive rescue was Thomas John Barnardo. In 1885 Barnardo claimed that there were forty-seven cases in his home's registers in which he had 'abducted children, in order to save them...in defiance of the law of the land, and by modes which [were] legally indefensible'. By 1896 W.T. Stead reported that the good doctor had been summoned to court eighty-eight times in custody cases for his self-proclaimed 'high-handed' methods. [24]   Two of these cases received particularly wide public attention between 1889 and 1891 and resulted in path-breaking legislation, the 1891 Custody of Children Act, to limit the previously incontestable right to guardianship of negligent parents.

In the spring of 1888 Mary Gossage, a widow, in a transaction during which several shillings changed hands, surrendered her eleven-year-old son, Harry, to two organ-grinders. Four months later these men deserted Harry in Folkestone. To save him from the workhouse, a local clergyman took the boy to Barnardo. The staff found his mother and secured her mark on a document recording that she and her relatives were unable to support the boy and that she wished 'that he should remain in this Home'. On 9 November the home's agreement form with the clause permitting emigration was sent to Mrs. Gossage. The next day 'a thoroughly well-to-do' Canadian named William Norton presented himself at the home and asked for a boy to adopt. Barnardo agreed to this request, and in order to avoid difficulties with 'impecunious or even vicious relatives' also consented to remain ignorant of the child's location in Canada. Norton selected Gossage and arranged to pick him up on 16 November. [25]

On 12 November a Catholic agency informed Barnardo that Mrs Gossage wished Harry to be transferred to St Vincent's Home, London. This letter enclosed ten shillings as a donation and commended Barnardo's great acts of charity. On 14 November the donation was acknowledged, but on 16 November the boy was sent off with Mr Norton. The correspondence between the mother's agents and the home continued, but not until 8 January 1889 was the boy's absence from England revealed. [26]

Mrs Gossage brought a writ of Habeas Corpus obliging Barnardo to return her son. She won this case, the court finding that Barnardo had no consent for Harry's emigration and had sent the boy away in order to evade restoration. Barnardo's appeal to this judgement was denied. Mrs Gossage did not, however, secure the return of her son. [27]

The second case concerned Martha Ann Tye, a girl of about 14, found in May 1888 by an official of Müller's Orphanage outside its gates in Bristol. Barnardo admitted the girl after discovering that the mother's lover, Francis Ward, had been convicted in April 1888 of assaulting Martha and that she had been sent by her mother into the streets to beg. [28] On 3 July the mother signed an agreement surrendering her daughter to Barnardo's care for two years, the agreement containing the customary emigration clause. [29] In September 1888, Mme Gertrude Romande, a Quebec-born widow, visited Barnardo's home, interested herself in Martha Tye and two other girls and agreed to return for them later. Margaret Ward married Francis Ward in September and on 14 December wrote to Barnardo asking that her daughter be returned through a friend who would call at the home. On the appointed day, 18 December, a woman with written authorisation from the parents arrived and was informed that Martha would not be surrendered to anyone but her mother. On 22 December Mme Romande called for the three girls and left with them, stating only that she would be in Cannes, France, about 20 February 1889. On the same day solicitors for the parents wrote to arrange for the return of the child. Not until the third reply to this request, dated 7 January 1889, was the fact that the child was 'not now in the United Kingdom' revealed. When the writ for Martha Ann's return was granted Mme Romande eluded searches on the continent and in Canada, and again the court suggested that Barnardo had sent the child away to evade lawful restoration to the parent. [30]

In neither of these cases did the judges or the press suggest that the parents were fit guardians. But in law even the signed agreement in the Tye case gave the home no grounds to defend the child against its parent. [31]

The 1889 Prevention of Cruelty to Children Act (52 and 53 Vic. C. 44, 5.5) allowed the courts to remove guardianship from parents committed for trial or convicted of wilful neglect. Appeals to the House of Lords in the Tye and Gossage cases brought a broadening of these stipulations in the 1891 Custody of Children Act to include instances in which guardians had allowed children to be brought up long enough at another person's expense 'to satisfy the Court that the parent was unmindful of his parental duties' (54 Vic. C. 3, s. 3). After 1894 youngsters whose custody had been transferred by magistrate's order could be sent abroad with the permission of the Home Secretary (Prevention of Cruelty to Children Act, 1894, s. 6, ss. 5). In 1896 the Mundella Committee argued that the latitude for emigration of the 'children of profligate parents' ought to be broadened. But by that time public sympathy for the now legitimate practitioners of preventive emigration was waning. Policy-makers argued for ever-open doors to adults' jails rather than children's institutions, for removing the cruelty rather than the children from families. [32] For the duration of the programme, however, agencies wishing to separate youngsters from unfit parents either met the cumbersome procedures of the courts and the Home Secretary or quietly continued to practise philanthropic abduction. Barnardo, Birt and Macpherson, at least, chose between these two procedures depending on the case.

Admission to a home removed all possibility of further free and casual contact between children and their kin. Most of the evangelical children's villages were placed some distance outside urban centres. Most city shelters were walled and guarded. Visiting privileges were granted selectively. Quarrier's issued visiting cards with which welcome callers might identify themselves at the gate. Special visiting facilities were maintained separately from the cottages where the children lived. All homes strictly controlled the times and intervals of visits. [33]

Emigration was thus merely part of a system of kinship management that began as soon as children were admitted to institutions. These controls applied to every girl and boy, not merely to the extreme moral rescue and philanthropic abduction cases. The guards and gates and censors were designed to prevent youngsters from being stolen away or urged to steal away by the more vicious of their old associates. As nineteenth-century 'evangelical clergymen almost always counselled those whom they converted to consort only with other serious people' to safeguard their conversion, [34] the revivalist emigration workers wanted their children to detach themselves totally from all previous connections. Their concern focused on the individual child. For each they wanted a fresh start in a new place in a new direction. Keeping the family at bay simplified and safeguarded the passage through moral and religious conversion. [35] It also, of course, caused pain.

Some part of that pain was inflicted unintentionally. Charitable homes were understaffed. In the struggle to clothe, wash, feed and train so many youngsters family links sometimes were not so much suppressed as lost sight of. One man remembered as the worst of his experience at Barnardo's in the 1940s a 'simple thoughtlessness...that made them take us apart, and just forget we were brothers, without so much as a word of explanation from them, or a good-bye from us'. [36]

The homes knew from sad experience that there was no room for such carelessness in the management of emigration plans. Families dreaded the event. The early nineteenth-century association of emigration with the transportation of criminal offenders to Australia lingered. Allowing a small boy or girl to go so far, alone and among strangers, shamed a family to the status of paupers. No visits were possible with children banished to the Dominions, and the hope of retrieving a youngster surrendered during a family emergency was forever extinguished. [37]

The Quarrier, Macpherson and Birt Homes made guardians' consent to emigration a precondition of admission. Parents were warned that once children entered the institution their 'ultimate disposal' would be decided upon by the home. Kin not satisfied with this state of affairs, for themselves or for their young relations, were told to leave with their offspring in tow. At Quarrier's, guardians who had agreed to emigration and then changed their minds were asked to reclaim their youngsters or else keep their peace.'[38]

Barnardo's position required considerably more delicate management. Neither admission nor emigration was made conditional upon parental consent, and children were rarely allowed to return to their parents. But with so many children constantly entering the home they were obliged to maintain a steady emigrant stream. There was always the chance that embarking youngsters who saw their relations might be dissuaded from the carefully instilled conviction that they would enjoy life in Canada. On the other hand those allowed no final visit might harbour the impression that they had been torn from loving kin. Neither kind of dissatisfaction helped the young emigrants deal with their new and difficult predicament.

The home therefore developed a selective notification policy for kin. [39] Some parents were informed well in advance of their children's departure and invited for a farewell visit to the home. On these occasions some were successful in postponing, if not preventing, emigration, others left resigned to the venture by the child-savers' insistence or their youngster's enthusiasm. [40] Before-sailing notices were sent for one-third of the girls at Barnardo's and to almost two-thirds of the parents described in the admission reports as respectable.

More often when kin were thought disreputable, to avoid confrontations and evade relatives' raiding attempts on travelling parties, Barnardo staff decided it 'best and quite simple just to take no notice' of letters enquiring about emigration plans. In 42 per cent of the cases of Barnardo girls, kin received only a printed after-sailing form posted a day after their daughter, niece or granddaughter left for Canada. The girls most effectively insulated from parental displeasure were the one-in-four whose relatives received no news at all. Of the children sent abroad before their parents were notified, 26 per cent had guardians the home's admission officer had described as 'not moral' or 'not respectable'. [41]

From the gates of securely walled British institutions, child-savers had been able to regulate carefully the contacts and reminders young wards might have of their previous lives. With emigration, their control in some ways strengthened. Grasping and battering relations could not reach across the broad Atlantic to reclaim their young. Preoccupied with new concerns, the children let their old attachments slip away. But not too far away. Memories, affections and loyalties lingered. The penny post, the prospect of winter passages paid with summer wages, crossings in cattle boats from Montreal or the soldiers' berths in the First World War kept the past alive. Freed from close scrutiny at the homes' gates, young emigrants and their kin were sometimes able if they chose to reach each other again. The tension continued between families' desires to keep together and the rescue workers' wish to keep them apart. Thus, emigration paradoxically weakened, even as it strengthened, the child-savers' hand. Seventy per cent of the parents of the Barnardo girls who received before-sailing notices remained in contact with their children; almost as high a proportion — 60 per cent — of parents who were sent after-sailing notices did so; and 22 per cent of parents who had been deprived of any knowledge of their children's emigration later succeeded in re-establishing communication with them. [42]

It would therefore have been unwise for emigration workers to let their guard down too far once youngsters were safely in Canada. Letters from home could be profoundly unsettling. Alternatively, they might blunt the homesickness that moved children to flight. Tampering with the mails thus became an important part of the Canadian work, at least in the Birt, Macpherson and Barnardo branches for which we have records.

'Write now. Write regularly'. 'Remember your important duty to keep mother advised of your progress and well-being', three-quarters of the Barnardo children of 'respectable' parentage were counselled. The English headquarters had a standard form with which to chastise poor correspondents for their neglect of filial responsibilities, [43] although the tenor of the painfully extracted responses may have been less than reassuring to anxious widows missing their boys.

James and Willie McGee were placed by Quarrier's near Dunsford, Ontario, in spring 1882. Their mother had not wanted them to emigrate, in fact the previous year had taken them from Bridge of Weir for a time, hoping to avoid losing them to Canada. In August

1883 James guiltily wrote home:

> Dear Mother,
>   I write you these few lines to let you know I am well. Hoping you are the same. I received your welcome letter on Tuesday the 8th. No one hindered me from writing; it was my own neglect. My missus often did ask me to write, but I wouldn't...I and William Thurston [another Quarrier emigrant] drew milk for a week and I saw Willie [the brother] every morning. He draws milk to the same factory, but I didn't ask him why he didn't write...You needn't be fretting about us not writing for it was our own neglect. Neither of us has been sick since we came. We are going to have a pic-nic. The crops are not very good this year, it has been such a wet spring. We have raised a lot of chickens this year. That is all at present. It is near dinner time and we have a big raspberry pudding for our dinner. I would like you to write soon and send me a songbook. James McGee. [44]

When the correspondence of British friends was suspect, it was censored. Dubious relations were given only the location of the agency in Canada. Old country addresses were removed and children instructed to reply through the homes. Offending passages — pleas to return or accounts of calamitous events at home — were deleted, and kin were warned that their correspondence must not be unsettling. [45] Messages from unregenerate troublemakers were intercepted entirely and rest to this day in the agency files. [46]

Young children remained none the wiser, which may have been for the best, especially when the homes' meddling merely speeded their separation from a past which offered them little but pain. For adolescents or young adults the policy is less easy to justify. Older emigrants who discovered deletions or suspected interceptions in their mail were furious. One such young woman, the illegitimate daughter of a domestic servant seduced by her master, had been removed at age 11 from the care of an aunt at the insistence of a lady frantic to save her from moral peril. The aunt was alleged to be a prostitute, and the letters she wrote to her niece were withheld. Eight years after the young emigrant arrived in Canada, now aged 21, she began to enquire of the home about her relations. Dissatisfied with the response of the Canadian staff, who claimed the aunt had not enquired of her for several years, she wrote to Barkingside headquarters insisting that, though the aunt 'was not what she ought to be', she wanted the address. Then, and to further enquiries until she was 28, the home replied only that the aunt was undesirable. She soon married and bitterly severed all connection with the home. [47]

Canadian conditions provided some natural barriers to correspondence. It was possible to move children up country and 'take care that the post-office was not too accessible'. Youngsters were short of pocket money for postage and had little quiet time to themselves for composition. Furthermore, rural masters and mistresses were likely to assume the worst about children's associates from old country slums and to discourage or interrupt contacts they thought would taint their young apprentices. [48]

To some extent siblings filled the gap left in young emigrants' lives by absent adult relations. A third of the Barnardo children had brothers or sisters in Canada. Almost always these youngsters maintained some contact. [49] Even as they frustrated queries after parents the homes fostered sibling attachments and tried to place newly arrived brothers and sisters near one another. [50] Children changed situations frequently as they grew older and although subsequent moves invariably took them to different regions, links between siblings often remained strong. In difficulty they sought each other out. Big brothers lobbied for better wages or better situations for little brothers. Sisters got rooms together when they could bear service no longer and looked for their first jobs in town. In hard times, when work failed or health failed or girls found themselves pregnant and alone, siblings offered shelter and sympathy. [51]

Ellen was 14 when she came with her 9-year-old sister Florence to Stratford, Ontario, in 1913 from the Hackney Union Schools. Florence was slow, and her first mistress was unkind. Ellen visited and complained, and on her urging a better place was found. By 1919 both sisters were in the west, Ellen on her own in Watson, Saskatchewan, Florence in Calgary with a family. When three boys raped Florence in a schoolyard and she became pregnant, she was despatched post-haste to the Salvation Army hostel at Saskatoon. There Ellen reclaimed her and saw her through term, vexed by the mistress, who 'don't know how to Mother her own children properly let alone somebody else's child', and hopeful that Florence had learned her lesson and 'will be a better girl for me'. [52]

But even this kind of solace was not always adequate. Fifty years after their arrival in Canada two brothers still remembered clearly their early longing to be home, the plans hatched to run away to the cattleboats at Montreal, the homesickness which afflicted them like a disease, sorely for a time and then slowly ebbing. [53] Youngsters who could not count on a loyal brother or sister to take the place of lost family in Canada kept alive much longer the fantasy of returning to Britain. Almost one-third of the Barnardo children did visit the Mother Country in their teens and twenties.[54] Many, once they had seen old friends or exhausted their Canadian savings, stayed in Britain, resuming the pattern of life of their parents. One of the most remarkable, Madge Gill, left her Toronto post as a nursemaid to settle again in East London, where she raised a family and through spiritualism and strange untutored paintings reviewed her troubled childhood. In all, 16 per cent of the Barnardo emigrants confounded the child-savers and made Britain their home as adults. [55]

The desire to return to family and childhood haunts easily over-powered the homes' exhortations to caution and thrift. A girl from Dover Union worked six years in Canada, first for a lawyer in Lindsay and then for a barrister in Colborne. Her brother and sister always wrote, but in 1912 when she was 19 and no longer bound to the home the satisfactions of life as a solitary servant knowing kin only through the mails began to pall. Dismissing warnings that Britain would seem a disappointment after 'her 'freedom and independence in Canada', she saved her wages and returned to her brother, a hairdresser's assistant in Ramsgate. She explained that she went only to have family near.

> My dear Miss Kennedy,
>   I am very sorry that you think I should stay hear but I have allways thought I would go back when I got enough money and I must go as it would be a very great disapointment to me and to my brother and sister that is interested in my welfare...dear Miss Kennedy I have nothing against Canada at all I think it is a lovely country and I would not return on enny other account lonely that I have a brother and sister and I want to see tham very badly and my brother said in the letter he wrote to me that there is lots of places I could get...my brother and sister have been wanting me to go home for some time...I must close for this time from one of your girls. [56]

Barnardo's, in exasperation, began in 1896 to escort winter excursions back to Britain for those who wished to visit friends, hoping at least to reduce the number of visiting youngsters unwillingly kept in Britain because they had lost or spent their return fare to Canada or had had it extracted from them by their kin. [57]

The alternative, of course, was family reunion in Canada. Barnardo's worked through the Salvation Army to bring out some widows and drew money from boys' wages to pay the fares of others. The Liverpool Sheltering Homes and its east London sister, the Home of Industry, made family resettlement a particular concern. Louisa Birt and Samuel Smith began their Liverpool work especially to care for the respectable kin of lost sailors, and their Canadian parties regularly included families travelling together and mothers working their way across to North America as matrons to join children already abroad. [58]

In preventive rescue cases the homes plainly disapproved of reunion of any sort. But such reunions did occur, despite the wages of apprentices, the broad Atlantic and many years' separation. For example, admission officers testified that John T. and his brother Willie were 'sturdy and healthy' when they came to Barnardo's but they refused to give credit for this to motherly care, describing Widow T. as 'feeble-minded and of loose morals', pregnant as an occupational hazard of 'working by night on the streets'. The boys seem to have dissented from these judgements. They came to Canada at ages 12 and 13, and by the time they were 19 and 20 had established themselves with their mother in a household in the tobacco belt at Tillsonburg, Ontario. One girl brought out the 'drunken and immoral' mother to whom the home had sent only an after-sailing notice, along with her two illegitimate half-brothers. Five brothers were separated on admission to the home. Three went to Canada, while their squabbling parents, a 'respectable baker' and his 'drunken, loose-living' wife, were left in charge of two others. The father was in ill health and may eventually have died. A decade later the mother and two brothers were at work in situations near Lindsay, Ontario, through the aid of the first emigrant there. [59]

Altogether an astonishingly high proportion of families separated by emigration kept track of one another. Ninety per cent of those Barnardo children who were urged to be dutiful correspondents were so, at least some of the time. One quarter of those emigrants counselled to sever their links with unworthy kin disobeyed. [60]

For many children emigration entirely closed the door on the past. Even for the best adjusted it was 'pretty hard sometimes to say you have no one nor don't know where you came from'. Emigrants raising their own families wrote with trepidation at middle life still puzzling over their 'vague memories' and anxious for the sake of their children to find out about their origins. They described 'terrible loneliness', the sense of exile, the shame of 'not being able to explain [their] reasons for being'. One man, described only as 'friendless', wrote to the Marchmont home:

> Now I am sure it would be of great benefit to me if it would not be too much trouble to you. If you would just answer my letter and let me know the name of my parents also if I have any brothers or sisters around the world, like myself or if I am all alone. Till you the truth I was left alone and never got any information at all. I should not like to be living hear alone and think I had a father and mother somewhere or a brother and sister of which I should be pleased to know...Hoping this is not too much to ask and that you will answer me as best you can.

Others chose to fill the yawning gap with fantasy, creating British brothers and sisters to satisfy enquiring Canadian friends. [61] The evangelical agencies prompting juvenile emigration recognised its powerful influence upon the links between children and their relations. They believed that in preventive or moral rescue cases no separation from kin could be too thorough and that in other cases qualities in Canadian life amply compensated for the losses emigrants incurred in leaving England.

In managing transatlantic communication family ties were circumscribed in order to expedite the child's moral and spiritual conversion. The degree of intervention between parent and child was more closely related to the homes' admission evaluation of the parent's character than to the immediate cause of the child's admission or to the stability of the child's pre-admission link with his or her guardian. In these circumstances, for good or ill, the emigrant child's understanding of the past was highly vulnerable to the homes' interpretation.

Much of the pain that home children felt as adults proceeded not from emigration itself but from leaving so young that the past was surrounded by a sense of mystery or of shame. A family income supplement, like the widow's allowance, would have kept many of those children admitted on economic grounds living in their own homes and saved mothers from resorting to prostitution. Better funding for charitable institutions would have reduced the pressure on limited facilities which made emigration essential to the expansion of the child-saver's work.

Only a change in the rescue workers' attitudes toward family life among the poor would have shaken the sturdiest underpinnings of the juvenile immigration policy, which equated poverty with negligence, intermittent unemployment with idleness, common-law union with viciousness. By the first decade of the present century that change was beginning. H.L.W. Lawson of the Emigrants' Information Office, testifying before the Departmental Committee on Agricultural Settlements in the Colonies in 1906, spoke for many others of his era:

> I maintain that even in cities, in most homes, there are good influences behind, and in most cases I should prefer to keep the parents and their family together and I think you would too. There is an evil psychological effect produced upon children who are separated from their parents. [62]

Notes

1. *Ups and Downs*, May 1927, p. 9.

2. 'Report on the maintenance and education of children in the Metropolis', *Br. P.P.* 1896, XLIII, vol. 2 (Mundella Committee), p. 360.

3. n = 900.

4. Paul de Rousiers observed such situations among the iron workers of Birmingham. See Paul de Rousiers, *The Labour Question in Britain* (Macmillan, London, 1896), p. 31; Liverpool 8, p. 13; Liverpool 4, pp. 7-10; Quarrier History 9, p. 255; Barnardo 433 B 7.01, 242 B 6.94, 364 B 7.99.

5. Barnardo 372 B 9.99, 269 B 6.95, 741 G 8.86.

6. Reginald Bray, 'Children of the Town', in Charles F.G. Masterman, *The Heart of the Empire* (T. Fisher Unwin, London, 1901), pp. 123-4.

7. George Sims, *How the Poor Live* (Chatto and Windus, London, 1883), pp. 24-5; Standish Meacham, *A Life Apart* (Thames and Hudson, London, 1977), pp. 63-4; Women's Cooperative Guild, *Working Women and Divorce* (David Nutt, London, 1911), pp. 4, 8; Charles Booth, *Life and Labour of the People of London* final volume, third series (Macmillan, London, 1902-4), pp. 41-2.

8. Barnardo 933 G 7.08.

9. Bray, 'Children of the Town', p. 124; Reginald A. Bray, 'The Boy and the Family', in E.J. Urwick (ed.), *Studies of Boy Life in Our Cities* (J.M. Dent and Co., London, 1904), pp. 80-1; Margaret Loane, *Next Street But One* (Edward Arnold, London, 1908), pp. 73-4; Alexander Paterson, *Across the Bridges* (Edward Arnold, London, 1912), p. 19; Booth, *Life and Labour*, IV, vol. 17, p. 42.

10. Quarrier History 9, p. 197; 32, p. 90; 29, p. 193; Barnardo 826 G 7.99, 832 G 9.99.

11. Barnardo 871 G 7.02.

12. Quarrier History 9, p. 36.

13. See Peter Laslett's evidence that historically children have been more likely to lose their fathers than their mothers and extremely unlikely, while children, to lose both parents. 'Parental deprivation in the past', *Family Life and Illicit Love in Earlier Generations* (Cambridge University Press, Cambridge, 1977), pp. 160-72.

14. Barnardo 824 G 7.99, 744 G 7.86, 868 G 5.02; Quarrier History 9, p. 96.

15. Barnardo 759 G 8.89, 738 G 9.85, 332 B 9.97, 338 B 4.98, 560 B 10.04, 628 B 5.06.

16. Barbara Hutchins, *Working Women and the Poor Law* (Women's Industrial Council, London, 1909), pp. 1-4; *Our Waifs and Strays*, April 1886, p. 4; Gareth Stedman Jones, *Outcast London* (Clarendon Press, Oxford, 1971), pp. 255, 275.

17. Samuel Smith, 'Social Reform', *The Nineteenth Century*, May 1883, p. 908; Helen Bosanquet, *Rich and Poor* (Macmillan, London, 1896), p. 72; National Society for the Prevention of Cruelty to Children, *Report* (1895-6), p. 55, (1898-9), p. 54; S.L. Barnardo and James Marchant, *Memoirs of Dr. Barnardo* (Hodder and Stoughton, London, 1907), pp. 376-9.

18. Barnardo 850 G 6.01, 915 G 7.04; 'Report on agricultural settlements in British Colonies', *Br. P.P.* 1906, LXXVI, vol. 2, p. 182; Alexander Michael Ross, 'The care and education of pauper children in England and Wales, 1834 to 1896', unpublished PhD thesis, University of London, 1955, pp. 160-1; Booth, *Life and Labour*, II, vol. 4, p. 365; F. Penrose Philp, 'Emigration to Canada of Poor Law Children', *Northern District Poor Law Conference* No. 5, 1903 (P.S. King, London, 1903), p. 209.

19. Quarrier History 9, p. 209; *Our Waifs and Strays*, April 1886, pp. 4-6; Barnardo 633 B 8.06.

20. n (boys) = 718; n (girls) = 259.

21. Pre-admission circumstances were coded as unstable when they included reports of desertion, repeated unsuccessful attempts at desertion or repeated movement among kin and/or foster parents. n (boys) = 620; n (girls) = 217.

22. n (boys) = 583; n (girls) = 218.

23. 'Emigration', *Children's Advocate*, October 1881, no. 22, p. 151; Smith, 'Social Reform', p. 908.

24. 'Is Philanthropic Abduction Ever Justified?', *Night and Day*, November 1885, pp. 149-52, reprinted in *The Christian*, 3 December 1885, pp. 9-10; *Night and Day*, 1902, pp. 63-4; 'Fulfil the law of Christ', *The Christian*, 8 December 1904, p. 21; 'Report on the maintenance and education of children in the Metropolis', *Br.P.P.* 1896, XLIII, vol. 2, pp. 359-60.

25. 'Sold to the Organ-Grinders', *Night and Day*, 1889, pp. 171-4; Barnardo Library, Queen vs. Barnardo, Judgement in the matter of Harry Gossage, an infant, in the High Court of Justice Queen's Bench Division, 30 November 1889, pp. 1-2.

26. *Night and Day*, 1889, pp. 175-8; Gossage Judgement, pp. 8-10.

27. Gossage Judgement, p. 8; Queen vs. Barnardo (Gossage), Appeal before Queen's Bench Division, *Law Reports* XXIV, 1890, pp. 283-303.

28. Barnardo Library, Queen vs. Barnardo (Tye), 'Copy Affidavits', Affidavit filed by Francis Wood, City of Bristol Assistant Magistrates Clerk, 21 January 1889, p. 19.

29. Barnardo Library, Queen vs. Barnardo (Tye) Interrogatories and answers of Dr T.J. Barnardo, Crown Side, 6 December 1889, pp. 1-2.

30. Tye Interrogatories, pp. 4, 6; 'Personal Notes', *Night and Day*, 1889, p. 84; Barnardo Library, Queen vs. Barnardo (Tye), Report of Master Mellor on the Interrogatories, 26 February 1890, p. 2; Barnardo Library, Queen vs.

Barnardo (Tye), Exhibits referred to in Affidavit, 17 June 1889, L1 to L5.

31. Robert Anderson, 'Morality by Act of Parliament', *Contemporary Review*, LIX, January 1891, pp. 80-1; W.T. Stead, 'Dr. Barnardo: Father of Nobody's Children', *Review of Reviews*, XIV, July 1896, p. 24; 'Children's rights against parental vice and cruelty', Howard Association, *Report*, 1890, p. 12.

32. Barnardo and Marchant, *Memoirs*, pp. 376-9; NSPCC, *Report* (1898-9), pp. 49, 57; (1895-6) p. 55; Bosanquet, *Rich and Poor*, pp. 72-3.

33. Glenbow-Alberta Institute, Wood Christian Home, Box 22, file 355, 'Orphan Homes of Scotland, Standing Orders', no. 24, pp. 8-9; Quarrier History 19, p. 51; 29, p. 153; PAC RG 76 32/724, Liverpool Sheltering Homes, printed brochure, c. 1893; Barnardo After Care Section, enclosure in girls' case history bundles for April 1903.

34. Ian Bradley, *Call to Seriousness* (Macmillan, New York, 1976), p. 70.

35. PAC RG 17 550/6566, Millie Sanderson to Department of Agriculture, 20 September 1887.

36. Leslie Thomas, *This Time Next Week* (Constable, London, 1964), pp. 57, 125.

37. Martha Vicinus, *The Industrial Muse* (Croom Helm, London, 1974), pp. 37-8; Edward Southwark, 'Introduction', to Alexander Paterson, *Across the Bridges* (Edward Arnold, 1912), p. 19.

38. 'Report on the maintenance and education of children in the Metropolis', *Br. P.P.* 1896, XLIII, vol. 2, testimony of Samuel Smith, p. 673; Liverpool Sheltering Homes admission form in Barnardo's After-Care section, 'Canada, General File'; Quarrier History 9, p. 234; Quarrier Emigration 5, pp. 31, 143, and 4, p. 35; exceptional cases in which parents' protests are ignored do exist. See Quarrier History 29, pp. 126, 146.

39. The breadth of this policy is difficult to determine. The type of notification employed is recorded in the girls' series for two-thirds of the emigrants in the sample (n = 182) but for only 26 of the 721 male sample members. It is unclear whether this results from a difference in record keeping, record preservation or a difference in policy.

40. Quarrier's account in *The Christian*, 17 July 1873, p. 8; Barnardo 803 G 9.97, 865 G 5.02, 920 G 9.04.

41. n = 182.

42. n = 190.

43. *Ups and Downs*, Sept. 1895, p. 4; Barnardo 907 G 5.04, 586 B 6.05; George Needham, *Street Arabs and Gutter Snipes* (Hubbard, Philadelphia, 1888), p. 292.

44. Quarrier Emigration 4, p. 35.

45. Marchmont 16, pp. 89, 93, 163; London and Stratford 27, p. 84; Liverpool 8, p. 97; *Night and Day*, April 1902, pp. 62-4; Barnardo 862 G 9.01, 905 G 5.04, 837 G 6.00, 972 G 7.07, 542 B 7.04, 79 B 3.88.

46. Barnardo 533 B 7.04, letter of November 1918 complaining of this policy in A.E. Struthers' Winnipeg office, 805 G 9.97, 831 G 9.99, 852 G 6.01, 750 G 10.86.

47. Barnardo 784 G 9.95, 805 G 9.97.

48. Interview with Sidney Chappel, Paisley, Ontario, 18 October 1975; *Night and Day*, April 1902, p. 64.

49. Percentage of Barnardo emigrants with emigrant siblings, 36 (n = 760); contact among siblings evident after emigration in 90.2 per cent of cases (n = 404).

50. Home's attitude toward contact with siblings (encourages) 58.5 per cent (n = 472); home's attitude toward contact with parents (encourages) 29.8

per cent (n = 404).

51. London and Stratford 7, p. 40; Quarrier Emigration 1, p. 316; Barnardo 819 G 9.98, 779 G 11.94, 758 G 9.88, 764 G 8.89, 426 B 7.01, 389 B 7.00, 255 B 11.94; on sibling placements by Fegan Homes see William Gooderham in *The Christian*, 20 January 1888, p. 7.

52. London and Stratford 32, p. 85.

53. Interview with William and Walter Knowles, Milton, Ontario, 4 October 1975.

54. Proportion visiting United Kingdom, 29%, n = 450.

55. n = 632.

56. Barnardo 954 G 8.06.

57. *Ups and Downs*, October 1897, pp. 4, 23; October 1900, p. 7; January 1900, p. 53; Barnardo 79 B 3.88, 459 B 7.02, 260 B 3.95.

58. Lillian Birt, *The Children's Homefinder* (Nisbet, London, 1913), pp. 205-9; *The Christian*, 8 Dec. 1904, p. 27; 'Report of the Department of Neglected and Dependent Children', *Ontario Sessional Papers* 1901, p. 86; PAC RG 17 90/8720, Robert Hagen, Moffat P.O., Halton Co., to Annie Macpherson, 4 July 1873; PAC RG 76 119/22857, Liverpool Sheltering Homes, 'English Orphans in Canadian Homes', c. 1894; Liverpool 8, p. 73; Barnardo 410 B 3.01.

59. Barnardo 798 G 6.97, 475 B 9.02, 485 B 3.03; note also Quarrier History 32, p. 197, mother repaying her son's passage money in order to terminate his indenture early and have him with her in Toronto.

60. n = 393.

61. Marchmont 16, p. 122, letter of 22 April 1918; Marchmont 16, p. 150; Barnardo Girls MT 7.04, IGC 9.01; *Loving and Serving*, March 1909, p. 8.

62. 'Report on agricultural settlements in British Colonies', *Br. P.P.* 1906, LXXVI, p. 234.

5 APPRENTICED OR ADOPTED

Doption, sir, is when folks gets a girl to work without wages. [1]

We are not so young and unsophisticated as to imagine that the farmers take our boys for love ... The primary object of the farmer in taking a boy is that his services be useful to him. [2]

It is not surprising that the child immigrants went to work when they came to Canada. They had worked when they were very young in their own families in Britain, and they had worked for neighbours, for distant relations and for their guardians in institutions. Naturally they would also work when older in Canadian households that sheltered them without claiming kin or community.

But if their work responsibilities were unexceptional for children of the labouring poor, and though their position as household rather than family members was a common one in their time, these British youngsters' status as aliens did set them apart. To be young, a servant and a stranger was to be unusually vulnerable, powerless and alone. Protecting such socially marginal children during the performance of the ordinary duties which made them welcome in Canadian homes required a legal, financial and administrative apparatus so conspicuous that it shattered all illusions that the young immigrant was like any other farm child. This dilemma confounded the best intentioned of child-savers, masters and mistresses and brought suffering to the most adaptable of children.

The experience of the rescue home children in Canada is well documented precisely because they found themselves as young immigrant workers, twice outsiders: beyond the help of kin and the solidarity of their own nationality. The detailed descriptions of their early years in Canada preserved in letters and visitors and inspectors' reports are enticing clues to that common yet anonymous stage of labouring life, apprenticeship, or 'service'. [3]

All Canadian farm children worked, and in Canada as in Britain the work load of children changed as they grew older and could bring more physical strength, dexterity and judgement to their tasks. An average 8-year-old boy began fetching wood and water for the house, gathering eggs from the hen-house, bringing cows in from the back fields, and feeding pigs. As he grew able he began to chop wood, hoe potatoes, dig turnips and help with the haying. In addition, he probably did some housework and child-care, especially when the adults of the household were away. In the west, boys 10 to 13 rode with the herds to keep browsing cattle from feasting on unfenced crops. In the east, boys 12 to 14 learned to milk and, like their western peers, to drive a gentle working team in the less demanding field tasks such as harrowing or raking. Boys 14 to 16 worked as men. They ploughed in spring and fall; in winter they threshed and husked corn and went to the bush to cut wood, to the traplines, or to the timber shanties of the Ottawa Valley or the road gangs and rail crews in the west. [4]

Girls became useful earlier, from age 6 minding members of the family younger than themselves. From 8 to 12 they also swept, did dishes, set the table and began to learn simple cookery. Although British-Canadian conventions generally kept them from the fields, these younger girls did some outside work, leading horses with loads of hay or hoeing and harvesting in market gardens. Like boys they worked hardest in spring and summer when the household chores were swollen by the laundry and large appetites of hired men. Hired girls aged 14 to 18 probably did more heavy housework, cleaning floors and grates and stoves, and washed more clothes than the other women of the house. They did simple cooking and as they grew more trusted by the family helped as well in the cash-earning dairy and poultry enterprises of the farm. [5]

Just as the sons and daughters of the British labouring poor, Canadian-born rural children grew up in families which functioned like firms. Children took from the enterprise in supervision, clothing and food and were expected to repay their debts through their labour. In the American mid-west near the Canadian regions where most rescue home children were placed, and in the agricultural hinterland of turn-of-the-century Hamilton, Ontario, adolescents owed their parents 'time'. They were expected to work for their father and mother or to surrender to them the proceeds of their wage labour until somewhere between ages of 18 and 20. This tradition reduced parents' need for hired help. Because older youngsters might be loaned to work without pay, it also earned parents the good will and esteem of their neighbours. Through the 'time' obligation parents were repaid for the burden of raising their young. [6]

Children's contributions to the farm were recognised at a further remove through inheritance. In agricultural Ontario wills often bequeathed the entire land holding undivided to one sibling but encumbered it with the responsibility of making 'equitable provisions' for brothers and sisters through mortgages of the current returns from the land.   The prospect of this share in the patrimony was distant and precarious. [7]

The inheritance system was not an appropriate means of payment for non-family members like the child immigrants. The family system left too much to chance in an arrangement which was a 'matter of business' and not a matter of love. [8] Inheritance functioned well when family solidarity kept relatives working together and in contact with each other until the cycle of payment and repayment was complete, and provided the bequest was fair-minded. The family system relied on parents' foresight to distribute work equitably among growing children with due concern for varying size, age and gifts and to portion out in just measure clothing, food, schooling, play, punishments and rewards.

Quite early British emigration agencies discovered that the family system of repayment was not suitable for their young wards. British children were not bound to Canadian households by family ties. To offer them informal familial adoption was deception. As household rather than family members British children needed the strict formality of an apprenticeship indenture. The child-savers were aware of the paradox in this position, that 'the idea of being bound has unpleasant suggestions, and the term falls harshly upon democratic ears'. [9] But formal apprenticeship indentures did more to define the rights of British immigrant children than to extinguish their liberties.

The indenture was clear and legally binding upon masters, mistresses, children and the homes. Through it a 'fair market value' for the youngster's services was struck and periodically revised so as to be neither too high to force children to work beyond their strength nor too low to pay them less than their worth. Both a master who did not pay on time and an apprentice who deserted before his term was up knew exactly what rule he transgressed and what consequences he might face in the courts. Good care would always be partly a matter of trust, but under indenture it could be encouraged through periodic scrutiny by a visitor whose loyalties lay with the child. Masters and mistresses who broke faith with the homes were thus liable to lose the labour of their charge. For the young stranger the formal apprenticeship system offered what the family system could not — fair payment, safeguards for fair treatment and resort to outside protection should fair play default.   These stipulations were necessary household substitutes for trust, solidarity and affection among kin. [10]

Nineteenth-century farm households often had working members who were not part of the family. In Peel County, Ontario, just west of

Toronto, between 1841 and 1871, 41 per cent of households included boarders, servants, labourers' apprentices or orphaned children. These household members were, like the child immigrants, usually young, single, landless and unskilled. Some worked just for the training, shelter and food. Adolescents placed by the Hamilton and Toronto Protestant Orphan Homes were paid small wages. In bordering American states, bound-out boys received board, clothing and schooling and some further perquisite at age 21, in the early nineteenth century a piece of land, later perhaps a horse saddle. Local hired girls worked by the week, young hired boys for monthly or yearly settlements. [11]

The uncommon feature among the child immigrants was that, unlike Canadian-born boarders, servants or apprentices, they did not stay with their own families or in an institution until they were 12 or 14 and near their adult strength. Nor did they begin their 'bound-out' time with the local child's rudimentary knowledge of the tasks at hand. The child immigrants' indentures therefore had to accommodate much learning and growth. Almost all the immigration homes did this by establishing stages in the indenture, each with separate apprenticeship articles. Barnardo referred to the three stages as 'boarding out', 'board, clothing and school' and 'wage'. Stephenson's National Children's Homes called them 'adoption', 'raising' and 'service'. In the Catholic agencies' terminology children were boarders, helpers, then workers. [12]

For each child 6 to 10 who was boarded out, the Catholic agencies and Barnardo's paid the Canadian master and mistress five dollars a month toward the child's keep. The boarding fees freed youngsters from large labour obligations and bought them time from the household for attendance at school. The other homes placed very young children, aged 3 to 8, in trial adoptions. When, as often happened, the family found they could not come to think of the British child as one of their own, the youngsters were moved on to the next stage in the agreements.

This was the barter phase. Children 11 to 14 were betwixt and between, not such burdens that their care need be paid for, not so useful as to be worthy of wages — just strong enough and experienced enough to earn their keep and some winter time off from chores for schooling. Most child immigrants — the Stephenson, Macpherson and Catholic agency children and the Barnardo girls — lived through this phase of their indentures with no substantial cash nexus to the Canadian household; they received only their board, clothing, some schooling and some pocket money in return for their labour, much like young family members.

From 14 on, young immigrants who were doing adult's work year-round with no time off for schooling contributed more to the household economy than they currently demanded in kind. Unlike their masters' sons and daughters, they had no outstanding obligations to the household. Their earliest debts had been extinguished by the boarding-out fees; their later wants had been satisfied in trade for their labour. At 14, the apprentices were therefore worthy of wages, and every agency but the Marchmont home at Belleville, Middlemore's near Halifax and Miss Rye's home at Niagara-on-the-Lake from this age on demanded cash payments for their young wards. For girls these were specified monthly, with yearly raises as their competence grew. For boys the term might be monthly or, as with the Barnardo and Stephenson youths, an accumulated sum of $100 to $200 paid at the indenture's end. These wages were the young woman's dowry and the young man's stake, their substitute for family support at the beginning of life as an independent adult. [13]

When they found their role was to provide young labourers rather than surrogates for loving kin the child-savers preferred apprenticeship to adoption. The stages of the indenture articles existed to limit the growing child's labour to his or her strength and secure for the grown child fair pay for work. By making the economic foundation of the relationship explicit, the formal contract offered the young worker legal protection from abuse.

What were the parallel constraints on the demand for these young immigrants' work? Why should the need for child labour have been so intense in certain parts of rural Canada in such comparatively recent times? What made a farmer or farm wife choose apprenticed labour over adult labour or family labour, accept certain terms of payment and reject others — in effect accept only children of certain ages, rejecting others?

The rural proportion of the Canadian population declined during the era of child immigration from 80 per cent in 1871 to 50 per cent in 1921. The impact of this decline was most marked in rural Ontario, where young men and women left their homes for better prospects in urban industry or the agricultural west. Arriving adult immigrants, following the example of the native-born, chose to stay in the cities or to work near available prairie homestead lands or, on reflection recanting their choice of Canada entirely, followed the well-worn path to more certain subsistence in the United States. While the exodus from rural Ontario progressed and wage rates rose, world wheat prices drifted hesitantly and then firmly downwards. Farmers who had mechanised to avoid high labour costs found their income lamentably unsteady but their annual capital commitments rising constantly. Switching from wheat monoculture to mixed farming, market gardening, dairy cattle or beef brought better returns but also entailed more onerous seasonal labour demands.

During this time of transition, characterised by high relative wage rates, new technologies and new crops, several distinctive niches for economically useful children occurred. The most conspicuous, that in frontier farming districts, was not new. In the late nineteenth century such regions of subsistence production still existed in eastern Canada in the shield district of Ontario — Muskoka, Haliburton and Nipissing — and in parts of western Quebec. Children had always been greater assets in new agricultural areas still outside the market system than in settled trading areas. As the staff at Barnardo's astutely reckoned:

> the money we had to offer for the maintenance of our young charges would go further and be more gratefully appreciated by the farmers in a recently settled region, where, amidst plenty of the necessaries of life, ready money is comparatively scarce, than in older settled localities, where so much more produce is raised that is convertible into cash. [14]

In economists' terms, frontier children were more valuable as producer goods and relatively cheap as consumer goods. Frontier families were too isolated to market much of their produce or buy much in town, so that the simple needs of children for food and shelter were satisfied from household produce, goods for which there was no other effective demand. The care of children cost families little because there were few market outlets for the farm wife's labour. In these struggling districts even the small cash payments for the care of boarded-out child immigrants were a 'great boon'. Children's labour at lighter chores freed adults for the initial onerous work clearing land and breaking soil, and for the heavy work in the fields that continued as long as stumps prevented the introduction of labour-saving machinery, as they did for one-third of Ontario farmers as late as 1880. Households which did not sell their produce for cash could not enter the market for hired labour and therefore searched for helpers who could not command wages. [15]

A different sort of child worker was sought in the newly forming mixed farming districts where fruit and vegetable production succeeded precarious specialisation in grain. There a demand arose for small nimble-fingered workers to plant and weed in May and to harvest berries and currants in June and peas, beans and tomatoes thereafter. Households facing these new labour requirements preferred children, especially child immigrants, who worked for their keep and could be sent away when they outgrew the limited demands of the work.[16]

Throughout the most settled parts of old Ontario, as farmers mechanised their field, dairy and house work, the labour demands of the farm contracted. The tasks were no longer so heavy that the services of fully grown hired men and women were needed full-time. Younger help who would work for smaller wages were recruited to substitute in the remnants of these roles.[17]

In western Canada the shift in southern Saskatchewan from grain growing to mixed wheat culture and beef cattle raising created a demand for herd boys. And in the newly opening Dauphin and Swan River districts of Manitoba homesteaders accepted untrained teenage labour when they could not afford to pay wages for men.

The needs of the immigrant children and of Canadian farmers and farm wives were brought together through market incentives. This is demonstrably so for the Barnardo boys and girls and probably the case for all children bound by their institutional guardians in multistaged indentures. The children's placements were determined by economic criteria. They were moved as their economic worth increased. They were not placed to meet the emotional needs of Canadian homes nor monitored by guardians who allowed emotional considerations to be paramount.

Thus child immigrants changed places often during the course of their indentures. Barnardo girls moved an average of four times during their first five years in Canada, Barnardo boys an average of three times.[18] The Macpherson, Birt and Marchmont patterns seem similar. There are clearly discernible patterns in these movements. Of the boys in the Barnardo sample who served boarding-out terms, three-quarters moved to a different county when the wage portion of their indenture began,[19] and 15 per cent were transferred from Ontario to the west. Of Barnardo's girl boarders 62 per cent changed counties for their initial barter placements;[20] 59 per cent of those who served barter terms moved yet again when they began to earn wages.[21]

When the agricultural productivity of these placement locations is examined it becomes clear that children were moved from poor farming districts to more prosperous regions as they grew older and more experienced, that is, as their market value as workers increased. The results are more striking for boys than for girls, agricultural productivity being a poorer indicator of effective demand for domestic than farm labour. But the trend across the indenture stages is statistically significant throughout, as Table 5.1 shows.

Table 5.1: Agricultural Productivity of Ontario and Rural Placement Locations for Barnardo Boys and Girls, 1882-1908

Sex	Indenture stage		
	Boarding out		Wage
Boys $\overline{X}$	22.3		61.2
s	17.9		50.6
n	146		505
	Boarding out	Barter/Board, clothing and school	Wage
Girls $\overline{X}$	39.5	47.8	52.0
s	35.9	42.1	47.3
n	58	138	189

Note: The difference between the mean agricultural productivity of boys boarding out and wage placements is significant at 5 per cent, t= 9.13, d.f.= 649. For girls this difference is also significant, t= 1.7, d.f.= 245.

The Barnardo records offer no information about the income of children's employers, but either post offices or county locations are always recorded. An estimate of the prosperity of individual agricultural employers has been drawn by inference from the agricultural productivity of the county in which they held land. No suitable contemporary ranking for this purpose was found; instead the derivation from the Canada Land Inventory Soil Capability results calculated by Reeds has been used. The CLI classes soils by their suitability for the production of common field crops with respect to climate, drainage and soil conditions. The weighted average for the agricultural prosperity of employers in each stage of the indenture was created using the formula

$$\overline{X} = \left[\Sigma\left[CLI\eta_{\hat{\imath}}\right]\right]/\Sigma\,\eta_{\hat{\imath}}$$

where $\overline{X}$ is the average agricultural productivity of placement locations/ indenture stage, n is the number of immigrants/indenture stage/county, and CLI is the percentage of land in soil capability classes 1 to 3 as calculated by Reeds. [22]
Source: Canada Land Inventory Soil Capability.

Children were moved in response to competitive demands for the services they could supply. They grew up in several households, incidentally because quarrels or household crises arose, but systematically because successive households outbid each other for the command of their labour.

The indentures brought the supply and the demand for child

Figure 5.1: Southern Ontario, Agricultural Productivity as Measured by Proportion of County Land Inventory Soil Capability Classes 1 to 3

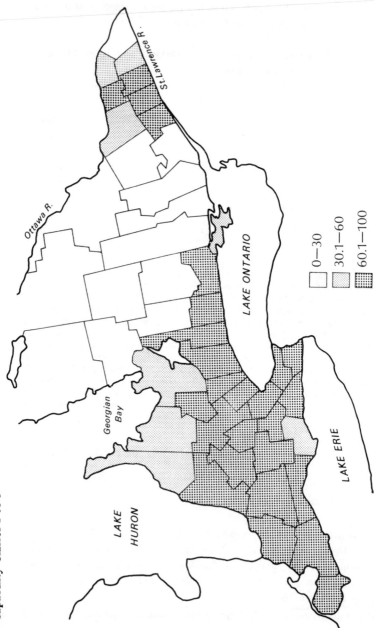

0—30

30.1—60

60.1—100

Source: Canada Land Inventory. *Land Use Capability for Agriculture* (1970).

immigrants' labour together in an economically rational way, but as arbiters of their social relationships within Canadian households the apprenticeship articles served the rescue home children less well. These structures, developed to protect British youngsters from exploitation and to get for them fair material compensation, did so at some social and psychological cost. The immigrant child thus protected was thereby also more starkly isolated, cast in a distinctive status, as a servant of the household separate from the siblings of the family. The few rescue homes that did not use indentures pandered to a vain illusion of equality between the newcomers and the native-born. They left their young wards in an ambivalent position in Canadian households, which occasionally might turn to their advantage but usually made them into drudges. The apprenticeship articles removed this ambivalence but in the process destroyed the illusion, the warm and welcome illusion of being 'like family', which every child immigrant must have at some time entertained.

The separation between servants and siblings was of course established in blood-ties and expanded through nationality, but it was elaborated upon for the apprentices in several other ways. The children of the family, like Topsy, 'just growed'. For the servants of the household, however, growing older meant moving on, moving away from the attachments of the household and the schoolroom, away from familiar surroundings, perhaps away from immigrant siblings who in the early days in Canada had been set to work nearby. There was 'grief and trouble' in the 'inevitable parting', one worker wrote of young children leaving their boarding-out homes, but 'it cannot be helped; the fledglings must leave their nest'.²³

At each stage in the child's maturation the pressure to leave the nest arose in a different way. Struggling families in marginal farm districts sent back their 11-year-old boarders and sent for new 8-year-olds from the Catholic homes and from Barnardo's. They needed the cash that a young child's care brought, and they did not have work for a child without pay. Families who could afford to give youngsters their keep and had work to be done took newly arrived school children from Macpherson or Fegan, Stephenson, Quarrier, Barnardo or Birt, but when the children became school-leavers and worthy of pay the families wrote to the homes to send them 'another, a year or two younger'. Or perhaps one of the family's own children left school and took the departing immigrant's place to save the parents the unwelcome drain on cash income entailed by wages. Adolescents then moved on to masters and mistresses who had cash to pay for their work. For boys from the Stephenson and Barnardo homes such later situations might be comparatively stable. The agreements for these young men specified that they were to stay until they were 18 with one master and then receive a lump-sum payment. But for girls from these homes and for youngsters from all others that drafted indentures the terms of wage agreements were less long and subject to revision. In consequence such placements were also often shorter, and hired boys and girls were regularly subject to recall. Some youngsters stayed in one place through their teens, but more likely at some time their master, when asked to grant a raise, took stock of his work load and decided that he no longer needed such high-priced help. [24]

Children were obliged to move on to new situations not only because the homes demanded terms their masters would not meet but also because their employers demanded work they would not or could not do. Displeased masters were within their rights to return apprentices immediately. Of an 11-year-old boy from Kilburn in London who had three places — one in Ontario and two in Manitoba — in his first year in Canada, his irritated guardian complained: 'he seems more like a child of six with no idea of anything but play'. Even youngsters from the Marchmont home at Belleville, which placed children casually and asked for no terms, were regularly returned as 'too small'. The records of all the rescue homes are peppered with such explanations for young people's return: 'no use to me', 'no good', 'not strong enough', 'too slow', 'too careless', 'not competent', 'not quick'. 'Working additions' who were physically, mentally or temperamentally unsuited for their work were promptly and in rapid succession sent on their way. [25]

But the young apprentices who might be sent on their way by their masters or mistresses or summoned away by their guardians from the homes could not of their own accord be on their way. They were bound. Under the terms of the Masters and Servants Act they could not leave without just cause until their indenture was complete at age 18. Runaway teenagers who were servants committed the offence of desertion, for which they were liable to jail or a fine. Such prosecutions were not common. [26] But restless young men and women were made clearly aware of the boundaries between genuine grievance and the daily irritations their status obliged them to bear. Demands to do dirty work or verbal abuse from the master's young kin were not just cause for flight. [27] 'I have received your letter telling me what is an old, old story to us here', a Toronto home's agent wrote to a 16-year-old who had walked out on his master in the midst of the harvest claiming ill-treatment:

I do not mean a story in the sense of being untrue, but hardly a week passes in our experience that we do not have to deal with exactly the same set of circumstances. The weather is hot, the flies are tiresome, the farmer is perhaps very keen on getting in some hay or some grain from the field and is driving himself and everybody else in the effort to do so. People's nerves and tempers get upset, some hasty expression is used, one word leads to another, the boy tells the farmer to do his work for himself and the farmer tells him to get the Hades out of it. Perhaps a blow is struck, and in the end the boy marches off claiming that he was abused and ordered to leave, and that he has a right to his wages, while the farmer claims that he was insolent and refused to work, that he had no excuse for leaving.

With sympathy and firmness the boy was informed by the agent that his desertion extinguished his claim through the courts, and was advised to return to his master, to see out his term, to 'keep a civil tongue' in his head and 'remember that if you wish to get on in the world, you must learn to give willing and faithful service to the employer with whom you have hired, who ever he may be'. [28] The indenture that secured a young child a place chafed as the teenager saw the other hired boys and girls of the neighbourhood move on independently when they disliked their employers or when opportunity offered.

The most emphatic way in which the indenture separated servants from siblings was the formal specification of what was owing them in cash or in kind. Families that sent for immigrant children solely for their labour might then provision them only with what the letter of the indenture required. Their great distance from the guardians in the homes and the infrequency of promised annual inspections invited less scrupulous masters to swindle their young charges in various and sundry ways the children felt but the home might never detect. One boarder got slippers for going to school while the children of the family got shoes and rubbers for winter. Macpherson's newly arrived children bound-out around Stratford, Ontario, in return for 'board, clothing and pocket money' kept being sent back when their clothes were worn out. Boys shivered through winters inadequately clad because heavy clothing cost more than masters counted their young hands' services worth. And sad Cinderellas who slept above the kitchen and ate apart when there were guests were clothed as the indenture required, but in dresses worn out by many wearings and wearers. [29]

The payment of wages particularly rankled — no other child in the household was paid — and negotiations for raises cost youngsters much. The rescue home visitor began by pointing out their growing ward's strengths, while master and mistress rebutted with litanies of weaknesses. The ensuing debate over faults in character, in strength and in training disturbed the slight security of the child's place by the hearth. The master then decided that on close observation the boy, who was a willing and useful lad through the busy harvest season, seemed too light for the work. Girls heard themselves described as ill-tempered, lazy and irresponsible by their mistresses while rescue home visitors praised their baking, decried their long hours and declared them 'indispensable' to the employers. The fight over the children's services continued by fair means or foul. Faced with the spring recall to secure better wages of a 17-year-old whose myriad failings she faithfully reported, one mistress replied:

> Now what I want to say is this, that I do not feel like keeping a girl all winter when there is not much to do and then giving her up this time of the year. I have taught her to do many things which is useful to me and do not approve of taking girls just to teach them and let some one else have the benefit. If I had thought of her leaving me now I would not have kept her through the winter when she never went to milk or do anything outside the door. [30]

Youngsters not claimed to be seriously flawed might emerge improbably in the midst of the bidding as one of the family's own. 'As to the statement of her wages', wrote a woman from central Ontario who had lost the maid to whom she gave neither good clothing nor place at table,

> we consider H. somewhat in our debt as we never agreed to any stated wages and beg to state that any household duties performed by her have been more than amply repaid not only by her clothing, gifts and spending money but by family privilages extended to her. Trusting the advantages of her future home will be as benificial as the one she is leaving. [31]

During this debate over their capacities under the threat of another move to another new place, young people underwent considerable stress, especially when the claim of family status was raised. There were child immigrants who quite desperately and understandably wanted continuity at all costs, who clung to certain hard work and abuse when urged to take a better situation, satisfied with low wages so long as their place in one houshold was secure. [32] For them the stability and the apparent family status a long association implied were enough. A girl of 17 from Lambeth Union Schools, in a farm home four years with a 'pale and frail' mistress, four children and inside and outside chores to do without help, wrote angrily to Stratford supporting her employer when the home's staff suggested in 1918 that she earn more than twelve dollars a month.

> I don't earn twelve dollars for the work is not in the house eight dollars is all I think I could stand just now anywhere. You may be sure if I thought I was overworked for nothing you would have know long before this for I have brains enough to stick up for myself . . . I really think that I would rather stay am quite contented getting along nicely if things were only settled. I will now close hoping to receive pleasant news . . . am I forced to go if I don't wish.

Immediate needs for security asserted themselves above the home's concern that their wards have savings against the day when their adolescent apprenticeship ended and independent adulthood began. In this case, when the visitors held firm they won the girl her fair wages without losing her her place. [33]

Youngsters who urged the travelling visitor to acknowledge their privileges in trade for part wages — time to read, to play the piano, for trips to town or day outings with friends — were pleading not only for substitution of time off for payment. They were also seeking the replacement of one status with another. They were accepting their employers' affective claim of their being 'as family' and rejecting the rescue homes' economic claims which would drive them from their actual home. [34]

In allying with their masters some children were acknowledging the special place they had actually been granted. But it seems more likely from their later letters and recollections that the apprentices willing to 'work for kindness' were hoping in vain to win a place in family affections they had to that time not been allowed. Another girl from Lambeth Union, this one a ward of Barnardo, stayed eleven years on one Hastings farm, refusing more than three dollars a month wages so that her mistress would have funds for the young children's schooling. In

1929 a widow with four children, she looked back with bitterness on the family which in crisis had closed ranks and left her, the servant, outside and alone. [35]

In refusing wages or raises or the offer of a new and better place, in siding with master or mistress in opposition to the rescue homes, the young apprentices gave their fantasies full flight. They were rejecting the swift reckoning of debts their indenture required as a matter of business and seeking instead the trust, sharing and solidarity they knew to characterise family concerns. They wanted what experienced child-savers knew would rarely, truly be theirs; status as family, as siblings not servants, adoptees not apprentices. Yet it was not their indentures or wages but their social circumstances that relegated them securely to a place outside the family. By birth, by background, by speech, by the physical and mental legacies of their early deprivations, the child immigrants were different from Canadian children, too different to plausibly claim kin.

Notes

1. 'Report of the President of the Local Government Board by Andrew Doyle, Local Government Board Inspector on the Emigration of Pauper Children to Canada', *British Parliamentary Papers* 1875, LXIII, p. 12.

2. *Ups and Downs*, Apr. 1900, p. 7.

3. Recent studies have discussed this stage of the life cycle under the rubric of semi-dependency. Michael Katz and Ian Davey, 'Youth and early industrialisation in a Canadian city', in John Demos and Saraine Spence Boocock, *Turning Points: Historical and Sociological Essays on the Family* (University of Chicago Press, Chicago, 1978), p. 88; Michael Katz, *The People of Hamilton, Canada West* (Harvard University Press, Cambridge, Mass., 1975) ch. 5; Harvey J. Graff, 'Patterns of Dependency and Child Development in the Mid-Nineteenth Century City: a sample from Boston 1860', *History of Education Quarterly* (Summer 1973), pp. 129-43; David Gagan and Herbert Mays, 'Historical Demography and Canadian Social History: Families and Land in Peel County, Ontario', *Canadian Historical Review* vol. 54 (1973), pp. 27-47.

4. *Children's Advocate*, 1896, p. 148; 'Homestead Adventure, 1883-1892: an Ayreshire Man's Letters Home', *Saskatchewan History*, vol. 15, (winter 1962), p. 33; Claude Theodore, 'The Story of My Life', *New Frontiers*, vol. 1, no. 3, pp. 22-4; *Ups and Downs*, April 1901, pp. 30-1, 54-5; Jan. 1904, pp. 35, 38, 40, 43; PAC RG 76 66/3115, G.B. Smart to J. Bruce Walker, 12 Feb. 1917; PAC RG 76 202/87308, Canadian Catholic Emigration Society, memo of 1899, article 11; Quarrier, Emigration 4, pp. 12, 20; Marchmont 16, p. 42; Barnardo 691 B 3.08, 536 B 7.04, 394 B 7.00, 244 B 6.94, 250 B 8.94, 511 B 9.03, 715 B 7.08.

5. PAC RG 76 66/3115, 'Parish of Fulham, Report of Miss M.C. Miles, Guardian of the Poor of the parish of Fulham, after her visit to the homes of the children emigrated to Canada by the Fulham Board of Guardians, 1903-4', p. 3; Helen Abell, 'The adaptation of the way of life of the rural family in Canada to

1.   Hope Place, London, 1911

3.   Boys with Meal Tickets

2.   Petticoat Lane, London, 1900

4. Boarded out Children at Cavan School, Durham County, Ontario, 1912

5. Girl in Service in Ontario, 1898 (Marchmont 23, p. 82)

6.   Boy, aged 13, Sawing Wood, 1894 (Marchmont 18, p. 15)

7.   Feeding Chickens, Hamilton, Ontario, 1912

8.   Hoeing Corn, 1912

technological, economic and social changes', *The Family in the Evolution of Agriculture* (Vanier Institute of the Family, Ottawa, 1968), p.16; David E. Schob, *Hired Hands and Plowboys* (University of Illinois Press, Urbana, 1975), pp. 191, 201; 'Report on the maintenance and education of children in the Metropolis', *Br. P.P.* 1896, XLIII, vol. 2, p. 693; Barnardo 897 G 9.03; Liverpool 16, p. 396; Jane Synge, 'Changing conditions for women and their consequences in the Hamilton area, 1900-30: an empirical study based on life history interviews', unpublished paper presented at the University of British Columbia symposium, 'The Working Sexes', Oct. 1976, pp. 14, 29, 44-6; Rosemary Ball, 'A Perfect Farmer's Wife: Women in Nineteenth Century Rural Ontario', *Canada, An Historical Magazine*, vol. 3, no. 1 (1975), pp. 3-21.

6. Schob, *Hired Hands*, pp. 171, 174-5; Synge, 'Changing conditions', pp.31a-4, 47; Jessie L. Beattie, *A Season Past, Reminiscences of a Rural Canadian Childhood* (McClelland and Stewart, Toronto, 1968), p. 10.

7. David Gagan, 'Indivisibility of Land: a microanalysis of the system of inheritance in nineteenth-century Ontario', *Journal of Economic History*, vol. 36, no. 1 (1976), pp. 129, 132, 136; David Gagan, 'Land, population and social change: the "critical years", in rural Canada West', *Canadian Historical Review*, vol. 59, no. 3 (1978), pp. 297, 303-7.

8. *Ups and Downs*, April 1900, p. 7.

9. *Ups and Downs*, March 1902, p. 7.

10. 'Special report on the immigration of British children', *Ontario Sessional Papers* 1897-98, no. 69, p. 23; 'Emigration of Pauper Children', *Br.P.P.* 1875, p. 20; PAC RG 17 511/56198, J. Wills to Minister of Agriculture, 4 Nov. 1886; PAC RG 76 202.87308, Canadian Catholic Emigration Society, memo of 1899, article 9: PAC, Charlotte Alexander Papers, MG 29 C 58 vol. 3, case of Jane Bushby; *Ups and Downs*, April 1900, p. 7; March 1902, p. 7; Barnardo 974 G 7.07.

11. Schob, *Hired Hands*, pp. 180-3, 206; Miriam Z. Langsam, *Children West: a history of the placing out system of the New York Children's Aid Society, 1853-90* (State Historical Society, Madison, Wisconsin, 1964), p. 18; David Gagan and Herbert Mays, 'Historical Demography and Canadian Social History: Families and Land in Peel County, Ontario', *Canadian Historical Review*, vol. 54, no. 1 (1973), pp. 45-6; Toronto Public Library, Protestant Orphan Home Papers; Hamilton Public Library, Hamilton Protestant Orphan Home Papers.

12. William Bradfield, *Life of Thomas Bowman Stephenson* (Kelly, London, 1913), p.143; PAC RG 76 45/1381, 'Dr. Stephenson's Children's Home', Terms; PAC RG 76 65/3115, 'Catholic Child Emigration to Canada', Liverpool 1902; PAC RG 76 119/22857, Dr. Barnardo's Homes, Boys Immigration Agency, 'Particulars'; PAC RG 76 32/724/3, copy of Knowlton agreement; Lillian Birt, *The Children's Homefinder* (Nisbet, London, 1913), p. 246.

13. PAC RG 17 392/42584, J. McGovern to John Lowe, 11 Feb. 1884; *Night and Day*, 1911, p. 8; 'Report on the maintenance and education of children in the Metropolis', vol. 2, pp. 347, 358; 'British Child Immigrants', *OSP* 1897-8, p. 87; PAC RG 76 51/2209, G. Bogue Smart, report on Barnardo work, Spring 1902; London and Stratford 27, pp. 112, 117, 120, 124; London and Stratford 12, pp. 141-2; Liverpool 4, pp. 25-6; Quarrier Emigration 3, p. 198; Marchmont 16, pp. 7, 16, 19, 27, 36, 65, 143.

14. Abell, 'Rural family', p. 17; D.A. Lawr, 'The development of Ontario farming, 1870-1914: patterns of growth and change', *Ontario History*, vol. 64, no. 4 (1972), pp. 241-4; William Tallack, *Penological and Preventive Principles* (Wertheimer Lee and Co., London, 1896), p. 370; Allan Bogue, 'The progress of the cattle industry in Ontario during the eighteen eighties', *Agricultural History*, 1947, p. 163; S.E.D. Shortt, 'Social change and political crisis in rural Ontario', in Donald Swainson (ed.), *Oliver Mowat's Ontario* (Macmillan, Toronto, 1972), pp. 212-14; *Ups and Downs*, Jan. 1897, p. 8.

15. *Ups and Downs*, Jan. 1897, p.8; Lawr, 'Ontario farming', p. 243; Marvin McInnis, 'Comment on paper by Gagan', *Journal of Economic History*, vol. 36 (1976), p. 144; Marvin McInnis, 'Childbearing and land availability: some evidence from individual household data', in Ronald D. Lees (ed.), *Population Patterns in the Past* (Academic Press, New York, 1979), pp. 205-6.

16. 'Immigration report for 1893', *OSP* 1894, p. 23.

17. Canada, Department of Labour, 'The Employment of Children', (King's Printer, Ottawa, 1921), p. 35.

18. n (boys) = 550, s (boys) = 2.2; n (girls) = 225, s (girls) = 2.9.

19. $\bar{X}$ = 75.5 per cent, n = 143.

20. $\bar{X}$ = 61.6 per cent; n = 52.

21. $\bar{X}$ = 58.4 per cent; n = 136.

22. Canada Land Inventory, *Soil Capability Classification for Agriculture* (Agriculture Regional Development Agency, Ottawa, 1965); Canada Land Inventory, *Land Use Capability for Agriculture* (Agriculture Regional Development Agency, Toronto, 1970); L.G. Reeds, 'The Environment', in Louis Gentilcore, *Ontario* (University of Toronto Press, Toronto, 1972) pp. 1-22.

23. *Ups and Downs*, Jan. 1897, p.8.

24. Barnardo 783 G 9.95, 799 G 6.97, 839 G 6.00, 905 G 5.04, 938 G 9.05, 933 G 8.05, 812 G 7.98, 883 G 4.03, 968 G 4.07.

25. Marchmont 27, p. 88; Barnardo 849 G 9.00; 931 G 8.05, 869 G 5.02, 379 B 3.00, 433 B 7.01, 196 B 3.93, 17 B 1.85, 612 B 9.05.

26. There are examples, however, of resort to the courts. Barnardo 539 B 7.04, 579 B 3.05; *The Christian*, 14 Sept. 1871, concerning 2 Macpherson boys, p. 4.

27. PAC RG 76 288/258859, letters of 11 May 1904 and 16 May 1904 between G. Bogue Smart and Alfred Owen.

28. Barnardo boys HDS 3.08 from microfilmed letters of 29 July 1914, 6 August 1914.

29. London and Stratford 17, p. 112; Barnardo 577 B 3.05, 951 G 8.06, 933 G 8.05, 973 G 7.07.

30. Liverpool 12, p. 40; London and Stratford 32 EP 14 Aug. 1913; London and Stratford 27, p. 138; Barnardo 958 G 10.06, 961 G 10.06, 719 B 10.08, 420 B 7.01, 636 B 8.06.

31. Barnardo 976 G 9.07.

32. Marchmont 16, pp. 27, 225; Liverpool 4, pp. 119-20; Barnardo 793 G 7.96, 845 G 7.00; PAC, Charlotte Alexander casebook, MG 29 C58 vol. 3, p. 11, Sarah Driscoll.

33. London and Stratford 32, p. 125.

34. Barnardo 974 G 7.02, 843 G 7.00, 874 G 9.00.

35. Barnardo 848 G 9.00, 726 G 7.84.

6 HOUSEHOLD AND SCHOOL

> At first, Matthew suggested getting a Barnardo boy. But I
> said 'no' flat to that. They may be all right — I'm not saying
> they're not — but no London street arabs for me . . . Give me
> a native born at least. There'll be a risk, no matter who we
> get. But I'll feel easier in my mind and sleep sounder at nights
> if we get a born Canadian . . . He can't be much different from
> ourselves. [1]

Marilla and Matthew Cuthbert, the adoptive parents of the most famous
of fictional Canadian orphans, Anne of Green Gables, decided to take
in a child when Matthew grew too old to handle the work on the farm
alone. Adult hired help was hard to find on Prince Edward Island, and
the Acadian boys of the district would work for a time but soon left for
the lobster canneries or the United States. Because local adults were
unavailable and local adolescents unreliable, Matthew suggested they
get a British apprentice from one of the distributing homes for child
immigrants at Halifax or Saint John.

Marilla, remembering local rumours, stoutly declined. A child that
sucked eggs, burned barns and put strychnine in wells would not live
in her household. Were not rescue home children unpredictable, untrustworthy, unlikely to adapt well, unsatisfactory in general because
they were not born Canadian? Marilla and her eagerly meddlesome
neighbour, Rachel Lynde, were firmly agreed; a London street arab had
no place in a Canadian home. [2]

In this, the first of the Anne books, written in 1908, Lucy Maud
Montgomery describes fears commonplace among Canadians of her
time. The Cuthberts were able to find a Canadian child through an
orphanage in Nova Scotia. If they had lived in Quebec, Ontario or
Manitoba, where competition for labour was keener, they might not
have been able to be so particular and might have had to tolerate a
British child in their midst. British child-savers were surprised that
their young people were only tolerated, not welcomed, in Canadian
households. They had expected a heartier greeting and a more thorough acceptance.

In the evangelical journal *The Christian,* through which revivalists
like Macpherson, Birt, Fegan, Quarrier and Barnardo shared their
concerns about many kinds of domestic and foreign mission work, the
word 'friends' often appears. It is a term used in eighteenth-century
British writings to describe the circle of household members and kin

to whom a person felt special obligations to give guidance and offer care. People who brought children to the British homes, even parents, are described without distinctions of blood relationship as 'friends' of the children. The evangelicals often added to their own families through adoption and preserved the traditions of household unity through worship in the home. In the early days of child emigration Annie Macpherson had described how servants were regarded as friends of the house in the pious Ontario farm homes where her children were placed. The hope that the rescue home children would find a place in a guiding circle of friends was never entirely abandoned, but the fact was inescapable that late nineteenth-century Canadian households were different from the eighteenth-century British ideal, at least for young servants of alien birth. [3]

In the late nineteenth century the rural inhabitants of eastern Canada encountered few recent immigrants. They suspected that slums were unsavoury places but were hazy about what life there was like. In consequence Canadians based their expectations about British boys and girls upon comparisons with the only youngsters they knew, rural Canadian children raised in families. They had an idea of how strong and skilled a 12-year-old was likely to be or how well a 10-year-old would get on with their own boys and girls and accordingly drafted their requests to the homes.

The young immigrants who disembarked at Halifax or Quebec and stood waiting alone with their boxes of possessions at village railway stations two weeks later were neither blank slates nor the products of the back concessions. They were British city children with eight or twelve years behind them in troubled families and neighbourhoods and a succession of institutions. Their pasts were short, but distinctive, and indelible.

The conflicts that made young immigrants fail in their situations were often peculiar to the master, the mistress or the child. Misfits in their first placement might do well in their second and thrive happily in their third. [4] And there were ways in which children adapted better than their parents or elder siblings might have. Still, patterns of temperament and training with roots in the lessons of infancy and early childhood bedevilled the adaptation of the group as a whole.

Children whose parents had died or deserted them and who had lost their sense of security as they moved through a succession of kin came directly to Canada from large understaffed institutions where attention and affection were necessarily thinly spread. Such children protected themselves by developing the passivity typical of the urban parish child. As one man observed, recalling his union school boyhood, 'I have often wondered to myself, in reading Dickens' works, am I, am I, the original Oliver Twist, but no it was not me that got up and raised his hand and asked for a second helping, it was the other fellows'. The reticence and self-containment the British slum children had learned in their previous lives was often interpreted in Canada as deceit. Lonely mistresses awaiting the affection and companionship of another 'wee bairn' in the house found immigrant girls in particular disappointingly 'dull' and 'unsociable', 'unresponsive to kindness' and still after several years in the household 'far from their affections'. [5]

The transition from institutional to domestic life taxed to the limit even the most stolid rescue home child's ability to endure through disruption. Many wrote later fondly of their time in the British homes and yearned to have those years back again, to be without 'trials and temptations. . . among the boys again'. By contrast, their years in Canada were filled with uncertainty and isolation.The two worlds were so different that their time behind walls inevitably left children unprepared both practically and emotionally for their Canadian roles, dashed their spirits and made them disappoint their Canadian masters and mistresses. [6]

The British philanthropic homes were crowded, busy places and, within the children's ranks, egalitarian as well. Children felt there a solidarity and community that as solitary servants to Canadian families they were unlikely ever to feel again. Even in urban England, workhouse girls who had always been accustomed to living in a crowd 'were frightened by the loneliness of long evenings . . . left entirely alone in the house'. In Canada farm houses were so much farther apart and households so much smaller that experienced British domestics remarked upon how 'most awful dull and quiet' was country life, how 'everything and everybody round here is got so stale I . . . feel such a modest young woman'. The monotony and lack of company made young people fractious, as their irritated letters to the home's offices show. One Barnardo boy wrote after five years in Canada in February 1912:

> Well sir my time is out this spring and I am not a bit sorry either I wish to ask you tonight if you are going to put my brother near me this summer I am getting awful lonesome here have to stay on the old farm nearly a whole year at a time without as much as going to Sunday school or any place . . .

P.S. how much money does it take to go to England answer quick.

Resentment with their confinement moved some to wander, seeking diversions, to behave in fact as Canadians feared such idle street arabs might.[7]

In large institutions children lived among their peers. Neither such surroundings nor their family life prepared them for the demeanour expected of servants. Boys raised in turbulent male environments clashed with farm wives over the conventions of deference and politeness required in the presence of ladies; often they could 'get on with the boss but not with the mistress'. Women put more store in the respectability and orderly functioning of their households and made plain their dissatisfaction with 'saucy', 'contrary' and 'impudent' lads. The evangelical homes dressed their girls in the manner of artisans' daughters, eschewing dreary uniforms and institutional cropped haircuts, aiming to prepare them for their eventual roles as Christian wives and mothers rather than for their intermediary position as maids. A girl used to sharing equally with others in her English cottage, if faced with a demanding mistress who treated her differently from the other children in the house, was more likely to respond with 'black looks' and insolence than with the compliance called for by her rank. [8]

These stresses, of course, varied with the Canadian family's perception of its social station. Children found readier acceptance in poorer households with fewer pretensions and more pressing needs for help. For younger girls officials sought plain rural and village homes where maids would work side by side with their mistresses under 'the strong hand of Christian sympathy' rather than having 'their moral sensibilities blunted' by the 'drudgery and toil of a gentleman's kitchen'. Nonetheless, inexperienced girls were placed with families aspiring to the status servant-keeping implied but lacking the funds to pay for more than an apprentice. Such mistresses were often 'too exacting and unwilling to make allowance for the youth and inexperience of the child'. Among the most consistent offenders in this respect were the wives of penurious clergymen whose requests the evangelical agencies could not easily refuse. Girls who found themselves waiting upon ladies in the front parlours of rural rectories learned too clearly their place and their failings and were rarely pleased with their lot.[9]

Even in plain homes the social exclusion of child immigrants was at times conspicuous. A rescue home child's being included in family excursions to town or to neighbourhood gatherings always merited special note in case records. Someone had to stay behind to feed the stock or the hired man, and that someone was naturally the immigrant child. Dour masters saw little reason why hired boys and girls should be granted Sundays off to ride about the countryside or should feel free to storm out of the house if excluded from table when family friends called. Many of the faults reported among young immigrants – listlessness, laziness, lack of ambition, untrustworthiness, untruthfulness, undependability – were common complaints against all hired help and derived from their status as servants of the household. Stronger-willed immigrant children excluded from privileges in the family and with no cash incentive to make the farm enterprise thrive might reasonably be unwilling to undertake great exertion voluntarily on their master's behalf. [10]

After the bustling variety and the comforting anonymity of life in a crowded institution in the company of their peers, farm life was a rude shock. No urban child could have anticipated the silence, the solitude, the daunting scale of the Canadian landscape. And children raised in a family or large village were not the eager pliant young people Canadians had been led to expect. Being raised by harried staff in ill-funded refuges did not make for finished servants. But when inspectors and employers spoke about young immigrants 'whose early training has been neglected' they referred to deficiencies more basic than that. [11]

It was common for children, particularly boys, to be returned from situations for lapses in personal hygiene described inexplicitly as 'dirty' or 'unclean habits', or for more particular complaints about 'night habits' and bedwetting. John Smith, the Dominion immigration agent at Hamilton, claimed in 1888 that two-thirds of the pauper boys he inspected were afflicted with enuresis. This estimate seems exaggerated by comparison with the Barnardo sample, in which persistent incontinence was reported in less than 10 per cent of cases. But the problem does appear repeatedly in the Quarrier, Birt and Macpherson files, and the trait was believed to be widespread among child immigrants. [12]

In part these problems stemmed from the children's pre-admission histories. Parents eventually forced to surrender family members to workhouses or refuges neglected or were unable to control their children's excretory habits. Institutions coped with this characteristic through frequent changes in linen and straw pallets and, Agent Smith alleged, by selecting children with this trait for speedy emigration. Possibly the anxiety of moving to Canada increased the incidence of bedwetting among young emigrants.

In so far as enuresis was brought about by stress, the pills regularly distributed by the homes' local branches were effective placebos, but for neither the young people nor their custodians was the problem as trivial as it might seem. Agent Smith claimed that bedwetters showed 'want of mental vigour . . . weak constitutions and want of physical development'. And as an inspector for the Salford Catholic Protection and Rescue Society reported in 1890,

> Too much importance cannot be attached to this matter. In Canada, such a case is regarded as evidence of bad moral lives on the part of the child's parents, and people are unwilling to become responsible for physical and religious moral conduct of such children.

Barnardo children reported incontinent were over-represented among those who failed in many situations during their first five years in Canada and those who never adapted well enough to any one place to complete an indenture. Boys and girls from Birt's Liverpool Sheltering Home were returned, and as a final expedient deported, if they could not conquer their kidney troubles. Canadian mistresses were understandably irritated by the increase in their own work caused by these nightly lapses. Such big children persisting in such childish habits were called stupid and wilful, and the connection between their low habits and their low beginnings was forcefully impressed upon them. [13]

A related problem developed for children who had not been introduced to genteel taboos concerning masturbation. Canadian masters and mistresses believed masturbation a cause of physical and mental weakness. In these attitudes they were supported by contemporary medical literature. And certainly there were a sufficient number of young apprentices gloomy, vacant and generally enervated for reasons quite independent of their sexual habits to lend this spurious correlation some force. It is possible that the emigrant children had been deprived of this taboo, as they had been deprived of many other things. At any rate, Canadian employers viewed the practice with respectable disdain and often demanded that immigrant children be removed from their midst, giving that as the reason. [14]

The rough language, clumsy table manners and unconcern with cleanliness or orderly dress typical of the apprentices made masters and particularly mistresses fear the example they set for other children in the house. The concern was not uniquely focused upon hired help sent by the British homes. Canadian clergymen concerned with the stresses increasingly besetting country life noted the 'personal penalties' that the employment of any immigrant labour entailed for the family, whatever the 'national compensations' in more rapid assimilation of alien workers. Midwestern American journals advised farmers to hire faithful moral hands, though they might be less physically strong, rather than risk their children's association with profane immoral men. The exceptional element in the accusations of impurity, bad influence or infectious bad habits made against rescue home children was that the protests rang with claims of promises betrayed. From the young wards of British Quakers and Plymouth Brethren salty language and aggressive or profligate posturing arrived quite unannounced. [15]

The immigrant apprentices may have failed to meet their employers' expectations in many ways, but they were often the only additional sources of help available to sorely pressed households. In these circumstances masters and mistresses might keep on children they found slow, stubborn, lazy or ill-tempered in the hope of amending their behaviour through discipline. The Criminal Code allowed masters to mete out 'moderate chastisement' on due provocation from recalcitrant servants — to punish young apprentices as they might chasten their own young.[16] But the frustrations born of these household relationships were not those of the family. The provocations offered by rescue home children were exceptional; the frustrations felt by masters were atypical; the moderating influences of blood ties were absent.

The cultural differences exhibited by young Britons in the household seemed failings in character, which could not be lightly ignored. In some boys and girls the drastic transitions of emigration evoked drastic responses — extreme anger and despondency unknown in local children — which masters interpreted as unbridled ill-temper and tried to govern by extreme means. Masters vexed with the futility of 'moderate chastisement' found little to constrain their own mounting anger. Apparently these young outsiders had arrived at the farm gate after being casually discarded at every station en route. No British institutions had cared even to keep them, while their Canadian guardians were incautious at best, satisfied with selections of situations through the mails, irregular and infrequent in their promised inspections. The children's welfare seemed of little consequence to anyone. The force of example counselled little care and suggested that the penalties for abuse would be small — as indeed they often were. [17]

For 9 per cent of boys and 15 per cent of girls in the Barnardo sample, evidence of excessive punishment exists. The home's officials set the threshold of excess much higher for boys than for girls, so that the difference between the sexes may not be particularly significant.

But reported and substantiated cases of abuse must certainly have been much fewer than the incidents of ill-treatment. [18] Among the Barnardo boys and girls the frequent changes in situations brought about by unacceptable personal or work habits are consistently associated with reports of ill-usage. Boys too restless or recalcitrant to complete their indentures were especially likely to encounter excessive abuse. [19]

Home officials became habituated to ill-treatment of their charges as an unfortunate consequence of their work. It was something they did not condone but could not control with the resources at hand. Pressed for details concerning the death four years previously of a badly treated child, Miss A.F. Proctor, the matron of a Catholic home in Montreal, wearily replied: 'Really there have been so many cases of ill-usage in the past that it would occupy the judges fully for some time if they could *all* be raked up.' Some rescue home personnel, particularly Robert Wallace of Marchmont at Belleville and the staff of the Middlemore home at Halifax, too readily acknowledged that their lads were difficult to manage and countenanced discipline so severe as to be, in the eyes of Bogue Smart of the Dominion Immigration Department, 'not only humiliating and discouraging but out of keeping with the times'. [20]

The occasional inspections that the small Canadian staffs could manage were inefficient in detecting ill-treatment, even if visitors were sympathetic to the children and assiduous in their duties. A man placed near Rapid City, Manitoba, at the age 13 in 1901 who was described in the visitors' reports as happy in his home and well treated wrote a warm letter to the rescue home in 1924 during a time when the provincial press were highly critical of Barnardo's work. He described his predicament as an apprentice in this way:

> I went through more than I ever want to go through again . . .
> I know myself that I often looked forward to the time for the man from the Homes to come, Mr. White, but when he did come I used to be too scared to say anything for fear that I got more after Mr. White had gone, although I must say The Mr. White done all he could . . . I would not want them to get any things on the Homes as the Homes had been too good to me for that. I have often said I would like to have my time over again in the Homes in England but not here. [21]

If the inspection system offered little protection and the children were reluctant to complain on their own behalf, the only other likely observers — neighbours — were reluctant to betray one of their community to relieve an outsider of dubious descent. Nor were the rescue homes keen to attract the adverse publicity that resort to the courts invariably entailed. Seldom were such prosecutions successful anyway, for witnesses to the event were rarely to be found. As a magistrate in a Renfrew County, Ontario, court recorded in his judgement after a young child's wounds were exhibited before him in 1905: 'there was no doubt that the boy had been most cruelly beaten by some person', but there was no way of reliably ascertaining the identity of that person. [22]

When children died from ill-treatment, prosecutions were more likely and their outcomes more successful than in other cases. Neighbours were moved to testify by the magnitude of the offence; autopsies allowed the nature of the abuse to be more reliably defined. The trials for manslaughter show the same patterns present in assault prosecutions. William White, a ward of the London Children's Aid Society, was placed in Grenfell, Assiniboia, in May 1892 at age 14 for his board and clothing. He began that autumn to be incontinent at night. Because of the smell, his master, James Wheelton Brown, had made him sleep in the stable, though temperatures reached 45 degrees below zero. The boy's feet froze solid, and he died on St Valentine's Day 1893 of gangrene after frost-bite — less through the absence of love than through a lack of 'ordinary care and reasonable interest'. William effectively had nowhere to turn. His habit inclined his institutional guardian to ignore him and his master to prefer to have him out of the house, and made it highly unlikely that neighbours recognising his plight would offer him protection. [23]

George Everitt Green came to Canada with limited intelligence and restricted eyesight. He was sent back by his first master because he could not see well enough to drive a team. His second employer, Helen Findlay, a spinster, had less latitude to be particular and kept him though he was 'stupid and slow and she feared he always would be'. She worked her land alone and needed to extract from the boy all the labour she could. After scolding and shoving she began to wield axe handles and pitchforks as incentives to George to stretch his limited strength. He may have died of these beatings; the doctors attributed his injuries to external violence. But the jury trying Findlay for manslaughter was less sure: a boy blind in one eye and hardly able to see with the other, neither physically robust nor mentally very quick, might well have had some disease 'inherent in his system' for years which developed in Canada to bring about his death. [24] It was not difficult in the case of a child immigrant to establish such reasonable doubt.

The children's typical responses to tensions in their situations — flashes of anger or stolid retreat, rebellious 'black looks' or unwillingness to work — went to widely publicised extremes. Some children acted out their anger. Boys retaliated against masters through cruelty to farm animals; girls resisted their housework by destroying household effects. Some apprentices put the torch to haystacks or houses, although a large proportion of the accusations of arson are suspect, winter fires in wood stoves being common in Canada and the only strangers in the neighbourhood being all too easily made scapegoats. There are only two examples of the most thorough revenge against masters. In one case a Fegan boy killed his master's adopted son; in the other the master himself was murdered by a Catholic Emigration Society apprentice. Although criminality was certainly not characteristic of the child immigrants, these episodes and the evil influences suspected lurking in their pasts fed speculation about their 'criminal natures'. [25]

Other young immigrants turned their anger and confusion inwards, rebelling not against subjection but against life itself. The instruments for suicide were near to hand on the farm. Children learned through their work that paris green, saltpetre and lye were poisonous, although contemplating the use of such strongly corrosive substances must have required considerable determination. There were also hangings and drownings, and one death by gas poisoning in a carefully sealed room. [26]

The schoolroom was the bridge between the household and the larger Canadian community, the place where immigrant children were compared and compared themselves most explicitly with local youngsters and where they first encountered local opinion about their own kind idly expressed in gossip and casual accusation. The emigrating agencies stressed the advantages that free schooling afforded their children in Canada, the opportunities for advancement it offered and the equality between newcomer and native implied by sharing a school bench.

But British apprentices were unlikely to have sustained contact with the Canadian educational system. English Local Government Board officials were convinced by the reports they received on their own wards that immigrant children were not being sent regularly to school. The young apprentices themselves often complained in adulthood that emigration ended rather than expanded their opportunities for schooling. A girl who went to southern Ontario through Annie Macpherson's Home of Industry in 1896 wrote as she entered middle life of her early experiences:

> excuse my poor writing and mistakes as I am poor hand to write
> letters I feel asham of myself . . . The people you let take me and
> raise as there child they would not sent me to school and mistreat
> me at reason I run away when I was 15 year old I wish I could see
> you. [27]

The rescue homes' definitions of sufficient schooling were eventually
upgraded substantially. In 1895 Barnardo's advised the young immigrant that he might 'perhaps have the privilege of attending school in the
winter months, and, if so, we hope you will make the most of the
opportunity remembering how important and valuable education is to
everyone who had to make his way in the world'; at the same time it
was suggested to masters that 'attendance at school during the winter
months is desired in the case of younger boys'. By 1907 their indentures explicitly specified the number of years an apprentice must attend
school for four months annually. After 1913 British and Canadian
government officials and the homes themselves insisted upon at least
five months' yearly attendance for all youngsters aged 14 and under. [28]
  Two-thirds of Barnardo's children aged 9 or younger when they
came to Canada received regular schooling, but three-quarters of his
emigrants aged 10 to 12 attended irregularly or not at all, and about the
same proportion of arrivals aged 13 to 14 never saw the inside of a
Canadian schoolroom. [29] The first compulsory school attendance bill
was passed in Ontario in 1871, although similar legislation was not in
place in western Canada until half a century later. Even in reform-
minded urban communities the broad adjustment in the 'rigour and
rhythm of work' required to free Canadian children for schooling came
very slowly. Apprenticed children usually lived in rural areas where
enrolments were much lower than in the cities. In Ontario as late as
1891 less than half the children registered in rural schools attended for
more than one hundred days annually, and trustees were obliged to
provide accommodation for only two-thirds of the school-age population. In the west, schools were fewer and further apart and often open
only when children could not be spared from work on the farms. For
many rural children, but especially for those from rescue homes, the
advantages of the common school system were usually ephemeral and
often entirely unavailable. [30]
  Until 1896 some rural trustees refused British apprentices access to
local schools on the ground that their guardians, the officials of the

English Local Government Board and the emigrating agencies, did not live in the school section, whose funds were exhausted in providing for local children. The 1897 Ontario legislation to protect British immigrant children — swiftly copied in Manitoba and Quebec — did establish for young apprentices the right to public education but stipulated no effective penalties for masters who denied them that right. 'Trustees being generally neighbours', James Burges of Quarrier's Brockville home reported, were constrained by community loyalties from intervening to secure adequate schooling for the young immigrant. [31]

Immigrants later remembered not only fewer opportunities to attend school than their Canadian-born peers but also the distinctive treatment they received in the Canadian classroom. Rural teachers did not welcome immigrant apprentices to the student body. Because the background and current circumstances of rescue home children differed from those of their Canadian classmates, they tended to disrupt the orderly functioning of the schoolroom. They were among that vexing group of infrequent attenders who forced the teacher monotonously to repeat old lessons, until, patience exhausted, she or he corralled the stragglers into a corner for special attention, dooming them to taunts as dullards in the yard outside. Because their farm work loads were heavy, apprentices were often found 'plodding to school a little late', soiled by barnwork or housework and dreading the stern public lecture on the vitues of punctuality awaiting them. Teachers were even less tolerant than mistresses of lapses in personal hygiene or manners, and rescue home children remember being used as cautionary examples of unclean, unChristian or unCanadian behaviour. [32]

Their frequent changes in situations markedly retarded the progress of apprentices in school. A master or mistress with a new servant on trial tested her thoroughly in domestic routine before releasing her to the classroom or delayed investing in textbooks until certain the hired boy would work out. Since the early years of many children in Canada were only a further series of trials after doing the rounds of a succession of British public and private institutions, a young immigrant of normal capacities could easily have fallen very far behind Canadian children of the same age. On the other hand there were immigrant apprentices, particularly those from the better-run workhouse schools, who came to Canada aged 11 or 12 equipped with as firm a foundation in basic skills as any rural school could offer. But the British philanthropic agencies never served their candidates for emigration very well, and most young emigrants disembarked in Canada with an educational handicap that the circumstances of their apprenticeship only intensified.

Not surprisingly, young immigrants labelled as dimwits and lectured for unsatisfactory personal and moral conduct found the rural school-room an unpleasant place. Some boys, like a Quarrier boy aged 12 of Annan, Ontario, having been struck with a stick in the play-hour and thrashed by his teacher in the classroom, simply refused to go to school, a circumstance that did not cause his employer great grief. Others showed such stubbornness or disinterest that exasperated teachers expelled them from class.[33] In the schoolroom as in the household, therefore, child immigrants strained Canadian forbearance. The rural schools did as much to isolate the immigrant apprentices as to ease their adjustment and reinforced rather than allayed local sus-picions of these strangers in their midst.

Among rural community members who neither employed nor taught them and therefore saw them only at a distance, the child immigrants were suspected of carrying hereditary or contagious diseases from 'the foul slums of the Old World' into the fresh countryside. It is true that the British communities from which rescue home children sprang were not conspicuously healthful. The fact that more than two-thirds of the young emigrants had lost a mother or father testified to the vulnerab-ility of urban, working-class physical constitutions. The residents of children's homes were typically undersized because of deprivation. In 1883, boys aged 16 from British industrial schools were found to be on the average only a fraction of an inch taller than boys aged 13 in the general population. Such youngsters were unlikely ever to recover fully from their slow start and to grow as tall or as strong as better-nourished children. The emigration institutions, moreover, often received the youngest or weakest members of families in trouble, and staff members observed that in many of these youngsters 'the intellect [was] not so bright nor the physique so energetic as in children more favourably nourished'. Ill-fed, ill-sheltered children were susceptible to pneu-monia, pleurisy or chronic bronchitis, and the institutions to which such youngsters were surrendered were ridden with infectious eye and skin disease.[34]

Of the Barnardo children who eventually came to Canada 24 per cent first arrived at the rescue home with serious health problems. During their stay in British shelters children partially recuperated from some of these chronic maladies. Those in severely weakened condition upon admission were detained longer before emigration than their more robust peers.[35] But the adverse effects of their slow start lingered; ringworm, catarrh and ophthalmia circulated continuously through the best-run institutions; the sea crossing was frequently hard upon weakened constitutions. It was exceptional for child immigrants to arrive in Canada in good health, notwithstanding the claims of pre-emigration medicals, doctors' certificates and dockside inspections and the philanthropists' affirmations that they sent abroad only the 'flower of their flock'.

The Barnardo emigrants were healthier during their apprenticeship in Canada than they had been upon admission in Britain, partly because they had been nursed to better health before being sent to Canada, partly because they lived in healthier environments in Canada than in Britain. Improvement was most marked in the active cases of the contagious diseases endemic to schools and shelters: the eye and skin diseases (Table 6.1).

Table 6.1: Physical and Mental Health in Britain and in Canada, Barnardo Sample 1882-1908

		Eyes, ears nose, throat	Skin	Lungs	Mental	General condition
Incidence	%	14.3	19.9	9.0	4.9	25.8
(British	n	115	160	72	39	208
admission						
medical)						
Incidence	%	5.6	2.0	2.4	8.8	17.5
(Canadian	n	45	16	19	71	141
medical						
history)						
Persistence	%	20.0	5.0	6.9	46.2	30.8
	n	23	8	5	18	64
Genesis	%	48.9	49.9	73.7	74.6	54.4
Missing	n	22	8	14	53	77
Data	n	191	192	193	192	190

Note: 'Persistence' measures the proportion of children who retained in Canada a health problem reported on admission. 'Genesis' measures the proportion of children with a Canadian health problem for whom a British medical history of that ailment was not noted. In all cases the rates of persistence are probably lower bounds, since the hurried physicians at the rescue homes could not reliably detect many problems, in particular latent lung disease and mental disturbance or deficiency.

Since the likelihood was at least 20 per cent that a child with a history of eye disease would continue to suffer from it in Canada and at least 30 per cent that a delicate child at admission would continue to be less sturdy than his fellows through his apprenticeship, was the emigration of such youngsters justified? It is clear that children without the sight, the hearing or the physical stamina to cope with work or with school did not do well in Canada. They were more often returned from situations as unsatisfactory, more often punished for failings they could not correct, more often injured in accidents in the course of their work than children without handicaps. Even those who overcame the physical deficiencies of their early deprivations bore scars. A child clearly marked by skin disease or bone disease was especially vulnerable to being labelled a British castoff. The label was readily generalised to denigrate all the rescue home children and thus led some masters and mistresses to think their apprentices cheap commodities, unworthy of better care in Canada than they appeared to have received in Britain.[36]

It is less clear that mental disturbances among young immigrants in Canada were legacies of their British pasts. Mental health problems seem to have become more common with emigration, though physical health improved. Almost half the children manifesting psychological problems or mental deficiencies on admission to the rescue homes continued to exhibit those symptoms in Canada. Nonetheless, children with longstanding problems represented only one quarter of the mentally hampered among the Barnardo apprentices in Canada. Some of these cases may merely have been overlooked in Britain; but there was much in the placement and inspection process in Canada which must have taxed the adaptability of the most stable child. Precipitate removal of young people from English boarding homes to which they had developed firm attachments, abrupt post-emigration despatch to Canadian families known to the homes only through correspondence and entirely unknown to the child, infrequent visiting of the children in their situations and lax removal procedures which left children for months and sometimes years in places where they were not well thought of or well cared for made some young apprentices fearful and despondent. These problems aggravated the stresses inherent in emigration: the transfer from hectic urban to isolated rural environments, the extinguishing of all reasonable hope of reunion with family and friends, the movement of apprentices through several situations as their capacity for work developed, and the problems of being treated as an outsider. Under such burdens it is not surprising that some young immigrants behaved in a way that led to incarceration or deportation. [37]

The more substantial results of their previous physical deprivations — small stature, weaker constitutions, greater susceptibility to infection — probably made the child immigrants marginally less useful as workers by comparison with their rural Canadian competitors and thus made them seem less valuable to the community as a whole. Assumptions current at the time about the unshakeable burden of heredity coalesced in the metaphor of 'bad seed'. The personal habits that proved irritating in the household and the schoolroom and the health problems that seemed to threaten the larger community were attributed variously to physical environment, previous training and parentage. In the popular mind it was a question of degeneracy. Masturbation, weak kidneys, lack of mental vigour and physical robustness, whatever their causes, were regarded by masters and mistresses as indications of a general deterioration within the social class from which child immigrants were drawn — a progressive degeneration individuals could not easily overcome and would very likely pass on to their children.

In rural Canada illegitimacy was commonly thought to be hereditary. Although only a small proportion of the child immigrants had been born out of wedlock, most were generally believed to be 'the product of illegitimate transactions going on between the father and mother' and thus predisposed to such moral lapses themselves. One of the most common requests of rescue home boys and girls later contemplating marriage was for evidence to refute allegations of uncertain paternity. Several of Miss Macpherson's wards in southwestern Ontario lost good homes after they reached puberty because their mistresses feared the 'great responsibility' of governing the sexuality of such girls. [38]

The rescue home girls were certainly more vulnerable for mistreatment than other young women in rural communities. Barnardo attributed this dangerous tendency to 'the very freedom of the life, its liberty', the fact that in rural Canada the hired servant 'and all the family are on the same footing. They eat at a common table and are very familiar and free in their intercourse with each other [which] creates evils which need be carefully provided against'. [39] But the immigrant girls and the family were in one important sense not on the same footing: hired girls lived inside the household but outside the incest taboo.

Several British agencies were so concerned about the risks for young women that they emigrated only boys or, following the example of the English Local Government Board, approved removal to Canada only for girls under age 10. Nonetheless many of the societies did place girls, among them many adolescents. One-third of Barnardo's Canadian apprentices were female, as were almost all of Miss Rye's wards. There were girls in each of the Macpherson, Birt, Quarrier and Manchester parties and among all the bands of Catholic children. [40] Some safeguards for these young women were established. Girls were not usually placed in households which did not also include an adult woman. Mistresses were instructed not to leave the girl at night when another woman was not present in the house. The official visitors carefully noted deficiencies in sleeping accommodation in their reports, the absence of interior locks on bedroom doors and windows, the lodging of hired help in a separate part of the house. But visitors called seldom and always by day. [41]

If rescue home girls were taken advantage of by hired men, masters or their sons, resorts to the courts were rarely successful either in prosecutions for rape or in suits to establish paternity. As usual in such cases the common impediment was the absence of corroborative evidence. In addition, girls were often vague about the exact date upon which the incident had taken place. In 1887 Miss Rye pointed out that two cases she had pressed, one involving a girl of 10 consistently abused over a prolonged period, had been dismissed for lack of proof of the girls' age. The Ontario protective legislation for British immigrant children treated this difficulty by establishing the information on disembarkation documents as sufficient approximation of the date of birth. A 1900 amendment to the Criminal Code made this provision Dominion-wide. Even so, the girls' marginal place in the community contributed both to their defencelessness and to their assailants' invulnerability before the courts. When a prominent New Brunswick Liberal arrested for the rape of a girl aged 12 from the Middlemore home fled in 1907, forfeiting his $1,000 bail, 'the judge remarked that the girl was only low English and that it was not a very important matter'. [42]

In the Barnardo sample, 11 per cent of the girls became pregnant while they were wards of the homes. The records suggest but do not confirm pregnancy in a further 2 per cent of the cases. Girls who arrived in Canada early in adolescence, aged 13 to 15, were, as the Local Government Board expected, the most vulnerable, comprising 35 per cent of the female emigrants but 46 per cent of the girls 'in trouble'. They were one-third more likely than those who disembarked at age 10 to 12, and four times more likely than those who arrived under age 10, to become pregnant during their apprenticeship. But since the apprentices who became pregnant in Canada had been in British rescue homes for shorter periods before emigration than those who did not, it is not clear that hurrying youngsters to Canada sooner after their admission would have affected their adolescent experience in this respect. [43]

There is no clear relationship between the ease with which girls adjusted to their position as apprentices and the likelihood that they would bear a child out of wedlock. Girls reported to have been 'in trouble' are only slightly over-represented among those with less stable work histories. On the other hand, the reasons given for admission to the rescue homes were linked to the likelihood of pregnancy during apprenticeship. Children admitted for principally moral reasons are over-represented among girls 'in trouble' by 44 per cent, as though experiences before admission or the effects of such labelling after admission made such a youngster more likely to 'lose her character'.[44]

By and large, it seems more reasonable to link the incidence of pre-marital adolescent pregnancy to the predicament of the group as a whole rather than to individual adjustment problems among its members. Emigration placed girls beyond the reach of their mothers' and sisters' counsel. Moving frequently between situations, young apprentices were unlikely to develop compensating relationships with Canadian women. Rescue home girls were in any case viewed as outsiders whose characters were suspect, and their 'moral falls' tended to confirm local beliefs rather than provoke local outrage against the supposed father.

The incidence of pregnancy in the Barnardo sample is not markedly higher than that among other Canadian women of similar ages in 1926, the first year for which comparable figures are available. Assuming that, on average, rescue home girls were under institutional supervision for four years after puberty, their pregnancy rate was about 33 live births per thousand a year. The comparable rate for women in the population at large aged 15 to 19 was 29 per thousand. [45]

But all the pregnancies among the Barnardo apprentices aged 18 or younger were to unmarried girls. Home girls were not free to marry until their apprenticeships were completed. The mean age of marriage among Barnardo girls was 21 years, which suggests that many preferred to postpone marriage until their trusteeship funds were released to them at age 21. Of course, many of the home girls' pregnancies resulted from involuntary liaisons with masters or hired men, which would not in any case have resulted in marriage. In the Canadian population as a whole in the 1920s the proportion of illegitimate births to total births among girls age 19 or younger was 13 per cent.

In 1921 the proportion of illegitimate births in rural Ontario, the principal place of residence of Barnardo home girls, was only 1.26 per cent. Thus the unfortunate vulnerability of the immigrant apprentice resulted in an illegitimacy rate much higher than that among Canadian adolescents as a whole and higher still compared with that of other rural residents of similar ages. [46]

Because the problem was not rare the rescue homes developed standard procedures for dealing with pregnant wards. When a 'moral fall' or 'loss of character' was reported, that is, an experience with coitus whose consequences were as yet unclear, either on the basis of the girl's confession or household suspicion, a visitor was sent to interview the apprentice and attempt to convince her mistress to let her remain in service until the diagnosis of pregnancy was possible. When a mistress was unwilling to keep the girl in the household she was taken to the distributing home or, in the case of Barnardo's, to a special shelter operated in conjunction with the Toronto headquarters, to be released to a new situation after three months if 'no consequences resulted from the act'. Barnardo's counselled their girls against Salvation Army homes in which their savings would be taken to pay for their keep. Thus as more girls emigrated the Barnardo maternity home grew from a small cottage in 1897 to the two-storey former boys' headquarters after 1905. Rye sent many of her pregnant wards back to England. Macpherson, Birt, Quarrier's and the Wallaces at Marchmont in Belleville used Salvation Army facilities or local Homes of Refuge. [47]

The rescue agencies accepted premarital adolescent pregnancy as one of the hazards inherent in the programme, a regrettable but reasonable risk in light of the better opportunities they believed awaited children in Canada. Although childbed deaths were often reported and the lot of the unmarried domestic who chose to keep her child was no easier in Canada than in Britain, in the better-run homes girls were guided through their confinements with sympathy and support, were counselled as they looked for employment thereafter and were no more likely than their luckier sisters to prematurely sever their links with the homes. [48]

Most immigrant youngsters were, by virtue of their short but distinctive pasts, too different in temperament and personal habits to establish common cause easily with Canadian families. Distrust of these differences and broader suspicion of their slum origins made masters and mistresses less sympathetic with youngsters' difficulties in their new circumstances than they might have been for Canadian-born young people. Perhaps the bonds between boys and girls hired from the neighbourhood and their employers were somewhat stronger and more encompassing. But the generalised notions of stewardship and guardianship which drew household and family together under the rubric of friends were almost entirely gone by the later nineteenth century, withered by the growth of the capitalistic labour market and the increasingly migratory character of labouring populations.

Because the children were widely scattered through the countryside they soon lost the group loyalties developed in the British homes and through the period of preparation and travel to Canada. Even when other British children were settled nearby, the sense of fellow feeling and mutual responsibility characteristic of urban family immigrant groups rarely arose among the alumni of the rescue homes. Isolated youngsters in households readily internalised community attitudes towards 'British workhouse brats' and 'slum offcasts' and therefore chose to deny their affiliations with the homes. Understanding little about the circumstances which had separated them from their families, many felt shame or resentment toward their own kin and hence animosity toward their own kind. These feelings made public, and even private, recognition of their common predicament an unpalatable prospect for many immigrant children long after they outgrew their status as apprentices.

Notes

1. Lucy Maud Montgomery, *Anne of Green Gables* (L.C. Page, Boston, 1908), p. 9.

2. Montgomery, *Green Gables*, pp. 8-10.

3. Alison Prentice, 'Education and the metaphor of the family: the Upper Canadian example', in Michael Katz and Paul B. Mattingly (eds.), *Education and Social Change: Themes from Ontario's Past* (New York University Press, New York, 1975), pp. 112-13; Harold Perkin, *The Origins of Modern English Society 1780-1880* (Routledge and Kegan Paul, London, 1969), pp. 44-51.

4. 'Report on the education and maintenance of children in the Metropolis', *Br.P.P.* 1896, XLIII, vol. 2, pp. 360, 675.

5. Barnardo 955 G 8.06, 970 G 7.07, 915 G 7.04, 941 G 4.06, 796 G 10.96.

6. Barnardo 435 B 9.01; *Loving and Serving*, Dec. 1908, p. 7; National Children's Home, *Report*, 1900-1, p. 35; *Highways and Hedges*, 1896, pp. 266-9.

7. Charles Booth, *Life and Labour of the People in London* (Macmillan, London, 1902-4), II, vol. 4, p. 215; Barnardo 656 B 2.07, letter of Feb. 1907 to A.B. Owen; Annie Macpherson, *Winter in London* (privately printed, London, 1872), pp. 53-6; 'Report of the department of neglected and dependent children',

Ontario Sessional Papers 1899, p. 81.

8. Barnardo 83 B 6.88, 542 B 7.04, 681 B 7.07, 659 B 2.07, 562 B 10.04, 11 B 1884, 903 G 9.03, 860 G 9.01, 841 G 7.00, 830 G 9.99, 828 G 9.99.

9. PAC RG 17 177/18369, Edwin Clay to the Minister, 8 Jan. 1877; PAC RG 17 173/17953, John Donaldson to John Lowe, 27 Nov. 1876; Barnardo 859 G 7.01, girl's letter of May 1907, 929 G 5.05, cleric's wife to Miss Kennedy, 15 June 1912, and cleric to Miss Kennedy 13 Sept. 1912; 762 G 8.89, removal from a manse for ill-treatment, 25 Nov. 1889; 749 G 10.86, failures in two clerical placements, Dec. 1886 and Sept. 1887; 869 G 5.02, report of Oct. 1902; similar difficulties in households of farmers in older settled regions, 976 G 9.07, report of 19 Nov. 1913 by Agnes Sillars and letter of 24 Dec. 1913 to Miss E. Taylor, Peterborough.

10. Liverpool 12, p. 84; Liverpool 16, p. 557; Quarrier Emigration 1, pp. 88, 390; Arthur Copping, *The Golden Land* (Hodder and Stoughton, London, 1911), p. 208; Barnardo 866 G 5.02, 875 G 7.02, 812 G 7.98, 851 G 6.01, 795 G 10.96, 758 G 9.88, 616 B 3.06, 266 B 6.95, 197 B 3.93, 429 B 7.01, 703 B 5.08.

11. PAC RG 17 395/42584, J.M. McGovern to John Lowe, 11 Feb. 1884; PAC RG 17 591/57417, John Smith to J. Small, 10 Dec. 1886; PAC RG 17 585/66105, John Donaldson to J. Small, 26 July 1888.

12. PAC RG 17 568/64018, John Smith to John Lowe, 6 Mar. 1888; Barnardo 97 B 3.89, 194 B 3.93, 270 B 6.95, 328 B 9.97, 344 B 7.98, 401 B 9.00, 644 B 8.06, 653 B 2.07, 695 B 3.08, 713 B 7.08, 410 B 3.01, 421 B 7.01, 444 B 3.02, 464 B 7.02, 546 B 7.04.

13. PAC RG 17 669/76286, Inspector Rossall, second report, 31 Oct. 1890 to the Salford Catholic Protection and Rescue Society; Liverpool 4, pp. 79-80; Liverpool 8, p. 138; Barnardo 942 G 4.06, 879 G 9.02, 721 B 10.08, 719 B 10.08, 294 B 4.96, 288 B 4.96, 94 B 3.89, 31 B 7.85, 22 B 1.85, 79 B 3.88, 297 B 7.96; PAC RG 76 491/761668, Report of R.W. Hillyard on the case of Robert Murphy from the Liverpool Sheltering Homes, ill-treated because of his unclean habits, 8 Feb. 1908.

14. PAC Charlotte Alexander Papers, MG 29 C 58, vol. 3, p. 71, case of Ethel Maclean; H. Tristam Englehart, Jr., 'The disease of masturbation: values and the concept of disease', *Bulletin of the History of Medicine*, vol. 48, no. 2 (1974) pp. 234-48; R.P. Neuman, 'Masturbation, Madness and the Modern Concepts of Childhood and Adolescence', *Journal of Social History* (Spring 1975), pp. 1-27; Robert H. MacDonald, 'The frightful consequences of onanism: notes on the history of a delusion', *Journal of the History of Ideas*, vol.28 (1967), pp. 423-31; Michael Bliss, ' "Pure Books on Avoided Subjects" ': Pre-Freudian Sexual Ideas in Canada', Canadian Historical Association, *Historical Papers* (1970), pp. 89-108; Barnardo 985 G 5.08, 333 B 4.98, 134 B 3.91, 127 B 5.90.

15. John MacDougall, *Rural Life in Canada* (University of Toronto Press, Toronto, [1973] 1913), p. 129; David Schob, *Hired Hands and Plowboys* (University of Illinois Press, Urbana, 1975), p.220; Marchmont 16, Richard Hampson; Quarrier Emigration 1, p. 318; Quarrier Emigration 2, p. 35.

16. PAC RG 76 66/3115/6, section 55 of the Criminal Code.

17. 'Report on the emigration of pauper children to Canada', *Br.P.P.* 1875, LXIII, p. 13; *Ups and Downs* Jan. 1904, p.43; PAC RG 17 385/41460 and 387/41470, Dr Edwin Clay's reports on the ill-treatment of James Francis, ward of the Liverpool Sheltering Homes in Nova Scotia, 1883; *Children's Advocate*, Oct. 1881, p. 149.

18. n (boys) = 604; n (girls) = 228; excessive punishment consists of substantiated charges of ill-treatment resulting in reprimand of the master or removal of the child.

19. n (boys) = 529; n (girls) = 204.

20. London and Stratford 27, p. 138; Barnardo 809 G 9.97, 42 B 6.86; PAC RG 76 343/364372, G. Bogue Smart to Rev. Robert Wallace, 13 June 1906; PAC RG 76 491/761668, R.W. Hillyard report on the Robert Murphy case, 8 Feb. 1908; PAC RG 76 32/724/3, R.W. Hillyard to G.B. Smart, 19 Mar. 1906 in the case of James Griffith ward of the Knowlton Liverpool Sheltering Home branch.

21. Barnardo 435 B 9.01.

22. PAC RG 17 629/71401, 'The Police Court, A Serious Case Dismissed', *Cornwall Standard*, 29 Nov. 1889, p. 2; PAC RG 76 324/318481, Cecil Arden, Catholic Emigration Association to G. Bogue Smart, 19 Nov. 1905, and clipping from the *Renfrew Journal*, approx. 17 Nov. 1905.

23. North West Territories, *Law Reports* 1893 (Queen vs. Brown) in L.G. Thomas, *The Prairie West to 1905* (Oxford, Toronto, 1975), pp. 164-8.

24. PAC RG 76 124/25933, manslaughter trial of Helen Findlay in the death of George Everitt Green, 1895; PAC RG 76 363/466418, manslaughter trial of James Kelly in the death of Arnold Walsh, 1906.

25. Barnardo 452 B 3.02, 586 B 6.05, 275 B 9.95, 149 B 8.91, 379 B 3.00, 162 B 3.92; Quarrier Emigration 4, p. 10; Liverpool 4, pp. 49-50; London and Stratford 32, p. 79; PAC Toronto Trades and Labor Council, Minutebooks, MG 28 I 44, 20 April 1888; PAC RG 76 65/3115, *Ottawa Citizen*, 7 June 1898; PAC RG 76 94/10216, Brandon Grand Jury, July 1893; 'Prison Reform Commission', *Ontario Sessional Papers* 1891, pp. 498, 515, 637.

26. Liverpool 12, p. 474; Quarrier Emigration 1, pp. 382; Barnardo 906 G 5.04; 814 G 7.98, 795 G 10.96, 771 G 10.92, 612 B 9.05, 323 B 6.97, 71 B 3.88, 17 B 1.85; PAC RG 76 378/523636, case of Lily Aldhouse from King's Norton Union and the Middlemore Homes; PAC RG 76 78/6648, Maria Rye to L. Periera, 2 Dec. 1893; 'Report of the department of neglected and dependent children', *Ontario Sessional Papers* 1899, p. 81.

27. *Children's Advocate*, Oct. 1881, p. 149; Barnardo girls K.A. 7.02, microfilmed letters; London and Stratford 17, p. 111.

28. PAC RG 76 119/22857, James Burges of Quarrier's, Brockville reply to 1895 circulars; PAC RG 76 63/2869, J.S. King, Middlemore, Halifax to Bogue Smart, 5 June 1913; PAC RG 76 64/3081, W.D. Scott to W.H. Merry, Macpherson Home, Stratford, 2 Mar. 1910; PAC RG 76 66/3115, J.J. Kelso to the secretary of each orphan home in the province of Ontario, 20 June 1910.

29. n = 724.

30. Ian E. Davey, 'Educational reform and the working class; school attendance in Hamilton, Ontario, 1851-91', unpublished PhD thesis, University of Toronto, 1975, pp. 228, 239, 240, 296; Terry Copp, *The Anatomy of Poverty* (McClelland and Stewart, Toronto, 1974), pp. 52-3; Beth Good Latzer, *Myrtleville* (South Illinois University Press, Carbondale and Edwardsville, 1976), pp. 155-6; similar patterns existed in English rural areas, see Jennie Kitteringham, 'Country work girls in nineteenth-century England', in Raphael Samuel, *Village Life and Labour* (Routledge and Kegan Paul, London, 1975), pp. 81-5.

31. *Canada Law Journal*, 1 Dec. 1896, XXXII, no. 19, 'Hall vs. School Trustees for sec. 2, Stisted'; PAC RG 76 530/803563, J. Young to J. Bruce Walker, 1 Dec. 1909; PAC RG 76 94/10216, James Burges to Secretary, Immigration Branch, 5 May 1894; *Ups and Downs*, August 1896, p. 4; June 1897, p. 2; Jan. 1898, pp. 1-2.

32. London and Stratford 7, Alice Edwards; Liverpool 12, p. 74; interview with Sidney Chappell, October 1975, Paisley, Ontario.

33. Quarrier Emigration 2, p. 163; Marchmont 1903, 1904, 1905, p. 7; Barnardo 942 G 4.06, 893 G 7.03, 435 B 9.01, 397 B 9.00, 391 B 7.00, 417 B 3.01.

34. n = 880; A Watt Smyth, *Physical Deterioration, its causes and the cure*

(John Murray, London, 1904), pp. 28-9; Children's Home, *Report* 1884-5, pp. 10, 14; 1886-7, p. 10; 1889-90, p. 16; 1895-6, p. 20; PRO, MH 32, vol. 92, Mason report for 1888, 3 Jan. 1889, p. 22; PAC RG 17 395/42680, Maria Rye to John Lowe, 12 Feb. 1884; Standish Meacham, *A Life Apart* (Thames and Hudson, London, 1977), pp. 155-6.

35. n = 898; admission data were taken from the medical report included in each printed case history. No information upon the child's health at point of emigration has been preserved. Canadian incidence was constructed using records from throughout the apprenticeship period. 'General condition' refers to the effects of malnutrition, bone disease and inherited social disease. Mental weakness and mental illness could not be partitioned. British observers did not make a clear distinction between retardation and illness and in the Canadian reports children who seem to have become severely depressed for a time are described as slow witted.

36. Barnardo 433 B 7.01, 85 B 6.88, 297 B 7.96, 314 B 3.97, 449 B 3.02, 193 B 3.93, 318 B 6.97, 304 B 10.96, 854 G 6.01, 891 G 7.03, 939 G 9.05, 924 G 5.05, 893 G 7.03, 900 G 9.03, 810 G 9.97, 911 G 7.04, 978 G 9.07, 304 G 10.96.

37. Liverpool 4, pp. 4-10; London and Stratford 32, Emma Pedder; PAC RG 76 63/2869, case of Dora Rooker, Aston Union and Middlemore Home, Halifax; PAC RG 76 78/6648, Maria Rye to L. Periera, 19 Dec. 1893; PAC RG 76 378/ 523635, Lily Aldhouse, King's Norton Union and Middlemore Homes.

38. Canada, House of Commons, *Journals* 1888, app. 5, 'Report of the select standing committee on agriculture and colonisation', pp. 10, 12-14; Liverpool 16, p. 12; 'First conference on child-saving', *Ontario Sessional Papers* 1895, p. 23; 'British child immigrants', *OSP* 1897-8, p. 11; PAC RG 17 395/42584, J.M. McGovern, Portland Maine to John Lowe, 11 Feb. 1884; PAC RG 76 32/72412, Miss E. Meiklejohn, Knowlton to Louisa Birt, 23 Sept. 1902; London and Stratford 22, p. 56.

39. 'Report on the education and maintenance of children in the Metropolis', *Br. P.P.* 1896, XLIII, vol. 2, p. 351.

40. For example 153 of the 271 emigrants sent to Canada by the Liverpool Sheltering Homes in 1883 and 1884 were girls; 148 of their emigrants for 1892-3 were female. See Liverpool 4, Liverpool 8.

41. Barnardo 870 G 7.02, 930 G 8.05.

42. PAC RG 76 94/10216, James Burges to Secretary, 5 May 1894; PAC RG 76 78/6648, Maria Rye to secretary, 25 Aug. 1893; PAC RG 76 65/3115, Edward de M. Rudolf to Clifford Sifton, 12 Mar. 1900; PAC RG 76 63/2864, Ada Francis case, 1907; PAC RG 17 649/73918, Edith Seymour case; PAC RG 17 555/62351, Maria Rye to John Lowe, 5 Nov. 1887; Marchmont 26, p. 89; Canada, Statutes, 63 and 64 Vic. 1900 c. 46 s. 701A.

43. Girls who became pregnant in Canada while apprentices are over-represented by 35 per cent among those who were in Barnardo's for less than 2 years before emigration; n = 187.

44. The relationship between provocation for admission and incidence of premarital pregnancy is significant, n = 176, chi-squared = .5389 with 6 degrees of freedom.

45. K.A.H. Buckley and M.C. Urquart, *Historical Statistics of Canada* (Cambridge University Press and Macmillan, Cambridge and Toronto, 1965), Series B1 – 14, p. 38.

46. s = 2.7, n = 123; Canada, Dominion Bureau of Statistics, *Vital Statistics* 1921-22, Table III; 1926, Tables VII and XIII, and XV and XVI.

47. The first indication of conception available to the farm wife was extramenstrual bleeding. In the 1890s the earliest confirmations of pregnancy available to an experienced medical practitioner were Chadwick's change in the

colour and Hegar's change in the compressibility of the cervix which appeared at ten weeks; J.R. Chadwick, 'Value of the bluish colouration of the vaginal entrance as a sign of pregnancy', *Transactions of the American Gynecological Society*, vol. 11 (1887), p. 399; A Hegar, 'Diagnose der schwangerschaftsperiode', *Deutsch. Med. Wschr.* 21.565 (1895); PAC RG 76 133/32405, McGovern report, 18 Mar. 1897; Archives of Ontario, RG 11 Box 14, 1880, 359, Maria Rye to D. Spence, 24 April 1880; London and Stratford 32, p. 113; Barnardo 985 G 5.08, 952 G 8.06, 951 G 8.06, 927 G 5.05, 872 G 7.02, 901 G 9.03, 883 G 4.03, 865 G 5.02, 862 G 9.01, 839 G 6.00, 822 G 9.98, 813 G 7.98, 792 G 7.96, 772 G 10.93, 770 G 10.92, 993 G 7.08, 808 G 9.97, 994 G 4.06.

48. $n = 212$, chi squared $= 81.9$ with 12 degrees of freedom.

7 ADULTHOOD

> Of those under our care fully eighty-five percent are permanently and definitely established on the land, making two potatoes grow where one grew before, and in doing so adding to the wealth and resources of the country. [1]

> If ... you send out lads and lasses of pluck and principle ... who from force of circumstances can never rise higher than common servants here, let them do as they will, ten to one in the years to come you'll hear such stories of success in life as might put the plot of many a fashionable novel to blush. [2]

The Canadian childhoods of British boys and girls were a mixed blessing, physically good for the growing body but isolating, disheartening, less favourable for resolving the mental struggle of growing up. If the childhood years alone were considered, the juvenile immigration policy was a dubious business. But the sponsors of the movement were not primarily interested in the child's early years. They looked past childhood inconveniences to the serious concerns of adulthood. If immigrants who had spent their youth in Canada adapted more readily, knew better how to get for themselves the best Canada had to offer, were more accustomed to Canadian ways and thus more contented to remain here, then, in the philanthropists' eyes, the apprenticeships, no matter how arduous, were justified. [3]

The best that Canada had to offer immigrants was the country life. Agricultural idealism led British philanthropists to prefer a rural environment for their wards, and settling immigrants in the countryside corresponded to contemporary Canadian conceptions of the national interest. The children's sponsors claimed that their wards were later 'to be found in nearly all walks of life' and gave special prominence to their evangelical success stories, the young men and women who were 'holding forth the Word of Life' in the ministry or in missions. But all contemporary reports from the emigration agencies and from the government departments that monitored their work insisted that juvenile immigrants of both sexes generally remained on the land as adults. Based on twenty years' experience with the programme, Bogue Smart of the Interior Department's Juvenile Immigration Division estimated in 1917 that 75 per cent of British apprentices graduated into agricultural occupations and intended to make farming their life's work. Young men were described as proprietors and intending proprietors of lands being opened in northern Ontario and the west or of 'humble holdings' in more settled eastern districts. Most rescue home girls were reported to be married to home boys or hired men or farmers' sons and happily engaged in the poultry and dairy work which would help raise their husband from renter or sharecropper to prosperous independent proprietor.[4]

Throughout the duration of the programme British child-savers measured the practical success of their mission by the proportion of young people they permanently separated from urban life and the labouring class, rescued from the chaos of the cities for the settled respectability of rural communities. These predispositions were strengthened from the 1890s onwards as Canadian government preferences for agricultural immigrants were increasingly sharpened by organised labour's insistence that newcomers be agricultural colonists and not industrial labourers. In response it became politic for officials from the rescue homes to shrink estimates of those who 'might be found in city factories or shops' to 'a handful ... so small that they could not by any conceivable possibility affect labour conditions generally'. Barnardo's Alfred Owen declared to a reporter from the Toronto *Globe* in 1909, 'they are not wanted in the cities and towns, and we do not want the cities and towns for them'. But did young men and women sponsored by the homes heed the advice of their elders? There may be more to the matter than the policies of their guardians and of the Canadian government imply. [5]

What happened to the young immigrants after their apprenticeship was over? The enthusiastic claims of their British and Canadian sponsors require closer scrutiny. Did stability and comfort later arrive to compensate the apprentices for their early troubles in Canada?

It is not easy to find out. My interviews with child immigrants often concentrated on the later years of their lives, but the men and women I spoke to in 1974 and 1975 were not typical child immigrants. Most of them had been members of the small parties which came to Canada in the 1920s, having received more British schooling than early home children had and facing different Canadian conditions. Those willing to be interviewed often described themselves as exceptional in the help they received either from Canadian masters and mistresses or from family and friends. The case files agree that they did seem to have been the lucky ones — those who felt neither pain nor shame as they looked back and were consequently willing to reminisce with a stranger.

The written records also pose difficulties. Even the homes that maintained regular contact with their young wards did not follow them systematically after they completed their indentures. The Canadian Interior Department's responsibilities for reporting to British Boards of Guardians ceased when pauper children were no longer wards of the state.

The extant communications of old boys and old girls with the British homes are commonly of three sorts. First, there were friendly letters from alumni sympathetic with the homes' work who subscribed to the homes' magazines or donated to their Christmas funds, some of whom wrote to the homes as they would have to kin. Second, the majority of enquiries came when former wards sought information about British kin or the proof of their birthdate required for membership in lodges, company pension plans or life insurance policies or, after 1926, for the old age pension. Third, the homes sometimes sent out circulars asking men and women who had completed their indentures to report upon their current circumstances.

Not all parts of this information are strictly comparable. As immigrants grew older they were less likely to retain contact with the agencies, so that for each successive stage in the life-cycle there is a contracting pool of information. The accumulation of work experience and of savings and the process of family formation make occupation strongly dependent upon age. Men severed their ties with the homes sooner than women. Only in rare instances did institutions hear at regular intervals from a former ward. Still, the Barnardo sample used here (Table 7.1) includes information on one-third of the women and one-fifth of the men twenty years after they graduated from the care of the institution.

How typical were the men and women who wrote to the homes? Those in the Barnardo sample emigrated younger than most, changed situations less frequently and more often completed their indentures. Unfortunately the follow-up records of the other agencies are not complete enough to allow generalisation beyond Barnardo emigrants. But it would seem that the men and women we know most about were the boys and girls who adapted most easily to the constraints of their apprenticeships. They were probably neither the most restless and ambitious — these men and women tended to deny their associations with the homes — nor the slowest and most defeated by their predicament.

When young single women wrote to the institutions at Knowlton, Belleville, Brockville and Peterborough they described their jobs, their wages and their boarding houses. The letters of married women reflect

Table 7.1: Proportion of Child Immigrants in Contact with the Homes, Barnardo Sample

Age		Men	Women
21 or over	%	57.3	60.4
	n	410	160
26 or over	%	35.8	44.5
	n	256	118
36 or over	%	21.2	32.1
	n	151	85
46 or over	%	13.5	20.0
	n	97	53
56 or over	%	8.1	11.7
	n	58	31
Reporting cases.	n	716	265
Average age at last communication with the homes		28.5	32.0

family rather than individual concerns — children's health and schooling, correspondence with kin, the progress of the domestic work of the season. Only occasionally did they mention their husband's work and share their hopes for the future with the ladies who had visited them during their apprenticeships. Whereas we have some information about adult occupation for 87 per cent of the Barnardo men, we have similar data for only 40 per cent of Barnardo women. But these letters do tell us several things which are helpful.

First, women who came to Canada through the juvenile immigration homes became urban dwellers. Girls left the countryside in greater numbers than did boys. They left sooner, and they made the break more dramatically. They passed over the small towns nearby for larger Canadian cities, notably Toronto, Hamilton and Montreal and rarely gave the back concessions a second look. [6]

By the time they had completed their indentures most home girls had had at least four years' introduction to Canadian domestic routine. Most were weary of other people's babies and other people's housework. They did not go to the city in order to exchange the informality of the farm household for the strict hierarchy of service in a large city establishment or the aprons of the country kitchen for the starched uniforms of the city parlour. They wanted their own room, their own wage and their own choice of what to do on Saturday night. Like Canadian-born girls, whose flight from rural life was also marked by comparison with their male peers, young immigrants lately released from the bonds of apprenticeship wanted some variety, some excitement, a few years' independence before marriage and enough free time after work to look about for a suitable mate. [7]

The few who entered the confined world of urban domestic service did not linger there. Barnardo's had a Toronto office through which old girls could find city domestic situations. All the homes counselled young women to 'let no temptation draw [them] away from the safe respectable and happy, though monotonous duties of the household' since no other employment would bring them the same affection and 'good name in the community', so secure and respectable a place in Canada or (it was implied) so respectable a spouse. One young woman of 20 who had served her indenture in a small town, worked as a domestic in two homes in Toronto and then taken a job in Eaton's for ten dollars a week was thus warned of the trials awaiting her:

I was pleased to again hear from you, and to know that you are well, and doing well. I think you know, Dorothy, that factory work never meets our approval for our girls, the close unhealthy atmosphere of the work-room is usually detrimental to health, and the life is not wholesome and uplifting. I consider our girls much happier and better off in domestic service, however, we are pleased to know that you are in a good safe boarding house. Your freedom is in your own hands, and I hope, dear girl, you will have the wisdom to use it properly.

Undaunted, most home girls finished their apprenticeships and left service as soon as opportunity offered. [8]

Few had difficulty finding jobs, although the places available for unskilled young women with limited schooling were rarely less physically demanding than those they had left behind on the farm, and they seldom paid well. There were rescue home girls who worked first in hotels, either as chambermaids or kitchen maids, still using their domestic skills but trading respectability for anonymity in the workplace. Some young women from Marchmont at Belleville and Mrs Birt's home at Knowlton, Quebec, graduated from service into the textile mills of the Eastern Townships Quebec, northern Vermont or eastern Ontario. But work in larger cities was more common — most often factory work — particularly in the plants run by large department stores, sometimes service work in restaurants, or sales work in shops. Hours were long, and the wages were not high. In the decade before the First World War Barnardo and Macpherson girls in such employments were making five to twelve dollars a week. From this they paid for their rooms in boarding houses and their clothing. There were some young women who managed to save enough during this period in their lives to return for a visit to Britain. Nonetheless there were few inducements to stay in such employments. Young women regarded their period as factory workers, shop clerks or waitresses as a temporary transition before they left the paid labour force to marry in their early twenties. [9]

There were, of course, other occupations labelled women's work which offered more status, if not always more pay. Bright adventurous daughters from prosperous farm families went into teaching, nursing or stenography after they finished school. Ambitious rescue home girls astutely reckoned that these professions were certain routes to respectability. For them, however, the path led very steeply uphill through junior school and high school to professional training beyond.

Home girls were less likely than home boys at any age to attend school. They were particularly less likely to be released from domestic demands as teenagers — young men's farm tasks being strongly seasonal but young women's work being relentless the year round. To complete the primary course of instruction and pass the entrance examinations for high school, girls needed an exceptional British background, unusually quick wits or a remarkably self-sufficient and sympathetic mistress. There were no high schools in the countryside. Rural teenagers who had passed their 'entrance' and wanted to work for their high school matriculation had to find a place to live in a nearby town. Local young people paid board or stayed with kin. Lacking either cash or connections, immigrant adolescents managed only if they were able to find situations where they could work for their board and go to school full-time — at the same time. [10]

Teaching was the least popular of these three options for the ambitious. There were several school teachers among the Quarrier girls. Both the Scots officials at the Fairknowe Home in Brockville and the Scots-Canadian families with which these young women were placed seem to have placed special emphasis upon education. But there are no women teachers in the Barnardo sample, and they are rare in the records of the Macpherson and Birt homes. Even the girls who worked as pupil-teachers before they emigrated did not pursue this profession in Canada. Finding money for living expenses while at model or normal school was an obstacle. Savings from the apprenticeship years would rarely suffice for that. But more important, the carefully monitored life of the respectable teacher shared the worst disadvantages of work in service, often requiring living-in on suffrance with the parents of her pupils and being poorly paid and obliged to conform to ideal, rather than conventional, local standards of behaviour. [11]

The training in nursing required less capital and less preparatory schooling but considerably more stamina. Some hospitals required students to buy their books and uniforms, a circumstance which locked several Barnardo girls in bitter disputes with the home over release of wages held in trusteeship funds. But other schools paid students a monthly stipend — which eased the economic barriers to entry — and kept the educational requirements for admission low to ensure a steady supply of working students for the wards. The course commonly took three years of twelve-hour days and six and a half day weeks, a test of endurance. But nursing provided a singular opportunity for rescue home girls to acquire professional credentials, and several rose to prominent posts in western Canadian and government hospitals. [12]

The most accessible route to respectability for former apprentices was the business college. Secretarial schools did not require high school certificates from their students, and they offered courses at night. Young women moved to the cities, found themselves temporary situations in domestic service and commenced 'learning stenography evenings to escape from housework' and from the stigma of being a rescue home child. At least 7 per cent of Barnardo girls qualified themselves in this way. [13]

By their mid-twenties most women from the homes had married and left the paid labour force. Few who wrote to the homes returned later in life to wage work. Their husbands, so far as we know, were drawn from the ranks of working men — machine hands in the railway shops, railway linemen, telegraph operators, mechanics, labourers, factory workers, stationary engineers, carpenters. For many the early years of marriage saw frequent moves. A bright and dependable woman, settled in Shanty Bay, Muskoka, at age 8, the wife of a carpenter and mother of two, wrote to Barnardo's:

> Owing to the labor we do not settle long in any one place so should you desire to reply, mail will always reach me at Shanty Bay ... We think seriously of returning to the States where there is a good

opening at present. I like it over there too. Wishing you success in 1929. [14]

There were a few farm wives among the home girls — wives of renters, sharecroppers, northern Ontario pioneers. One woman married a Barr colonist, another completed her household science degree at the Ontario Agricultural College and became mistress of a farm in a prosperous rural district. [15]

Most young immigrant maids did not heed their guardians' advice. They left both the countryside and domestic service very soon after their apprenticeships were over. Most worked for a few years in city factories, restaurants or shops. Less than 15 per cent secured the clerical or professional training that ensured success in the labour force. Most were married in their twenties to working men; few married farmers.

Were they better off than their mothers or their sisters? It is impossible to say. Begging letters are extremely rare in the after-care files. There is only one instance of an old girl asking for the admission of her own child to one of the homes. But the experience of their male peers carries us somewhat further.

A few boys from the homes grew up to be the settled, prosperous agricultural proprietors the philanthropists praised (Table 7.2). Many more left the land and became urban labourers, factory workers, artisans and clerks — exactly as Canadian labour leaders had glumly prophesied. In its own terms, the movement to rescue the sons of city wage workers from the city and from wage work failed.

Young men moved rapidly out of agricultural labour after their apprenticeships were over. Only 11 per cent of the Barnardo men last known to the homes between the ages of 27 and 36 were employed in this way. By middle life 16 per cent of the boy immigrants who wrote to their former guardians were farming their own land, but 67 per cent were working for wages in towns and cities. Why did so many leave the parts of Canada they knew best, the places where they would seem to have had an advantage? In forsaking the back concessions did they also leave behind the head start the philanthropists had promised in return for a Canadian childhood?

Young men left the countryside because they found there neither the sense of community nor the 'opportunity for substantial advancement' which philanthropists expected would capture their imagination and bind them to the soil. Looking toward the bright city lights was of course a common preoccupation among farm youths of the time. The

Table 7.2: Occupations, Barnardo Men, all years

Occupation		Age at last contact with the homes, years			
		15-21	22-26	27-36	37 or over
Unemployed	%	14.9	7.8	7.4	4.8
	n	34	11	7	7
Agricultural labourer	%	54.4	37.1	10.6	5.5
	n	124	52	10	8
Other labourers, extractive, seasonal [a]	%	14.0	15.5	23.2	18.5
	n	32	22	22	27
Unskilled service [b]	%	4.8	7.1	13.8	10.3
	n	11	10	13	15
Factory labour [c]	%	4.8	7.1	14.9	16.4
	n	11	10	14	24
Artisan, foreman, clerk	%	2.2	9.2	11.5	20.5
	n	5	13	11	30
Police, RCMP, firemen, military	%	2.2	5.0	2.1	1.4
	n	5	7	2	2
Sharecropper, renter in agriculture	%	0	0.7	5.3	2.7
	n		1	5	4
Agricultural proprietor	%	2.6	8.6	6.4	15.8
	n	6	12	6	23
Professionals	%	0	1.4	2.1	4.1
	n	–	2	4	6
Reporting cases	n	228	140	94	146

Note: The highest status occupation closest to the expectation of the movement's sponsors was chosen when more than one adult occupation was recorded.
a.   Labourers in logging, mining, fishing, lakeboats; railroad hands, seasonal labour in several sectors.
b.   Domestic service, waiter, postman, stableman, truckdriver, janitor, street railway worker, telephone or electrical line man.
c.   Railroad foreman, conductor, telegraphist, skilled craftsmen including engineers, blacksmiths, mechanics, carpenters, barbers, painters; clerk, secretary, salesman.

rural population of Ontario reached its peak in the decade between 1891 and 1901 and thereafter declined. By 1911 there were already fewer country-dwellers in the province than there had been in 1871. This movement was not a flight from marginal lands: new townships were still being opened to settlement in Ontario, and county population declines bear no clear relationship to local soil quality. [16]

Young men, like young women, left the farm to escape the monotony, the loneliness and the quietness of the work, and the dullness of the life.   Contemporary commentators blamed rural parents and employers for the rural problem, for burdening young men with the menial work on the farm, excluding them from management decisions, harassing them with a continual succession of petty tasks which made a ten-hour city working day seem leisurely and condemning them to a separate status within the household which made the autonomy of cramped urban lodgings seem liberty. Rural teachers and preachers were increasingly drawn from urban backgrounds and seemed inclined to think their country charges a dreary apprenticeship for better - city - things to come. The future was city clothes, city manners, city wealth. Young men listened and left. [17]

If there were social and cultural incentives to leave the land, there were also economic compulsions to do so. No man could make his fortune as an agricultural labourer. Very few men who did not already possess a small fortune could hope to establish themselves as agricultural proprietors. The very most a young man could expect to have saved at the end of his apprenticeship was $150. Even in the earliest days of the juvenile immigration movement the least he would need for shelter, stock and implements on Manitoba grant land was $500. By 1907 the stock and implements alone cost at least $1,000. [18]

It was easier to enter farming in some places than in others. Over one-third of the Barnardo men who took up land did so in rural Saskatchewan. Most of them had emigrated in the 1890s and completed their indentures during the time when grant land was most readily available in that province. Those who persisted on the land did so by taking seasonal wage jobs to sustain them through the years before their farms began to pay. One 10-year-old immigrant from Hammersmith, boarded out by his mother from birth and rejected by his stepfather, went west with his Ontario master at age 15. They both took up homesteads at Islay, Alberta, in 1911, the young man working on his own land on his own account and his employer's land for wages. He enlisted in 1916, returned three years later with an English wife, and by 1924 was well established on his half section with fifteen milk cows. But those who persisted were few. [19]

There was still grant land available in Ontario early in the twentieth century, in the fertile pockets of the northern shield then called New Ontario. Some men from the homes took up such land, but the region was not well endowed for farming. [20] In southern Ontario, particularly in the eastern counties where Macpherson and Quarrier boys grew up, there were graduating apprentices who tilled rented farms for years, working at odd jobs in winter, saving and waiting until they were able to enter the land market; others in southwestern Ontario waited in the same way while raising cash crops on shares. Sydney Mills worked rented land until, at age 44, he bought land the federal government had repossessed for tax default and was selling to increase wartime food production. A few men inherited farms through their wives or from their employers. But no more than 8 per cent of the men in the Barnardo sample ever tried farming, and an even smaller proportion were able or inclined to make farming their life's work. [21]

Nevertheless, young men did not usually leave the countryside with the abruptness characteristic of young women's flight to the city. Through their mid-twenties half of the Barnardo men were still doing labouring work outside the towns, in agriculture or in logging, on the lakeboats or railroad lines. One bright, studious 18-year-old went to England for the winter in 1909 and spent the next year working for his former master. The following summer he was sailing on the lakes between Toronto and Collingwood. The next spring he was constructing lines for the telephone company, and the year after that went west as a fireman on the Grand Trunk Railway. The next fall he left the countryside, in the ambulance corps of the first Canadian contingent to France, returning shell-shocked five years later to settle in as an employee of the telephone company. [22]

Seasonal combinations of employments were particularly common adaptations to the rigid demands of the Canadian climate and to young men's tastes for variety and independence. Many immigrants spent the decade after their apprenticeships trekking from winters in the shanties along northern rivers or in work-trains clearing track to summers on the lakes or on the land. They found intermittent work in rural industry, in saw mills, grist mills, or cheese and butter factories, travelling, using their wits and their motley accumulation of skills through Ontario, the border states and the west. [23]

A few men stayed in the seasonal labour market all their working lives. These were sturdy British street arabs grown to rugged wandering men who never seemed to crave more security than they had had as boys. In 1950, George Black of Barnardo's Toronto office made notes on the file of a 'jovial' 70-year-old, 52 years in Canada, 'a seasoned old fellow, as tough as nails, in more ways than one, [who had] been a farm hand, lumberjack, prospector, labourer, sailed to New Zealand and Chile'. He was visiting the agency to leave a donation and rail against 'the Jews, capitalists and Governments' for cutting off his old age pension because he had been doing winter construction work for good wages. [24] More usually, men settled by their mid-thirties. A steady proportion, about one in five of Barnardo men reporting to the homes after age 27, were living in rural Ontario. This group included the agricultural proprietors, the renters, the sharecroppers, but also a large number of rural home owners raising families and working by the week on the farms and the roads and whatever else offered itself nearby. [25]

In these years, the movement of immigrant men in their late twenties and early thirties into urban centres became marked. The proportion of Barnardo men of these ages known to be in rural areas declined by one-third, while the proportion in Ontario towns and small cities and in Toronto, Hamilton and Ottawa doubled. Some of these were experienced section men and foremen for the railways, marrying and choosing one town in their district in which to settle down.[26] But the drift to the towns and cities usually also implied a shift from the agricultural and extractive sectors into service work and manufacturing. The proportion of Barnardo men in these urban employments was twice as large for 27- to 36-year-olds as for those 22 to 26. The trends towards residence in towns and cities and work in factories and service industries persisted among middle-aged and older men. By this stage in life, one in twenty of those reporting were agricultural labourers and one in six were agricultural proprietors while half were urban wage workers.

Deterred from agricultural proprietorship by city preferences and lack of funds, their tastes for change dulled by several years shifting through the seasonal labour market outside the towns, men from the homes turned to factory labour for precisely the feature their philanthropic guardians thought them least likely to find there — security. In substantial measure the Quarrier, Macpherson, Birt and Barnardo men whose middle years as manufacturing employees we know about do seem to have achieved this aim. Most settled not in Canada's large metropolitan centres but in towns and smaller cities. Thus boys not only moved into urban areas later than girls, they experienced urban life on a markedly smaller scale. Only one in ten Barnardo men settled in Toronto, Hamilton, Montreal or Ottawa, by contrast with one in four Barnardo women.

The typical urban dwellers among men from the homes worked as labourers, foremen and craftsmen in tariff-sheltered secondary manufacturing. They were woollen mill workers in Almonte, Paris and Hespeler. They made agricultural machinery for Cockshutt, Verity or Waterson's in Brantford. Perrin's employed them making biscuits in London; McClary employed them making stoves. While workers in the agricultural and extractive sectors faced difficulty during the

1930s, these men remained on the job, many buying their own homes, some being promoted to supervisory posts. The proportion of foremen, craftsmen and white-collar workers doubled among reporting Barnardo men between their early thirties and middle life. [27]

For men who had neither extraordinary gifts nor extraordinary opportunities, who possessed satisfactory health and as they grew older developed steady habits of work; in other words for the average rescue home boy, Canada did hold some promise. Let us take an example, a boy from the London slums, admitted to Barnardo's with his sister in August 1892, his two brothers having entered the home six months earlier. His father was dead after a prolonged illness. His mother had a bad leg which limited her earnings doing washing. He was four when he went to the rescue home and twelve when he went to Canada. His first master left farming soon after he was placed. He stayed with the second master four and a half years near Springfield, Ontario, in return for $100 cash and two terms of winter schooling; he worked the next season for another farmer in the district and at age 19 in 1908 went west. Within the year he returned, and in the next six years he worked as a carpenter, as an agricultural labourer and as a hand on the Michigan Central Railway in Ontario, with one more trip to Saskatchewan in 1912. He enlisted early in the war and after demobilisation married at age 33 and got a job in the Ford plant near Windsor. He fathered three children and after nine years in factory work joined the Canada Customs service in 1927. During the 1930s he bought a house in Windsor, and in 1949, when we last hear of him, he was still living there with his wife, working at the border crossing and worrying about his children's education. [28]

In the first half of the twentieth century the most prosperous region in Canada was southern Ontario, and one of the least vulnerable sectors of the economy was government-protected secondary manufacturing. If British apprentices were likely anywhere to find economic security, found a family and join a community in Canada, it seems to have been here: not in the old settled farms of the east, nor the new homestead lands of the west, not in commerce or the professions, but in the factories and in the railways, the electric companies and the government services which supported them.

Prospects for British immigrants in Canada have always been mixed. In the nineteenth century Britons did about as well, but only as well, in Canada as they might have done had they never left Great Britain. After 1900 the outlook for such immigrants in the Dominion seemed, if anything, even gloomier. Few observers outside Frank Oliver's

Department of the Interior and the most high-minded imperial circles expected Britons to be able to hold their own against competitors in Canada. James Shaver Woodsworth, a Methodist mission worker among the immigrants of north Winnipeg, faulted the English for their 'lack of adaptability', found them so wanting in enterprise and in useful skills that their presence was becoming a serious problem in Canadian cities. In the Montreal immigrant community in the 1930s Britons as a group were not moving upwards socially, while British craftsmen and other workingmen after emigration generally slipped downwards into the ranks of the unskilled and casually employed. Until the Second World War British birth did not seem to make immigrants more assimilable in Canada. After 1945 this pattern changed. By the 1950s Britons who arrived in Canada were in a few years earning more and holding down better jobs than other new arrivals of similar education and duration of Canadian residence. In postwar Canada, rather late for the child immigrants, the nineteenth-century prophecies came true. Britons were preferred for responsible positions. They improved their social and economic standing during a period when other entering groups were suffering declines in status. [29]

Although they came when, at least in retrospect, times were not especially propitious for Britons in Canada, the child immigrants were usually separated from their countrymen as a special case. Their sponsors described them as the select few from among the ranks of refuge children, the 'flower of the flock', boys and girls who would have done better than their peers had they stayed in Britain and who with the advantages of a colonial apprenticeship would outdo British city-dwellers encountering Canadian ways for the first time as adults. The friends of the movement thought their young protégés twice blessed, with the advantages both of British birth and a Canadian education, favoured by comparison with other Britons and indisputably superior to the 'unsavoury concourse of Poles, Polish and Russian Jews, Italians, Galicians, Syrians and other races of Southern and Eastern Europe that form the bulk of the present emigration both to Canada and the United States'. [30]

Others were unimpressed by either the process of selection or the transforming power of a Canadian apprenticeship. J.S. Woodsworth thought the child immigrants' pasts 'too great a hardship', their 'inherited tendencies too evil', too engrained, to be susceptible to change. Canadian labour leaders were convinced young immigrants had been chosen for their weaknesses and not their strengths. Edward de Montjoie Rudolf of the Church of England Waifs and Strays Society saw his young people as 'rolling stones', drifting 'from one occupation to another without making progress at all', endowed with 'neither the intelligence nor the physique to enable them to work out a career for themselves'. [31]

The 1931 Census of Canada is the earliest to report jointly on occupation and nativity, and then only nationwide rather than by region. This date is too late to be ideal for comparison with prewar Barnardo immigrants, and the data would not show the concentration of Barnardo men in Ontario. Furthermore, since census data cannot be controlled for age the Barnardo men are younger than the larger groups with whom they are compared. Nevertheless, Table 7.3 suggests how rescue home boys fared in relation to their peers.

The effects of the boy immigrants' apprenticeships are plainly apparent in these comparisons, though probably exaggerated somewhat in this rendering by the relatively young age, 28.5 years on average, at which most adult occupations in the Barnardo sample were filed. The over-representation of men from the homes in farm labour by comparison with each of the other three groups, and their under-representation among agricultural renters, sharecroppers and proprietors would be less marked among Barnardo men a decade or two older. Their life-cycle pattern of movement away from being hired hands and to a lesser extent into farm ownership makes this clear. But there is no reason to conclude that child immigrants were more likely than other immigrants to find independence and security in agriculture. However, by virtue of their early Canadian experience they were more often able to avoid the precarious and arduous existence in northern mining, logging and construction camps into which so many newly arrived Europeans were forced. In cities and towns they took up places midway between those of the British and Canadian groups. They were more likely than Canadians to be urban service or factory workers, less likely than other Britons to be trapped in the most poorly paid of city jobs. Their truncated Canadian education did, however, have its price. Barnardo men were starkly under-represented among the professional classes by comparison with Canadians, other Britons and the European-born. Because their British industrial training was cut short, they were also less likely to find a place among the ranks of the highly skilled manual workers, artisans, foremen and clerks where so many of their countrymen thrived.

Yet the child immigrants were materially better off in Canada than they would have been in Britain. Most girls from the homes would have been sent into service; boys would have taken up labouring jobs or

Table 7.3: Adult Occupations, All Barnardo Men Reporting, Canadian-, British- and European-born Men Gainfully Occupied, 1931

Occupational Group	Barnardo %	Canadian born %	British- born %	European- born %	ratio Barnardo/ Canadian- born	ratio Barnardo/ British- born	ratio Barnardo/ European- born
Agricultural labourer	36.6	19.3	10.3	12.8	1.9	3.6	2.9
Other labourers, extractive, seasonal	18.7	20.8	17.8	33.5	0.9	1.1	0.6
Unskilled service	8.8	6.5	14.1	4.1	1.4	0.6	2.1
Factory labourer	10.5	8.2	13.9	5.8	1.3	0.8	1.8
Artisan, foreman, clerk	10.5	11.9	17.2	9.4	0.9	0.6	1.1
Police, RCMP, fireman, military	2.9	0.5	1.3	–	5.8	2.2	–
Agricultural proprietor, sharecropper or renter	10.1	22.2	13.8	26.4	0.5	0.7	0.4
Professionals	2.1	10.7	11.7	8.0	0.2	0.2	0.3
N	626	2,130,009	530,531	389,763			
Missing data	95	264,668	66,355	18,392			

Note: Census occupational categories have been regrouped to conform with the Barnardo categories. Barnardo profiles have been recalculated excluding the unemployed. Census data do not distinguish between agricultural proprietors, renters and sharecroppers.

Source: Canada, *Census of 1931*, VIII, Table 44, pp. 310–21.

joined the ranks in the navy or army.[32]   As sons and daughters of semi-skilled and unskilled manual workers in Britain their prospects were not bright. About half of Britons with similar backgrounds found themselves in the same poor jobs as their parents, with the prospect that their own children would face the same severely circumscribed opportunities. Men who were not in the same predicament as their fathers were doing less well. While upward mobility was characteristic of prosperous Britons in the first half of the twentieth century, less privileged people tended to be drifting downwards rather than gaining ground.[33]   By contrast among the Barnardo immigrants, 31 per cent of those reporting adult occupations broke away from unskilled service and labouring work and from military service. Nineteen per cent achieved the relative security of commercial, industrial or agricultural proprietorship or of foreman, artisan or clerk at some time in their working lives. The gains are clear, whether or not they compensated for the hardships entailed in early emigration. They were, however, far smaller than the reformers had predicted.

Notes

1. PAC RG 76 51/2209, A. de B. Owen to A.M. Burgess, 24 April 1895.

2. *Night and Day*, 1884, p. 30.

3. Canada, House of Commons, *Journals*, appendix 8, p. 10.

4. PAC RG 76 30/674, Robert Wallace to Superintendent of Immigration, 2 July 1901; *Christian*, 13 April 1905, p. 24; PAC RG 76 66/3115, G. Bogue Smart to J. Bruce Walker, 12 February 1917; PAC RG 76 202/87308, Southwark Catholic Emigration Society pamphlet, 1898; Arthur Copping, *The Golden Land* (Hodder and Stoughton, London, 1911), p. 205; PAC RG 76 200; *Ontario Sessional Papers*, 'Immigration', 1888, p. 14; 'Neglected and Dependent Children', 1903, p. 118; 1907, p. 116.

5. *Ups and Downs*, XI, 2, June 1905, p. 10; *OSP*, 'British Children', 1898, p. 23; 'Neglected Children', 1905, p. 76; 'Neglected Children', 1909, p. 96; PAC RG 76 202/87 308, Southwark Catholic Emigration Society prospectus, 1898.

6. Adult Locations,   Barnardo sample, women – Toronto, Hamilton, Ottawa, 26.5%; Southern Ontario, cities less than 50,000 (1901), 12.3%; Southern Ontario villages, 14.6%; n = 268.

7. John MacDougall, *Rural Life in Canada* (University of Toronto Press, Toronto, [1973] 1913), p. 39; W.R. Young, 'The Countryside on the Defensive: agricultural Ontario's views of rural depopulation', unpublished MA thesis, University of British Columbia, 1971, pp. 31, 41; Goldwin Smith, *Canada and the Canadian Question*, (University of Toronto Press, Toronto, [1971] 1891), p. 28; Lloyd Reynolds, *The British Immigrant* (Oxford University Press, Toronto, 1935), pp. 185-6; Peter Stearns, 'Working-Class Women in Britain, 1890-1914', in Martha Vicinus, *Suffer and Be Still* (Indiana University Press, Bloomington and London, 1973), p. 110; Genevieve Leslie, 'Domestic Service in Canada, 1880-1920', in *Women at Work, Ontario, 1850-1930* (Canadian Women's Educational Press, Toronto, 1974), pp. 85-9; Leonora Davidoff, 'Mastered for Life: Servant, Wife and Mother in Victorian and Edwardian England', *Journal of Social History*, vol. 7, no. 4 (1974), pp. 406-22.

8. Barnardo 868 G 5.02, letter of 6 May 1912, 852 G 6.01, 917 G 9.04; *Ups and Downs*, Jan. 1901, p. 59; Oct. 1900. p. 84; *Christian*, 19 Feb. 1880, p. 14.

9. Mean marriage age (Barnardo girls) 21.2 years, s = 2.7, n = 123; Quarrier Emigration 1, pp. 98, 105; Barnardo 761 G 8.89, 788 G 9.95, 824 G 7.99, 868 G 5.02, 882 G 9.02, 917 G 9.04.

10. Liverpool 12, Annie Moss; Barnardo 899 G 9.03, 864 G 9.01.

11. Doris French, *High Button Bootstraps* (Ryerson, Toronto, 1968), pp. 20, 21, 25; Elizabeth Graham, 'Schoolmarms and early teaching in Ontario', in *Women at Work*, pp. 180-7; I am grateful to Alison Prentice for sharing her research in progress on Ontario school teachers with me.

12. Quarrier History 29, p. 193; Judi Coburn,'"I see and am silent": a short history of nursing in Ontario', in *Women at Work*, pp. 140-4; Barnardo 846 G 9.01, 784 G 9.95, 826 G 7.99, 853 G 6.01.

13. Barnardo 781 G 9.95, 863 G 9.01, 894 G 7.03, 967 G 4.07, 971 G 7.07.

14. Liverpool 4, pp. 87-8; Quarrier History 19, p. 8; Barnardo 779 G 11.94; 780 G 11.94, 829 G 9.99, 832 G 9.99, 902 G 9.03, 923 G 10.04, 948 G 5.06.

15. Quarrier Emigration 1, pp. 30, 48; Emigration 2, p.35; Barnardo 799 G 6.97, 990 G 7.08.

16. J.W. Watson, 'Rural depopulation in south-western Ontario', *Annals of Association of American Geographers*, vol. 37 (1947), pp. 147-8; Jacob Spelt, *Urban Development in South-central Ontario* (McClelland and Stewart, Toronto, 1972), p. 179.

17. E.A.W. Gill, *A Manitoba Chore Boy* (Religious Tract Society, London, 1912), p. 74; *Highways and Hedges*, Feb. 1898, p. 27; Reynolds, *British Immigrants*, pp. 58-9, 269-72; Richard Allen, *The Social Passion* (University of Toronto Press, Toronto, 1973), pp. 23-4; Young, 'Countryside', pp.44-9, 76, 84, 190-1.

18. *Christian*, 20 Dec. 1883, p. 15; *Highways and Hedges*, Feb. 1898, p. 27; David E Schob, *Hired Hands and Plowboys* (University of Illinois Press, Urbana, 1975), pp. 267, 271; John Herd Thompson, 'Bringing in the Sheaves: the harvest excursionists, 1890-1929', *Canadian Historical Review*, vol. 59, no. 4 (1978), p. 488.

19. Barnardo 519 B 3.04, 488 B 3.03, 351 B 9.98; 280 B 6.95, 332 B 9.97, 7 B 1884, 519 B 3.04, 279 B 6.95, 394 B 7.00, 699 B 5.08, 590 B 6.05, 411 B 3.01, 67 B 8.87, 680 B 7.07; Quarrier Emigration 1, pp. 462-3; Thompson, 'Bringing in the Sheaves', pp. 468-9, 471, 487-9

20. Barnardo 340 B 4.98, 344 B 7.98, 525 B 3.04.

21. Interview with Sydney Mills, Paisley, Ontario, 18 Oct. 1975; interview with Sidney Chappell, Paisley, Ontario, 18 Oct. 1975; Liverpool 16, Herbert Laing; Barnardo 694 B 3.08, 38 B 3.86, 603 B 8.05, 694 B 3.08, 281 B 6.95, 278 B 6.95.

22. Barnardo 505 B 7.03.

23. Claude Theodore, 'The Story of My Life', *New Horizons* vol. 1, no. 1 (Winter 1952); Liverpool 4, pp. 219-20; Liverpool 8, p. 97; Liverpool 12, p. 474; Marchmont 16, p. 42; Schob, *Hired Hands*, pp. 150, 166, 255; Barnardo 553 B 13.04, 542 B 7.04, 599 B 8.05, 278 B 6.95, 656 B 2.07, 551 B 9.04.

24. Barnardo 361 B 7.99.

25. Children's Home, *Report*, 1899-1900, p. 34; Barnardo 542 B 7.04, 606 B 8.05.

26. Liverpool 8, p. 73; Quarrier History 9, p. 69; Barnardo 680 B 7.07.

27. London and Stratford 27, p. 138; Marchmont 1903, 1904, 1905, p.7; Barnardo 198 B 3.93, 255 B 11.94, 336 B 4.98, 342 B 7.98, 413 B 3.01, 440 B 9.01, 466 B 7.02, 502 B 7.03, 626 B 5.06, 656 B 2.07, 669 B 4.07; see similarly, Chad Gaffield and David Levine, 'Dependency and Adolescence on the Canadian

Frontier: Orillia, Ontario in the Mid-Nineteenth Century', *History of Education Quarterly*, vol. 18, no. 1 (Spring 1978), pp. 38-9.

28. Barnardo 413 B 3.01.

29. John Porter, *The Vertical Mosaic* (University of Toronto Press, Toronto, 1965), p. 62; James Shaver Woodsworth, *Strangers within our Gates* (University of Toronto Press, Toronto, [1909] 1972) pp. 54-5; Reynolds, *British Immigrants*, pp. 82-3, 270-1; Anthony H. Richmond, *Post-War Immigrants in Canada* (University of Toronto Press, Toronto, 1967), pp. 69, 78, 125.

30. 'Report of the department of neglected and dependent children', *Ontario Sessional Papers* 1904, p. 82; *Night and Day*, 1884, p. 30; 'Report on the education and maintenance of pauper children in the Metropolis', *Br. P.P.*, 1896, XLIII, vol. 2, p. 352.

31. Woodsworth, *Strangers*, pp. 61-2; 'Agricultural settlements in British colonies', *Br. P.P.*, 1906, LXXVI, vol. 2, pp. 69-70.

32. National Children's Home, *Report*, 1888-9, p. 9; *Night and Day*, 1884, p. 30.

33. Ramkrishna Mukherjee, 'A study of social mobility between three generations', in D.V. Glass (ed.), *Social Mobility in Britain* (Routledge and Kegan Paul, London, 1954), pp. 266-87.

8 TWENTIETH-CENTURY POLICY

A free open air life, in a healthy invigorating climate, and, among an energetic vigorous people, not afraid of work, is likely to restore, to some at least of our nation, that stamina and energy which we seem of late years to have so largely lost.[1]

What right has anyone to take a child away from its own parents simply on the ground of poverty? There must be some extremely slipshod social work going on in England if that is permitted. To cut off a child from his own family group is a most serious matter.[2]

Through the early years of the twentieth century the character of the child emigration movement changed. Several of the evangelical founders of the rescue homes died, and with their passing the revivalist aims of the movement became less prominent. The goals of the child emigration homes became more secular, their missions more imperial than proselytising. Youngsters were removed from British slums because working-class neighbourhoods were considered unhealthy rather than evil environments, and they were placed in Canada more to acquire physical strength than to achieve spiritual salvation. During the Edwardian period more British children were assisted to Canada yearly than ever before.

In the wake of the Boer War child emigration became commonly associated with national efficiency and imperial unity. The poor health of working-class recruits for South Africa suggested that a widespread deterioration in the national physique had occurred. Birth rates were declining among the propertied classes, but they remained high among the poorer communities from which the debilitated enlisted men had come. The 'future progress of the Anglo-Saxon race' thus seemed to depend increasingly upon boys and girls raised 'in the twice-breathed air of the crowded quarters of the labouring classes', children who must grow into healthy men and women 'fit to be a strength, and not a burden to the nation' if the empire were to be preserved.[3]

Social investigators such as Helen Denby Bosanquet, Benjamin Seebohm Rowntree, Reginald Bray and Charles Masterman attributed the arrested physical, mental and moral development of 'the town child' to urban environments. They described 'a characteristic *physical* type of town dweller; stunted, narrow-chested, easily wearied', produced by inadequate nourishment, unwholesome work and overcrowding.[4] They also claimed to detect a typical urban temperament, 'shallow and without reserve', mercurial, easily discontented,[5] which they attributed to the urban inhabitant's artificial isolation from the 'repose, silence and beauty of nature'. [6] Writers in the small journals published by children's homes with emigration branches shared this preoccupation with environmental influences. Barnardo cautioned his readers against 'obsession by the nightmare of heredity'. He reminded them that just as diphtheria and tuberculosis, once thought to be all-powerful and incurable, were now 'amenable to treatment', so in 'the moral and spiritual realms' as 'in the physical realm' heredity was not fate. He claimed that, granted certain conditions, a 'good environment' would neutralise the effects of 'tainted parentage'. [7] Officials from the rescue homes described Canadian farms as the best environments in which the nation's weakened children could be placed for rehabilitation.

Sending youngsters abroad became more compatible with nation-building as the identification of the British national interest with the imperial interest strengthened. In the years immediately before the First World War child emigration became an imperial work. In church weeklies, in the *Christian* and in the publications of the rescue homes charitable Britons were urged to combine their philanthropy with imperialism, [8] their 'love of children with a love of empire', [9] to think of child emigrants as 'Bricks for Empire-Building' [10] and of the un-settled lands of the Dominion as the 'natural heritage of the British race'. [11] The pamphlet conversion testimonials of earlier years were replaced by saccharine novels and travel accounts such as Walter Cranfield's *John Bull's Surplus Children* and Arthur Copping's *Smithers, a true story of private imperialism* and *The Golden Land,* [12] which featured rescue home children, inured to hardship by their early lives in Britain, serving as models of Anglo-Saxon pluck, persistence and fair play in the outposts of empire. [13]

For the first time child emigration received enthusiastic government support in Britain. The Imperial Conferences of 1907 and 1911 urged greater migration within the Empire and specifically commended child emigration. The Dominions Royal Commission of 1912 set about to find ways in which empire settlement could be raised above 'the accidents of private enterprise and the makeshifts of impecuniosity' to become an officially sanctioned arm of imperial policy, an 'imperialism of peace'. Members of the Royal Colonial Institute saw emigration as the foundation of a new imperial strategy to defend Britain by strengthening the economies of the Dominions and to raise the standard of living at home by expanding the productive capacities of Britain's possessions overseas. Representatives of the child emigration homes participated actively in the deliberations of the institute and of the Dominions Royal Commission, lending their philanthropic experience to the formulation of new imperial policy. [14]

The State Children's Association, which favoured wider use of boarding-out programmes for parish children in England, began in 1900 to lobby the Local Government Board directly for larger-scale publicly sponsored child emigration. They suggested in circulars to the chairmen of Boards of Guardians and in memorials ·to Whitehall that the central authorities take over the cost of emigration from the parishes so that greater numbers of the more than fifty thousand children receiving indoor relief at the time in barrack schools and workhouses could benefit from the good environment and healthy family life of the Dominion and help to secure the 'vast acres lying barren' in Canada for the British race. [15]   In 1903 the Local Government Board itself declared emigration 'one of the best means of providing satisfactorily for the orphans and deserted children under the care of the Guardians'. [16] Several Boards of Guardians despatched their own investigators to Canada to visit workhouse children in their rural homes.   These delegates returned from their short visits satisfied that child emigration met current English standards and willing with few reservations to send more children abroad. The committee appointed to enquire into Rider Haggard's plans for colonisation in the Dominions, and T.J. Macnamara, parliamentary secretary to the Local Government Board who had been commissioned to study the progress of children under the poor law, reached similar conclusions. [17]

This favourable climate of public opinion in London encouraged several new agencies to enter the emigration work: the Smyly Mission Homes and Ragged Schools of Dublin, which in 1905 established a home and agricultural training facility at Hespeler, Ontario; the Dakeyne Lads' Club of Nottingham, which sent boys to its farm near Windsor, Nova Scotia; and the Cossar Farm School which developed at Lower Gagetown, New Brunswick. [18] Arrangements were made for a small number of children from the Irish Local Government Board to be received in numbers in Canada for the first time. [19] And although the Canadian Interior Department refused requests for a more liberal welcome for reformatory children on probation and continued to admit such youngsters only at the discretion of the Canadian Emigration Commissioner in London, [20] the emigration of children from industrial schools increased. [21] All these new participants in the programme followed the philanthropic methods developed during the 1880s and 1890s.

There were, however, Britons whose enthusiasm for systematic imperial colonisation led them to suggest innovations. The most widely publicised of these new proposals urged the English Local Government Board to establish rural cottage complexes in Canada to which publicly dependent toddlers could be brought for the first sixteen years of their lives. The plan received the endorsement of several London parishes and gained enough financial support to purchase a farm in New Brunswick and bring several dozen children to Canada. But officials of the Canadian Interior Department thought the project too costly to be practical. In consequence the Local Government Board withheld its approval of the plan, and the New Brunswick property fell into disuse. [22] The second proposal envisaged colonial orphanages under English administration into which pauper children of boarding-out age could be moved for training before they were placed in Canadian households. This plan foundered on the long-standing Local Government Board fiscal stipulation that the rates should not be used for the maintenance of children outside England. [23]

Whereas between 1903 and 1914 the central authorities at the Local Government Board supported greater use of philanthropic agencies to place youngsters from workhouse and district schools in Canada, and baulked only at the administrative and financial burden that separate overseas facilities would entail, the Boards of Guardians, which regulated relief of the poor in individual parishes, became increasingly sceptical about the merits of child emigration. This was particularly true in the north, where socialist representation in municipal government was strong. The members of local committees who selected children from nearby workhouse facilities for placement in Canada were promised annual reports of their young wards' progress overseas. Procedures for such inspections had been established by agreement between the Canadian Immigration Branch and the English Local Government Board in 1887, but the process was cumbersome and the reports skimpy and out of date. During the Edwardian period, as labour sympathisers became more prominent in parish administration, Guardians became more conscious of the rights of parish boys and girls to protection during their childhoods. Protests about the inadequacy of cryptic year-old notes affirming only that youngsters were 'of good character' or 'in a good home' as evidence that state children were receiving proper care in Canada became more frequent. [24]

The first British local initiative to curtail child emigration came in a Manchester parish in 1910. The Chorlton Board of Guardians had sent Miss Olga Hertz, chairman of their Cottage Homes Committee and a woman of long experience in institutional care for children, to Canada to investigate the current circumstances of a large group of Chorlton youngsters placed by Reverend Robert Wallace through the Marchmont Home at Belleville in eastern Ontario. Miss Hertz was critical of the child immigrants' restricted opportunities for school attendance. She also thought that the quality of the Canadian inspections for workhouse children might be improved if a woman visitor were added to the staff of the Immigration Branch. But by and large, she reported, she was 'more than ever convinced that by sending children to Canada we are giving them happier and healthier surroundings than we can provide for them at home'.[25]

After considering the substance of her findings and the current sheaf of visitors' reports from Canada, the elected members of the Chorlton Board arrived at a considerably harsher appraisal of the child emigration policy. Several Guardians immediately observed that 7- to 10-year-old English children placed in Canada from Poor Law Unions 'were sent to work for their livelihood at an age which would not be tolerated' in Britain, and speculated that parish youngsters were welcomed only because 'child labour was allowed there'. They found the terms of the rescue homes' apprenticeship indentures more like forced labour than free labour contracts.[26] One board member made the ideological configuration of the debate explicit in a letter to the editor of the *Manchester Guardian*:

> We Socialists do not condemn (and never have done) Canada nor emigration there; what we do condemn is the robbing of young children, because they are poor, of their childhood, the depriving them of the educational advantages of their native country...No one can deny that the policy is one of economy bought at a fearful price — the price of a child's toil, for their work is compulsory, and therefore differs entirely from that of the child who in its play-hours works in its own home.[27]

In the ensuing debate in Manchester papers through the spring of 1910 critics repeatedly argued that child emigration denied distinctions between childhood and adulthood which ought to apply to all Britons.

A special correspondent to the *Weekly Times* who claimed to have lived for a time in rural Ontario insisted that 'the humanity that sends the strong man forth, as pioneer, into untried lands, becomes inhumanity when it allows little children to follow, almost unattended, in his wake'. [28] That autumn the Chorlton Board decided to discontinue sending school-age children to Canada. The Guardians of St Mary's, Islington, who had also employed child emigration extensively, soon followed the Chorlton example. [29]

In general, however, in Edwardian Britain the imperialist lobby to increase child emigration was more influential than socialist opposition to the policy on welfare grounds.

In Edwardian Canada it had begun to matter that the child immigrants were British. Until the Liberal government of Wilfrid Laurier came to power in 1896, non-British immigrants to eastern Canada and the prairies had been inconspicuous. Relationships between the ethnicity of newcomers and their success in adapting to new circumstances had not been readily apparent. Nor had the relative merits of British and non-British entrants arisen prominently in policy discussions. Clifford Sifton, Laurier's first minister responsible for immigration, welcomed eastern and southern Europeans to Canada between 1896 and 1905 because they were experienced agriculturalists. Many of these groups were allowed to take up bloc settlements in the territories that became Saskatchewan and Alberta. But as these distinctive Doukhobor, Ukrainian and Hungarian communites grew and prospered in western Canada, assimilation became an issue of urgent concern.

In eastern Canada Conservatives with strong imperial sympathies were troubled by the determination with which non-English-speaking and non-Protestant immigrants maintained their traditional cultures in their new prairie settlements. Lord Strathcona, one of the principal financiers of the first Canadian transcontinental railway, friend of Sir John A. Macdonald and later High Commissioner in London, told the committee investigating Rider Haggard's plan for overseas agricultural settlements in 1906 that Canadians preferred immigrants from the Mother Country because they were better fitted 'to become good settlers in a shorter time than the others — those from the Continent, the Galicians, the Doukhobors and others'. [30] 'Good British immigrants' were described as the 'leavening' with which to raise other newcomers to high Canadian standards of citizenship, the agents who would help 'diffuse an affection for the Motherland and deepen the determination ... to resist Americanisation'. [31] Sifton's successor, an Alberta newspaperman named Frank Oliver, shared these views and recruited prospective immigrants from all classes in the British Isles during the later Laurier years. After the Conservatives returned to power in 1911, advocates of imperial unity gained even greater influence. [32] Among those fearful of the diverse religious and political traditions of continental immigrants and those eager to strengthen Canada's imperial connections, the class backgrounds of the child immigrants were less important than their ethnicity. Like Emily Ferguson Murphy, a prairie police magistrate who called Barnardo boys part of 'the world's brown bread', these groups insisted that knowing how to play proper football and rally round the flag gave young men from the rescue homes important advantages and made their future prospects brighter than those of European immigrants. [33]

However, a decided sentiment against British immigration was developing in other quarters in Canada. New settlers with agricultural experience on the plains of Poland or the Ukraine preferred to take up prairie homesteads rather than urban wage work. The Dominion Trades and Labor Congress accepted that 'honorable, frugal and industrious agriculturalists' were required to develop the west and expand national markets for eastern manufactures. Canadian-born workingmen did not want the brutalising jobs in transportation and extractive industries which European immigrants endured to finance their beginnings in agriculture. But the central Canadian artisans and craftsmen who dominated the organised labour movement were not prepared to welcome British urban immigrants who took up city employments in direct competition with Canadian workers. Union leaders were most vigorously opposed to Canadian Manufacturers' Association recruitment of strikebreakers in Britain and to the gargantuan emigration schemes of the Salvation Army. But English immigrants had gained a reputation as dilatory, indifferent and complaining co-workers, inclined to be 'uppish', restless and unreliable. And suspicions of British immigrants became more general after legislation was passed in Britain in 1905 which offered unemployed workingmen subsidies to emigrate in search of work. [34]

When in 1908 a winter of high unemployment in England coincided with a year of poor crops and strained financial conditions in North America, the Canadian government bowed to public protest. The Department of the Interior published a report by J. Bruce Walker, a senior officer with the Immigration Branch, which described emigrants sent to Canda by British charitable and philanthropic societies as undesirable citizens, unsuited to Canadian requirements and unlikely to 'succeed in any great numbers. . .even under the most favourable conditions'. [35] They then implemented new regulations requiring that adult-assisted emigrants be screened for mental, moral and physical failings by Canadian emigration officers in London. [36] The same year Ontario embarked upon an independent programme of deportations for publicly dependent immigrants who had been in Canada too long to qualify under the Dominion Immigration Act. In 1908, 70 per cent of Ontario deportees were English-born. [37]

In rural areas an unfavourable impression of the rescue home children coloured the reputations of all British immigrants. The Prince Edward Island convenor of the National Council of Women reported in 1903 that troublesome experience with Middlemore and Barnardo boys and girls, the only immigrants arriving in the province, made Islanders wary of other immigration experiments. [38] Robert Mills, who grew up on a farm near Petrolia, Ontario, before the First World War, remembered identifying all English people with neighbourhood Barnardo boys who were 'away below the standards of farm boys brought up around here', 'to the point that, from my very limited knowledge, I didn't rate English people very high'. [39] By contrast, urban observers, who had less direct experience with child immigrants, attributed to boys and girls from the rescue homes the criminal tendencies and moral and physical degeneracies which were increasingly presumed characteristic of all sponsored English arrivals. [40] Popular opinion of the character and prospects of the child immigrants declined markedly during the first years of the twentieth century.

The Dominion civil servants who oversaw the child emigration programme from Ottawa were an exception to this pattern. Under George Bogue Smart, a Baptist from Brockville, Ontario, with business experience in Molson's Bank before he entered the service of the Immigration Branch in 1899, the section of the Interior Department deputed to inspect English parish children developed close links with the charitable British agencies which placed immigrant boys and girls in Canada. [41] Smart made frequent visits to Britain to attend conferences of the Reformatory and Refuge Union and adopted the attitudes towards child welfare work of English and Scottish philanthropic institutions. Believing that the existing charitable programme benefited both the child immigrants and the empire, Smart acknowledged only those flaws in the policy which could be overcome through more stringent regulation. [42]

Through both the Laurier and Borden governments Smart was given latitude to expand the supervisory role of the Dominion department. He began to urge smaller agencies to follow the more rigorous placement and supervisory practices of the larger rescue homes. [43] The inspectors who carried out the visits to workhouse children were chosen with more care from experienced field staff in the Interior Department, reminded that 'the primary objective of the inspection is to certify that everything is all right with the child' and provided with guidelines for this work which conformed to English Local Government Board regulations for boarding-out inspections. [44] The medical certificates required before embarkation were regularised. Physical examinations and attempts to discern mental deficiency at the port of entry were made more rigorous, particularly for contagious skin and eye diseases — developments not altogether welcomed by the sponsoring agencies but useful in reducing the number of conspicuous misfits who injured the reputation of the work as a whole. [45]

While the quality of government supervision increased, the Immigration Branch resisted urgings from private institutions that official inspections be extended to philanthropically assisted children and from members of its own staff that the frequency of inspections be increased. If standards of after-care for immigrant youngsters were improving absolutely, they were nonetheless falling steadily behind the best practice for Canadian children. [46] The first aim of the Dominion Immigration Branch was plainly to expand the child immigration programme as 'an important source of supply for farm and domestic help'. This priority dictated a supervisory programme which did not allow an excessively fastidious concern for the British children's welfare to compromise the satisfaction of Canadian labour requirements. [47]

Yet in the prewar years Canadian child-savers were not often critical of the British rescue homes. In 1909 the Ontario government closed the Liverpool agency through which prospective child immigrants had been screened. J.J. Kelso, the superintendent of Neglected and Dependent Children for the province, who had been instrumental in developing the 1897 legislation to protect rescue home children, justified the decline in provincial regulation on the ground that Smart and his staff were doing the work better from Ottawa.

During the war, hazards at sea interrupted the movement of children to Canada. Wartime attitudes accentuated the empire-building aspects of the juvenile immigration work, and the high incidence of enlistment among rescue home boys eager to serve and see home again vindicated claims that the movement was strategically important to the Empire. To ensure that the philanthropic agencies remained solvent and ready to resume their work when hostilities ended, the Interior Department provided each rescue home with an annual stipend for the duration of the conflict. [48]

But by 1919 the British division of opinion upon the merits of child emigration had become more marked. Initial postwar financial and industrial dislocation gave a certain credibility to surplus labour arguments for assisted emigration. Lord Milner, Secretary of State for the Colonies, likened Britain's predicament in 1921 to that at the close of the Napoleonic Wars and suggested a similar remedy: 'state-aided settlement of British subjects within the Empire'. [49] The Empire Settlement Act of 1922, which set out the administrative and budgetary structure through which British adults and families could be assisted to the Dominions (12, 13 Geo. V c. 13), included juvenile emigration clauses which provided for per capita grants of £14 10s to cover transportation expenses contributed jointly by the Imperial and Dominion governments and additional British support to philanthropic societies to defray placement and after-care costs. Outside the provisions of the Empire Settlement Act, 1,600 children were sent to Canada in 1920, 1,200 in both 1921 and 1922, and 2,100 in 1923. [50]

And yet by the early 1920s proposals for sending British boys and girls overseas seemed increasingly anachronistic. A Rhodesian Rhodes Scholar named Kingsley Fairbridge began to execute the plans laid in Oxford common rooms before the war for farm schools in Australia. Child emigration still had its parliamentary champion in Sir Charles Kinloch-Cooke. But there was an air of absurdity attached to such schemes, a quirkiness amusingly caricatured by John Galsworthy in his portrait of the ageing country gentleman, Sir James Foggart, and the callow, isolated novice MP, Michael Mont, who advanced the combined doctrine of child emigration and agricultural improvement called Foggartism. [51]

After the immediate crisis of demobilisation passed, the longer-term realities of lives lost on continental battlefields and falling birth rates undermined claims that Britain was overpopulated. The Adoption Act of 1920 and subsequent provision of mother's allowances to single parents further reduced the numbers of orphaned and deserted children who might be candidates for apprenticeship abroad. [52] The policy had become redundant.

It was also becoming morally repugnant. Parliamentary critics of the Empire Settlement Act compared assisted emigration to the old remedy of bleeding, 'weakening the already weakened'. Labour members described the programme as an expedient to distract attention from 'the real problem at home', inequities in the distribution of wealth which could be remedied only by a fundamental reorganisation of British society. They were particularly emphatic that workingmen had not fought the war 'to make a home for heroes in Australia', but for 'opportunities in their own island'. They ridiculed the rhetoric of citizenship in the Empire and condemned the 'complete disregard... paid to the natural feelings of these people who have to be moved from here to the ends of the world'. [53]

The stress emigration placed upon young people was dramatically underlined during the winter of 1923-4 by reports of three suicides among rescue home boys in Canada and five similar deaths among British teenagers in Australia. Only one of the Canadian cases resulted in a criminal conviction against a master, that of Charles Bulpitt, a 16-year-old emigrated by the Southampton Board of Guardians under the auspices of the Liverpool Sheltering Homes. Bulpitt had hanged himself a few days before what would have been his first Christmas in Canada. His master, J. Benson Cox of Goderich, Ontario, was sentenced to two months for assault after a coroner's jury linked the fatality with the boy's loneliness, his unsuitedness to farm work and the physical punishment he had received. The second incident, also a hanging, took place in Omemee, Ontario, in January at the same time as the Bulpitt inquest was receiving wide press coverage. Five months later a Marchmont boy living near Belleville who had been retrying his high school entrance examinations ate Paris Green and died. [54] No ill-treatment was alleged in either of the latter cases. Indeed, Bulpitt had been less harshly used than many boys whose deaths had passed unremarked upon before the war.

But sensibilities had changed in the 1920s. The Labour party was in power in Britain. The anxiety to 'emigrate other people's children' to places where 'they were apparently not wanted' had become questionable. By late February 1924 George D. Hardie, son of Keir Hardie, was demanding explanations on the floor of the British House of Commons. Robert Parr, director of the National Society for the Prevention of Cruelty to Children, was insisting upon reform of the programme from Mackenzie King, the Canadian prime minister. Sixty-one Boards of Guardians addressed protests to the Dominion immigration authorities. In response, in the spring of 1924 a delegation was appointed to investigate the Canadian child emigration system. [55]

The delegation consisted of Margaret Bondfield MP, parliamentary secretary to the Minister of Labour and formerly an organiser for the Women's Trade Union League and the National Federation of Women Workers, and two members of the Oversea Settlement Committee established to administer the Empire Settlement Act, Mr G.F. Plant, its secretary, and Mrs F.N. Harrison Bell, the appointee of the Trades Union Congress. Under Bondfield's leadership the group travelled for two months in Canada in the autumn of 1924 interviewing immigration officials, social workers, representatives from labour, farm and women's organisations, staff from the rescue homes and child immigrants themselves. By and large they approved of the programme and accepted that the boys and girls had better prospects in Canada than in the United Kingdom. But the delegation was emphatic that as the children were clearly sent to Canada to work they ought to be of working, that is to say school-leaving, age before they emigrated. [56]

In March 1925 the Dominion Immigration Branch ruled that no children under 14 years of age who were not accompanied by parents would be admitted to Canada for the next three years. During this period the Social Service Council of Canada and the Canadian Council on Child Welfare lobbied forcefully against Canada's 'nation-building on the backs of children'. [57] In 1928 the ban was made permanent and, although exceptions to the regulations were made from time to time thereafter, the British child emigration movement had ended. The boys and girls who came to Canada through the 1920s and 1930s were teenagers searching for their first paid jobs who had completed their schooling and made their own decisions to leave home and family and begin a new life abroad. [58]

Notes

1. Elinor Close, 'Scheme for the benefit of pauper children and for the reduction of the rates' (1904).

2. General Secretary, Toronto Neighbourhood Workers Association to editor, *Christian Guardian*, 26 Jan. 1923, in PAC, Canadian Council on Social Development (MG 28 I 10), vol. 26.

3. Charles Masterman, *The Heart of the Empire* (T. Fisher Unwin, London, 1901), pp. 7-8; John Gorst, *Children of the Nation* (Methuen, London, 1906), pp. 7, 12, 16; A. Watt Smyth, *Physical Deterioration* (John Murray, London, 1904), pp. 4, 62.

4. Masterman, *Heart*, p. 8.

5. Reginald Bray, *The Town Child*, (T. Fisher Unwin, London, 1907), pp. 29, 52; Benjamin Seebohm Rowntree and May Kendal, *How the Labourer Lives*

(Thomas Nelson, London [1913] 1917), p.15.

6. Helen Denby, 'The children of working London', in Bernard Bosanquet (ed.), *Aspects of the Social Problem* (Macmillan, London, 1895), pp. 31-3; Jack London, *People of the Abyss* (Macmillan, London, 1904), p. 280; Rowntree and Kendal, *Labourer*, p. 14; Reginal Bray, 'Children of the Town', in Masterman, *Heart*, p. 122.

7. 'Heredity versus environment', *Night and Day* (1902), p. 177; 'About heredity', *Night and Day* (1904), pp. 8-9.

8. *Methodist Times* (London), 8 May 1913, in PAC RG 76 3115/6.

9. Edward de Montjoie Rudolf in the *Canadian Mail*, 29 Apr. 1911, in PAC RG 79 6648.

10. *Night and Day* (1912), p. 60, (1911), p.8.

11. Charles Kinlock-Cooke, 'The Emigration of State Children', *Empire Review*, vol. 9 (April 1905), p. 215; also *Night and Day*, (1904), p. 21; *Christian*, 22 Apr. 1909, p. 28.

12. Walter Thomas Cranfield (pseud. Denis Crane), *John Bull's Surplus Children* (Horace Marshall, London, 1915); Arthur E. Copping, *Smithers, a true story of private imperialism* (Hodder and Stoughton, London, 1913); Arthur E. Copping, *The Golden Land* (Hodder and Stoughton, London, 1911).

13. See also, Cyril Fitzgerald, *The School-boy in Canada* (Northern Printers London, 1914), pp. 2-3; E.A.W. Gill, *A Manitoba Chore boy* (Religious Tract Society, London, 1912), pp. 41-65.

14. W.A. Carrothers, *Emigration from the British Isles* (P.S. King, London, 1929), pp. 243, 257; Cranfield (Crane), *John Bull's*, pp. 19, 35; G.F. Plant, *Oversea Settlement* (Oxford University Press, London, 1951), pp. 61-4; T. Sedgwick, 'Boy Emigrants', *The Standard of Empire*, 2 Dec. 1910; PAC, Canada House London (RG 25 A 7 vol. 499), 'Society for the Furtherance of Child Emigration'; PAC RG 76 66/3115, J.R. Boose, Royal Colonial Institute to Canadian High Commissioner London, 13 Apr. 1912.

15. State Children's Association, 'The emigration of Pauper Children', leaflet no. 30 (c. 1900).

16. 'Report of a conference held at the board room of the Lambeth Guardians to consider the subject of the emigration of poor law children, 29 June 1903', in PAC RG 76 65/3115; Lillian M Birt, *The Children's Homefinder* (James Nisbet, London, 1913), p. 198; PAC RG 76 65/3115, W.R. Preston to Walter Long, 13 Dec. 1902.

17. Parish of Fulham, 'Report of Miss M.C. Miles, Guardian of the Poor of the Parish of Fulham after her visit to the homes of the children emigrated to Canada by the Fulham Board of Guardians, 1903-1904', in PAC RG 76 65/3115; 'Report on agricultural settlements in British colonies', *Br. P.P.* 1906, LXXVI, vol. I, p. 20; 'Report upon children under the poor law by T.J. Macnamara', *Br. P.P.* 1908, XCII, pp. 7-12.

18. PAC RG 76 353/373725, 'Smyly Homes', 615/911864, 'Dakeyne Farm'; Kathleen Heasman, *Evangelicals in Action* (Bles, London, 1962), p. 94.

19. PAC RG 7 G 21 vol. 309 no. 926, A.R. Barlas, Secretary, Local Government Board, Dublin to Harcourt, Colonial Office, 22 Mar. 1912 and Canadian order in council in reply, 13 May 1912.

20. PAC RG 76 66/3115, W.D. Scott to J. Obed Smith, 13 May 1908; Smith to Scott, 9 Mar. 1909; Scott to Smith, 23 Mar. 1909; G.B. Smart to Frank Oliver, 15 June 1909, Scott to Smith, 17 Sept. 1909.

21. 'Report on agricultural settlements in British colonies', *Br. P.P.* 1906, LXXVI, vol. II, p. 262; PAC RG 76 65/3114, 'Industrial School Children'.

22. PAC RG 76 323/312973, Elinor Close, 'Scheme for the benefit of pauper children and for the reduction of the rates'; 514/800163, G.B. Smart to Edwin Davy, Islington Board of Guardians, 21 Apr. 1908.

23. Kinloch-Cooke, 'The Emigration of State Children', pp. 208-36.

24. See PRO, MH 20, vol. 11 for 1903 *et seq.* and also PAC RG 76 324/318481 for 1903, 1904 and 1905.

25. 'Report to the Chorlton Guardians on a visit to emigrated children in Canada by Miss O. Hertz of the Cottage Homes Committee', PAC RG 76 66/3115 (1910).

26. *Manchester Guardian*, 19 Mar. 1910, 4 Apr. 1910.

27. *Manchester Guardian*, 19 Apr. 1910.

28. *Weekly Times* (Manchester), 23 Apr. 1910.

29. PAC RG 76 66/3115, Olga Smith to J. Obed Smith, 7 Sept. 1910; J. Bruce Walker, Emigration Commissioner, London, to W.D. Scott, 6 June 1917.

30. 'Report on agricultural settlements in British colonies', *Br. P.P.* 1906, LXXVI, vol. 2, p. 148.

31. Emily Weaver, *Canada and the British Immigrant* (Religious Tract Society, London, 1914), p. 245; *Montreal Star*, 2 Dec. 1904.

32. Birt, *Homefinder*, p. 189; Carl Berger, *Sense of Power* (University of Toronto Press, Toronto, 1970), pp. 49-51; R.C. Brown and R. Cook, *Canada, a nation transformed* (McClelland and Stewart, Toronto, 1974), pp. 72-4; Marilyn Barber, 'The Assimilation of Immigrants in the Canadian Prairies, 1896-1918: Canadian Perception and Canadian Policies' (unpublished PhD thesis, University of London, 1975), pp. 48-52.

33. Emily Ferguson Murphy, *Janey Canuck in the West* (J.M. Dent, London and Toronto, 1917), pp. 155-6; Gill, *Chore boy*, p. 41; *Ups and Downs*, Nov. 1903, p. 5.

34. Dominion Trades and Labor Congress, *Report*, 1899, 1902, 1903, 1908; PAC, Toronto Trades and Labor Council, Minutebooks, 25 Aug. 1904, 29 Sept. 1904, 20 Oct. 1904, 21 Mar. 1907; James Shaver Woodsworth, *Strangers within our Gates* (University of Toronto, Toronto, 1972); 'The Englishman in Canada', *Morning Citizen* (Ottawa), 4 Sept. 1907, in PAC RG 76 463/708666; see also correspondence and clippings in PAC RG 76 516/801171.

35. J. Bruce Walker, *Aims and Methods of Charitable Organisations Promoting Emigration to Canada from the British Isles* (Interior Department, Ottawa, 1908).

36. PAC RG 76 510/79812, Otto Zimmer to Frank Oliver, 2 Apr. 1908; *Loving and Serving*, March 1908, pp. 2-3; Sept. 1908, p. 2; *Night and Day* (1908), p. 62; Barber, 'Assimilation', pp. 53-8; John Porter, *The Vertical Mosaic* (University of Toronto Press, Toronto, 1965), pp. 64-6.

37. PAC RG 76 537/803777.

38. National Council of Women, *Yearbook* (1903), p. 32.

39. Daphne Read, *The Great War and Canadian Society* (New Hogtown Press, Toronto, 1978), p. 75.

40. *Mail and Empire*, 23 July 1909; *Toronto World*, 18 June 1914; PAC RG 76 311/292601, protests from George W. Stephens, January 1904; RG 76 63/2869, reporting of Alfred Smith case, January 1905; *Ontario Sessional Papers*, 'Report of the Department of Neglected and Dependent Children', 1910, p. 64; 1911, pp. 114-15.

41. PAC RG 76 200/83981, personnel file, George Bogue Smart.

42. G.B. Smart, *Juvenile Emigration to Canada* (King's Printer, Ottawa, 1903); Smart, *Juvenile Immigration* (King's Printer, Ottawa, 1905); Smart, *A Visit to Great Britain and Ireland in 1905* (King's Printer, Ottawa, 1906); Smart,

A Visit to Great Britain in 1911 (King's Printer, Ottawa, 1912); 'Report before the Manchester Conference of Managers and Superintendents of Child-Saving, Reformatory and Industrial Institutions' (p.p., London, 1908), pp. 36-43; G.B. Smart, address before the International Council of Women, June 1909, in PAC RG 76 66/3115.

43. PAC RG 76 78/6648, Smart to E. de M. Rudolf, 12 Mar. 1906; 100/ 13204 and 324/318481, 'Bristol Emigration Society'.

44. PAC RG 76 324/318481, Smart to Thomas Cory, Homestead Inspector, Gladstone, Manitoba, 22 Apr. 1905; 66/3115, 'General Instruction for guidance of inspectors', 29 Jan. 1914.

45. PAC RG 76 392/542902, J.D. Page, Medical Superintendent, Quebec to P.H. Bryce, 8 August 1906; 58/2571, Page to Scott, 25 May 1907 and Greenway to Page, 29 May 1907; 285/252093, Page to Scott, 30 Sept. 1908; 66/3115, Smart to Scott, 13 June 1910; 32/724, A.C. Hawkins, Medical Superintendent, Halifax to F.W. Annaud, 5 Mar. 1910.

46. PAC RG 76 66/3115, J.B. Walker to G.B. Smart, 4 Jan. 1910, 11 Nov. 1909; W.B. Scott to Walker, 18 Nov. 1909; 78/6648, G.B. Smart to Rudolf, 5 Sept. 1905; Neil Sutherland, *Children in English Canadian Society* (University of Toronto Press, Toronto, 1976), pp. 34-5.

47. PAC RG 76 66/3115, J.J. Kelso to G.B. Smart, 16 Sept. 1909; PAC RG 7 G 21, vol. 309 no. 926, G.B. Smart to W.D. Scott for the information of the Governor-General, 7 May 1917.

48. *Red Lamp*, April 1915, p. 6; Sept. 1915, pp. 6-7; *Highways and Hedges*, April 1915, p. 52; *Ups and Downs*, XXI, no. 5, May 1920, p. 1; PAC RG 76 353/ 373725, Arthur Pullam, Smyly Homes, Hespeler to G.B. Smart, 6 Dec. 1915; 66/3115, W.D. Scott to W.W. Cory, 31 May 1916, A.B. Owen to Scott, 20 June 1916, L. Birt to Scott, 7 July 1916, J.W. Fegan to Scott, 17 July 1916, Order in Council of 31 Oct. 1916, W.W. Cory to the Secretary of the Governor-General, 9 May 1917.

49. PAC RG 76 32/304771/1, Milner to Duke of Devonshire, 7 Jan. 1921.

50. PAC MG 28 I 10 vol. 6, F.C. Blair to Charlotte Whitton, 4 July 1927.

51. Great Britain, Parliament, House of Commons, *Debates* 1922, vol. 154, c. 914; 1925, vol. 187, c. 148; John Galsworthy, *The Silver Spoon* (Charles Scribner, New York, 1926).

52. Ivy Pinchbeck and Margaret Hewitt, *Children in English Society II* (Routledge and Kegan Paul, London, 1973), p. 581.

53. See for example Great Britain, Parliament, House of Commons, *Debates* 1922, vol. 154, c. 914; 1924, vol. 174, c. 552-3.

54. PAC, Canada House Records, RG 25 A-2 vol. 204, I 45-57; PAC RG 76 67 3115 13, Fred Temple coroner's report, 30 June 1924; Bulpitt suicide coverage, *Times*, 2 Feb. 1924, *Globe* (Toronto), 18 Jan. 1924, 19 Jan. 1924, 23 Jan. 1924.

55. Great Britain, Parliament, House of Commons, *Debates* 1924, vol. 170 c. 57; 1925, vol. 187 c. 148; PAC RG 76 67 3115 11, Robert Parr to Mackenzie King, 27 Feb. 1924; RG 76 67 3115 12; PAC RG 7 G 21 vol. 309, no. 926, telegram of 14 Feb. 1924, Secretary of State for the Colonies to the Governor-General.

56. Plant, *Oversea Settlement*, pp. 131-5; Carrothers, *Emigration*, pp. 281-2; J. Breckenridge McGregor, *Several Years After* (Canadian Council on Child Welfare, Ottawa, 1928), pp. 6-9; Pinchbeck and Hewitt, *Children* (1973), p. 581; 'Report of the delegation appointed to obtain information regarding the system of child migration and settlement in Canada', *Br. P.P.* 1924-25, XV; PAC RG 7 G 21, vol. 309, no. 926.

57. PAC RG 76 200 85203, resolutions of the Canadian Council on Child Welfare, Sept. 1923; Social Service Council of Canada, *Canada's Child* (p.p., Ottawa, 1925); Canadian Council on Child Welfare, *Annual Conference Report* (1923), pp. 199-205; (1925), pp. 172-95; PAC Canadian Council on Social Development MG 28 I 10, vol. 6, vol. 26; *Canadian Child Welfare News*, I, 3 (Aug.-Oct. 1924), p. 53; McGregor, *Several Years After.*

58. PAC RG 76 200 85203, vol. 1; RG 76 63 2869 6, F.C. Blair to W. Egan, 1 Nov. 1927; RG 76 52 2209 4, 27 Mar. 1931.

This study is based upon the case records of the philanthropic institutions which brought the child emigrants to Canada. Case records were developed by Christian mission workers in the last third of the nineteenth century to screen applicants for assistance, avoid duplication of relief and monitor the spiritual and moral effects of charitable intervention. Annie Macpherson, one of the evangelical pioneers of the child emigration movement, accounted for her own meticulous record-keeping in this way:

> As a missionary band, we prayerfully wished to take a life long interest in those we sought to assist, recording their well-doing or their ill-doing upon our books, assisting the weak and sick, rewarding the industrious, and giving wholesome advice to those who fall back on their old habits. [1]

In later years professional social workers adapted the casework methods of the revivalist charities to the secular pursuit of uniformity and rationality in the implementation of government policy.

Case records generated by public and philanthropic social welfare institutions provide a special opportunity for the social historian. It is true that case files do not yield information about as many people as census, assessment and parish records. The clients of such agencies are not, for most periods, representative of the population as a whole. Only with careful qualifications can their experience be generalised to describe substantial groups among the poor. But this narrowing of focus allows for considerable sharpening in detail. Case files systematically include personal information rarely available elsewhere. With the records accumulated by beadles, bailiffs and the benevolent to manage the lives of patients, inmates and the destitute, it is possible to draft collective biographies to supplement the depth of the census and the breadth of literary sources and add a dimension available through neither.

The case histories of the child emigrants are exceptionally detailed by contemporary standards. In order to discharge their responsibilities as legal guardians of boys and girls placed in Canada, British philanthropic homes and parish authorities demanded written reports from their representatives in the Dominion. Emigration was so radical a child-saving measure that British officers of these institutions needed evidence to prove to their critics that the work was being competently managed. And the success of the programme in Canada depended so crucially upon local co-operation and sympathy that the Canadian staff were obliged to create adequate internal branch records upon which to base decisions about legal prosecutions, discipline and deportations.

Although record-keeping practices varied among rescue homes, the case notes for child emigrants commonly include a family history, a physical description of the youngster at admission, the location and terms of Canadian placements and visitors' reports for a portion of the apprenticeship period. The most complete series have, in addition, admission and emigration photographs, medical records, letters from the child, relatives, masters, mistresses and information about the apprentice's occupation and circumstances in adulthood.

I gathered information from the case histories in two ways: by reading as widely as possible in the files and making notes in the conventional manner and by drawing a sample of individual immigrants from one rescue home and grouping the information about sample members into comparable categories — a fifty-two-variable codebook — for computer-assisted analysis. I hoped in this way to preserve the texture of the narrative in the case files and find evocative examples of common predicaments while also developing reliable estimates for the frequency with which similar experiences occurred among such children.

The statistical sample included only boys and girls from Dr Barnardo's Homes. One-quarter of all the child emigrants came to Canada under the auspices of this one agency, the largest among the more than fifty engaged in such work. By the 1890s Barnardo's dominated the juvenile immigration movement, and their methods were studied and imitated by many of the other rescue homes. Barnardo's maintained branches in Ontario and Manitoba, and their children were more widely dispersed throughout rural Canada than those of any other agency. They emigrated both boys and girls, from toddlers to adolescents. As a result, their wards' experiences are more representative of the range of circumstances in which child emigrants found themselves in Canada than those of smaller, more localised agencies. Because the last Barnardo branch survived in Canada until 1963, their records on former wards' lives as adults are more complete than those of agencies that closed their doors soon after emigration ended.

The sample consists of every twentieth child included on the sailing party lists of approximately twenty thousand boys and girls emigrated through Barnardo's from 1882 to 1908. The sailing lists are not alphabetical and include Boards of Guardians' children seconded to the rescue homes for emigration as well as Barnardo's own wards. Each of the four record series retained by the institution was searched for all references to the 997 sample members. I drew up the codebook only after I had completed summary dossiers for all members of the sample.

Developing a system of comparable variables from the descriptive notes in case files requires some care. The biases of the record-keepers are a more serious issue with case files than with census, assessment or parish records, and there are large variations in the ages of youngsters seeking help, the duration of their contact with the rescue homes, and the consistency of record-keeping.

The evangelical child-savers shared little in class background or experience with the youngsters they sought to help. As a result their accounts of working-class life are often unreliable. The case notes on parents' characters, motivations and attachments to their children are especially untrustworthy. But because the judgements of the staff crucially affected the children's welfare, they bear note. They also demand careful comparison with less malleable details from the files.

I established variables in pairs in areas in which I suspected the reporters. One set of categories described the record-keeper's subjective evaluation. The other noted relevant conflicting or corroborating circumstances. For example, the variable recording the child-saver's opinion of the parent as guardian was always used in conjunction with a separate reckoning of family stability as measured by parents' continuity of co-residence with their offspring. A similar cluster of variables was used to analyse the children's attempts to maintain contact with their families. Cross-tabulations upon such pairs helped to define patterns in the record-keepers' judgements.

Some children entered the rescue homes soon after their births. Others were not admitted until their early teens. Some retained regular contact with the emigration branch until they died at an advanced age. Others disappeared from view soon after they arrived in Canada. Clearly occupational information about a 22-year-old is not strictly comparable with a similar report for a 40-year-old. The school attendance record of a child who arrived in Canada at age 5 cannot be evaluated by the same criteria which would apply to a girl or boy who emigrated at age 12. Therefore it seemed important to link information in the case files with stages in the life-cycle so that comparable groups could be selected for analysis. This was done by introducing eight chronological benchmarks into the codebook – age at admission, emigration, entry into each indenture stage, marriage, last communication with the home and death – and conducting the study by age cohort.

Individual case files vary markedly in their completeness. Deficiencies in record-keeping mask the incidence of a certain event in one record and accentuate it, by dint of absent qualifying statements, in another. In the child emigrants' files, information about premarital pregnancy in adolescence was particularly vulnerable for variations in the thoroughness and specificity of record-keeping. In this instance, variable categories which would accommodate differences in the quality as well as the content of the report suited historical conventions better than a classification which noted only the presence or absence of an illegitimate birth. The variable used ranked references to 'loss of character', 'moral fall', being 'in disgrace', or 'in trouble', and admissions to a refuge for periods of varying duration as well as explicit reports of a confinement and birth. A corollary variable ranked the completeness of other parts of the records. Variables reporting differences in the reliability and completeness of information between individuals are imperative if the codebook is to be an accurate representation of the original descriptive source. [2]

To preserve confidentiality each member of the Barnardo sample is cited in the text in the following form: 222 B 10.93, indicating the identifying number assigned the sample member, whether the emigrant was a boy or a girl and the month and year in which he or she emigrated. A key linking the identifying numbers with names has been filed with the librarian at Barnardo's headquarters. References to children from other homes are by record group, volume and page: London and Stratford 16, p. 241; Quarrier History 27, p. 4.

Case records are cumbersome documents. The transformation of descriptive accounts into machine-readable form is not without its hazards. But handled with care case histories provide an intricate and intimate view of a part of the past rarely glimpsed through other sources. [3]

Notes

1. 'Report on the emigration of pauper children to Canada', *Br. P.P.* 1875, LXIII, p. 5.
2. The codebook is reproduced in G.J. Parr, 'The Home Children: British Juvenile Immigrants to Canada, 1868-1924', unpublished doctoral dissertation, Yale University, 1977, pp. 129-34.
3. See also G.J. Parr, 'Case records as sources for social history', *Archivaria* (1977), no. 4, pp. 122-36.

I. Manuscript Collections

(a) Case Records

Dr Barnardo's Homes
  Barnardo Girls. 1. Notes and Correspondence, vols. A-X, 1883-1912
                   2. Registers
                   3. Bundles, Girls Canada Histories
                   4. Microfilm After-care files, 113 reels
  Barnardo Boys. 1. Canada Party, vols. 1-86, 1882-1915
                   2. Microfilm After-care files, 145 reels
Home of Industry — Annie Macpherson
  Home of Industry, Spitalfields, vols. 1-10, 1870-1924
  London and Stratford History Books, vols. 1-33, 1871-1914
Liverpool Sheltering Homes and Knowlton, Quebec — Mrs Birt
  History Books, vols. 1-18, 1872-1915
Marchmont Home, Belleville, Ontario
  History Books, vols. 1-27, 1870-1914
Quarrier's Homes
  1. Orphan Homes of Scotland, History Books, vols. 1-59, 1872-1938
  2. Canadian Register, 1872-1931
  3. Emigration Books, vols. 1-5, 1872-83
  4. Scroll Diaries, vols. 1-59, 1885-1938
Public Archives of Canada
  Charlotte Alexander Papers, MG30 C60, 3 vols., 1885-93

(b) Other

Public Records Office
  Colonial Office, Canada, Original Correspondence, CO 42, 1868-1922
  Colonial Office, Emigration, Original Correspondence, CO 384, 1868-96
  Colonial Office, Canada, Original Correspondence, Supplementary, CO 537, 1868-98
  Ministry of Health, Government Offices, Correspondence and Papers, MH 19, vols. 5-11, 22, 1835-92
  Ministry of Health, Assistant Poor Law Commissioners and Inspectors, Correspondence, MH 32, vols. 20, 92, 1871-88

Public Archives of Canada
 Aberdeen Papers, MG 27 1 B 5, 1847-1934
 P.R. Bengough Papers, MG 30 A 47, 1924
 Canadian Council on Social Development, MG 28 I 10, 1925-7
 Church of England Waifs and Strays Society
  Emigration Agenda Minute Book, 1910-32
  Register, Emigration Parties, 1925-31
 J.J. Kelso Papers, MG 30 L 2, vol. 5, 1880-1935
 John Lowe Papers, MG 29 E 18, 1868-74
 John A. Macdonald Papers, MG 26 A 1868-73
 Martha Morgan Papers, MG 29 C 85, 1892-3
 Toronto Trades and Labor Council, MG 28 I 44, 1887-1914

 Department of Agriculture, Correspondence and Letterbooks, RG 17, 1868-92
 Department of External Affairs, Canada House, London, Correspondence with Canadian and British Government Departments, 1880-1945
 Governor General's Numbered Files, RG 7 21, vol. 309, 1886-1925
 Department of the Interior, Dominion Lands Branch, RG 15 B-1a, 1891-6
 Immigration Branch, RG 76, 1892-1942
 Public Service Commission, Historical Personnel File, RG 32 C 2

Archives of Ontario
 William Kirby Collection
 Department of Immigration, Correspondence, 1872-96, RG 11

Glenbow-Alberta Institute
 Wood Christian Home
 Butler Library, Columbia University
 Toronto Emigration Office Records, vol. 22, Report of Inspection of Children, 1875, 1886, 1892

II. Government Documents

Great Britain. Parliamentary Papers
'Report to President of Local Government Board by Andrew Doyle, Local Government Board Inspector, as to the emigration of pauper children to Canada' 1875 LXIII
'Reply of Mr Doyle to Miss Rye's report' 1877 LXXI

'Letter addressed by Miss Rye to President of the Local Government Board referred to in Mr Doyle's reply' 1877 LXXI

'Report of the Departmental Committee appointed by the Local Government Board to inquire into the existing systems for the maintenance and education of children under the charge of managers of district schools and Boards of Guardians in the Metropolis' 1896 XLIII

'Report of the Interdepartmental Committee on the employment of school children' 1902 XXV

'Report by the Departmental Committee appointed to consider Mr Rider Haggard's report on agricultural settlements in British colonies' 1906 LXXVI

'Report upon children under the poor law by T.J. Macnamara,' 1908 XCII

'Report of the Royal Commission on the poor laws and the relief of distress' 1909 XXXVIII

'Report on children in receipt of poor law relief' 1910-11 LII

'Second report on infant and child mortality' 1913 XXXII

'Report of the Oversea Settlement Committee' 1923 XII, 1924 X

'Report of the delegation appointed to obtain information regarding the system of child migration and settlement in Canada' 1924-5 XV

Great Britain, Parliament, House of Commons
Debates, 1922-5

Canada, Parliament, House of Commons
Debates, 1868-1924

Ontario, Sessional Papers
'Report of the Commission appointed to enquire into the prison and reformatory system of the province' 1891 no. 18
'Proceedings of the Ontario conference on child-saving held October 18-19, 1894' 1895 no. 29 (Appendix)
'Special report on the immigration of British children' 1897-8 no. 69
'Report of the commissioner of immigration' 1873-1923
'Report of the department of neglected and dependent children' 1892-1925

III. Contemporary Works

(a) Serials

Dr Barnardo's Homes. *Annual Report* 1881-1924

Night and Day 1877-1906
Ups and Downs 1895-1949
Canadian Child Welfare News 1924-8
Canadian Conference on Child Welfare. *Proceedings and Papers* 1925, 1926, 1927
The Christian 1870-1912
Church of England Waifs and Strays Society. *Annual Report* 1882-7
    Our Waifs and Strays 1884-1906
The English Woman's Journal 1858-63
Fegan Homes. *The Christian Shield* 1877, 1879
    The Rescue 1892-1901
    Loving and Serving 1905-13
    The Red Lamp 1913-15
Howard Association. *Report* 1867-1907, 1912
Home of Industry. *Occasional Emigration Papers* 1869-74
Manchester and Salford Boys and Girls Refuges. *Annual Report* 1886
National Association for the Promotion of Social Science. *Transactions* 1857-84, 1886
National Children's Home. *Annual Report* 1879-1914
    The Children's Advocate 1871-87
    Highways and Hedges 1895-1915
    The Children's Hour 1889-99
National Council of Women. *Yearbooks* 1894-1928
National Society for the Prevention of Cruelty to Children. *Report* 1895-99
Ragged School Union Magazine 1850-2
Reformatory and Refuge Union. *Conference Report* 1853-1930
    Journal 1861-1936
Miss Rye's Emigration Home for Destitute Little Girls. *Report* 1879
Social Service Council of Canada. *Report* 1914

(b) Books

Acorn, George *One of the Multitude* (Heinemann, London, 1911)
Alden, Margaret *Child Life and Labour* (Headley Bros., London, 1908)
Barnardo, S.L. and James Marchant *Memoirs of the late Dr. Barnardo* (Hodder and Stoughton, London, 1907)
Bell, Florence *At The Works* (Edward Arnold, London, 1907)
Binnie-Clark, Georgina *A Summer on the Canadian Prairie* (Edward Arnold, London, 1910)
Birt, Lillian M. *The Children's Homefinder* (James Nisbet, London, 1913)

Bondfield, Margaret *A Life's Work* (Hutchinson, London, 1949)

Booth, Charles *Condition and Occupations of the People of the Tower Hamlets, 1886-87* (Edward Stanford, London, 1887)

Life and Labour of the People in London (Macmillan, London, 1902-4)

Bosanquet, Helen *Rich and Poor* (Macmillan, London, 1896)

Social Work in London 1869-1912 (John Murray, London, 1914)

Bowley, A.L. and A.R. Burnett-Hurst *Livelihood and Poverty* (G. Bell, London, 1915)

Brace, Charles *The Dangerous Classes of New York* (Wynkoop and Hallenbeck, New York, 1872)

Bradfield, William *Life of Thomas Bowman Stephenson* (C.H. Kelly, London, 1913)

Bray, Reginald A. *Town Child* (T.F. Unwin, London, 1907)

Bready, J. Wesley *Doctor Barnardo, Physician, Pioneer, Prophet* (George Allen and Unwin, London, 1930)

Chance, William *Children under the Poor Law* (S. Sonnenschein, London, 1897)

Church of England Waifs and Strays Society *The First Forty Years* (privately printed, London, 1922)

Handbook for Workers (privately printed, London, 1895)

Copping, Arthur E. *The Golden Land* (Hodder and Stoughton, London, 1911)

Improved Ontario Farms for Old Country Farmers (Department of Interior, Ottawa, 1912)

Smithers, a true story of private imperialism (Hodder and Stoughton, London, 1913)

Cranfield, Walter *John Bull's Surplus Children* (Horace Marshall, London, 1915)

Davies, Margaret *Life as we have known it* (Hogarth, London, 1931)

Dickens, Charles *Oliver Twist* (Chapman and Hall, London, 1895)

Dunlop, O. Jocelyn *English Apprenticeship and Child Labour* (T. Fisher Unwin, London, 1912)

The Economics Club *Family Budgets* (P.S. King, London, 1896)

Edmondson, William *Making Rough Places Plain* (Sherratt and Hughes, Manchester, 1921)

Findlay, J.J. *The Young Wage-earner and the problem of his education* (Sidgwick and Jackson, London, 1918)

Freeman, Arnold *Boy Life and Labour* (P.S. King, London, 1914)

Fullerton, W.Y. *J.W.C. Fegan* (Marshall, London, 1930)

Gammie, Alexander *William Quarrier and the story of the Orphan Homes of Scotland* (Pickering and Inglis, London, 1936)

S.J. Gibb, *The Problem of Boy Work* (Wells Gardner, London, 1906)

Gill, E.A. Wharton *A Manitoba Chore Boy* (Religious Tract Society, London, 1912)

Gorst, John E. *Children of the Nation* (Methuen, London, 1906)

Greenwood, Arthur *Juvenile Labour Exchanges and After-Care* (P.S. King, London, 1911)

Le Play, P.G.F. *Les ouvriers européens* (L'imprimerie imperiale, Paris, 1855)

Loane, Margaret *The Next Street But One* (Edward Arnold, London, 1908)

The Queen's Poor (Edward Arnold, London, 1910)

London, Jack *The People of the Abyss* (Macmillan, London, 1904)

Lowe, Clara *God's Answers, a narrative of Miss Macpherson's work* (James Nisbet, London, 1882)

Masterman, C.F.G. *The Condition of England* (Methuen, London, 1909)

The Heart of the Empire (T. Fisher Unwin, London, 1901)

In Peril of Change (B.W. Huebsch, New York, n.d.)

Money, L.G. Chiozza *Riches and Poverty* (Methuen, London, 1905)

Things that Matter (Methuen, London, 1912)

Montgomery, Lucy Maude *Anne of Green Gables* (Isaac Pitman, London, 1908)

Morgan, George E. *A Veteran in Revival, R.C. Morgan* (Morgan and Scott, London, 1909)

Needham, George E. *Street Arabs and Gutter Snipes* (Hubbard, Philadelphia, 1888)

Newsholme, Arthur *The Elements of Vital Statistics* (S. Sonnenschein, London, 1899)

Osler, William *The Principles and Practice of Medicine* (Pentland, Edinburgh, 1894)

Paterson, Alexander *Across the Bridges* (Edward Arnold, London, 1912)

Pember Reeves, M.S. *Round About a Pound a Week* (G. Bell, London, 1914)

Peterson, William *Planned Migration* (University of California Press, Berkeley, 1955)

Plant, G.F. *Oversea Settlement* (Oxford University Press, London, 1951)

Raymond, Allan M. *The Laws of Ontario relating to Women and Children* (Clarkson James, Toronto, 1923)

Reynolds, L.G. *The British Immigrant* (Oxford University Press, Toronto, 1935)

de Rousiers, Paul *The Labour Question in Britain* (Macmillan, London, 1896)

Rowntree, Benjamin S. *Poverty, a study of town life* (Macmillan, London, 1901)

Rowntree, Benjamin S. and May Kendal, *How the Labourer Lives* (Thomas Nelson, London, 1913)

Russell, Charles E.B. *Manchester Boys* (University Press, Manchester, 1905)

St John, Edward *Manning's Work for Children* (Sheed and Ward, London, 1929)

Sims, George R. *How the Poor Live* (Chatto and Windus, London, 1883)

   Living London (Cassell, London, 1902-3)

Smith, Goldwin *Canada and the Canadian Question* (Macmillan, London, 1891)

Smyth, A. Watt *Physical Deterioration* (John Murray, London, 1904)

Spaulding, Thomas Alfred *The Work of the London School Board* (P.S. King, London, 1900)

Sykes, Ella *A Home Help in Canada* (Smith Elder, London, 1912)

Urquhart, J. *The Life story of William Quarrier* (Partridge, London, 1900)

Weaver, Emily *Canada and the British Immigrant* (Religious Tract Society, London, 1914)

Webb, Sidney and Beatrice *English Poor Law History* (Longmans, London, 1906)

   English Poor Law Policy (Longmans, London, 1910)

Woodward, Kathleen *Jipping Street* (Harper, New York, 1928)

Woodsworth, James Shaver *Strangers Within Our Gates* (University of Toronto Press, Toronto, 1972)

(c) Pamphlets

Bans, E. and Arthur Chilton Thomas *Catholic Child Emigration to Canada* (privately printed, Liverpool, 1904)

Barnardo, Thomas *Preventive Homes and the Work done in them* (Haughton, London, 1878)

   A City Waif (J.F. Shaw, London, 1885)

The True Story of a Young Thief (J.F. Shaw, London, 1885)

Bilbrough, Ellen Agnes *British Children in Canadian Homes* (privately printed, Belleville, 1879)

Cruikshank, George *Our Gutter Children* (Wm. Tweedie, London, 1869)

Grainger, Allerdale *Charges made against Miss Rye* (privately printed, n.p., 1874)

Hertz, O. *Copy of report to the Chorlton Board of Guardians on a visit to emigrated children in Canada* (privately printed, Manchester, 1910)

Logan, Ellen and Annie Macpherson *Emigration: the only remedy for chronic pauperism in East London* (privately printed, London, 1869)

Macpherson, Annie *Canadian Homes for London Wanderers* (privately printed, London, 1870)

   The Little London Arabs (privately printed, London, 1870)

   The Little Matchbox-Makers (privately printed, London, 1870)

   Summer in Canada (privately printed, London, 1872)

   Winter in London (privately printed, London, 1872)

McGregor, J. Breckenridge *Several Years After* (Canadian Council on Child Welfare, Ottawa, 1928)

Philp, F. Penrose *The Emigration to Canada of Poor Law Children* (P.S. King, London, 1903)

Rye, Maria S. *Emigration of Educated Women* (Emily Faithfull, London, 1861)

   What the people say about the children and what the children say about Canada (James Wade, London, 1871)

Social Service Council of Canada *Canada's Child Immigrants* (privately printed, Ottawa, 1925)

(d) Articles

Alder, Nettie 'Children as Wage-earners', *Fortnightly Review* vol. 73 (May 1903), pp. 918-27

Anderson, Robert 'Morality by Act of Parliament', *Contemporary Review* vol. 59 (Jan. 1891), pp. 77-88

Bracebridge, C.H. 'On the Emigration of Boys', *Transactions of the National Association for the Promotion of Social Science* (1859), p. 545

   'Juvenile Emigration', *Transactions of the National Association for the Promotion of Social Science* (1866), p. 793

Bray, Reginald 'The Boy and the Family', in E.J. Urwick (ed.), *Studies of Boy Life in Our Cities* (J.M. Dent, London, 1904)

'Children of the Town', in C.F.G. Masterman (ed.), *Heart of the Empire* (T. Fisher Unwin, London, 1901)

Brookes, J. Rowland 'Should the Consent of Parents be necessary in dealing with the emigration or other destination of incorrigible children?' *Transactions of the National Association for the Promotion of Social Science* (1883), pp. 224-30

Dendy, Helen 'The Children of Working London', in Bernard Bosanquet (ed.), *Aspects of the Social Problem* (Macmillan, London, 1895)

Kinloch-Cooke, Charles 'The emigration of state children', *Empire Review*, vol. 9 (April 1905), pp. 208-36

Manning, H.E. and Benjamin Waugh, 'The Child of the English Savage', *Contemporary Review*, vol. 49 (1886), pp. 687-700

Rye, Maria S. 'On Assisted Emigration', *English Woman's Journal*, vol. 5 (June 1860), pp. 235-40

'On Female Emigration', *Transactions of the National Association for the Promotion of Social Science* (1862), p. 811

'Female Middle Class Emigration', *English Woman's Journal*, vol. 10 (July 1862), pp. 20-30

'The Colonies and their Requirements', *English Woman's Journal*, vol. 8 (Oct. 1861), pp. 165-71

Smith, Samuel 'Social Reform', *Nineteenth Century*, vol. 13 (May 1883), pp. 896-912

'The industrial training of destitute children', *Contemporary Review*, vol. 47 (Jan. 1885), pp. 107-19

Stead, W.T. 'Dr. Barnardo: the Father of "Nobody's Children" ', *Review of Reviews*, vol. 14 (July 1896), pp. 17-36

IV. Recent Works

(a) Books

Allen, Richard *The Social Passion* (University of Toronto Press, Toronto, 1973)

Anderson, Michael *Family Structure in nineteenth century Lancashire* (Cambridge University Press, Cambridge, 1971)

Aries, Philippe *Centuries of Childhood* (Random House, New York, 1962)

Beattie, Jessie L. *A Season Past* (McClelland and Stewart, Toronto, 1968)

Bliss, Michael *A Living Profit* (McClelland and Stewart, Toronto, 1974)
Blythe, Ronald *Akenfield* (Penguin, Harmondsworth, Middx, 1969)
Bradley, Ian *The Call to Seriousness* (Macmillan, New York, 1976)
Cardinal, Roger *Outsider Art* (Praeger, New York, 1972)
Carrier, N.H. and J.R. Jeffery *External Migration, 1815-1950* (HMSO, London, 1953)
Carrothers, W.A. *Emigration from the British Isles* (P.S. King, London, 1929)
Corbett, David C. *Canada's Immigration Policy* (University of Toronto Press, Toronto, 1957)
Demos, John *A Little Commonwealth* (Oxford University Press, New York, 1970)
Findlay, James F. *Dwight L. Moody* (University of Chicago Press, Chicago, 1969)
French, Doris *High Button Bootstraps* (Ryerson, Toronto, 1968)
Gillis, John R. *Youth and History* (Academic Press, New York, 1974)
Greenwood, Walter *Love on the Dole* (Jonathan Cape, London, 1935)
    There was a time (Jonathan Cape, London, 1969)
Hann, Russell *Farmers Confront Industrialism* (New Hogtown Press, Toronto, 1975)
Heasman, Kathleen *Evangelicals in Action* (Bles, London, 1962)
Heren, Louis *Growing Up Poor in London* (Hamish Hamilton, London, 1973)
Hewitt, Margaret *Wives and Mothers in Victorian Industry* (Rockliff, London, 1958)
Holcombe, Lee *Victorian Ladies at Work* (David and Charles, Newton Abbott, 1973)
Houghton, Walter *The Victorian Frame of Mind* (Yale University Press, New Haven, 1957)
Inglis, K.S. *The Churches and the Working Classes in Victorian England* (Routledge and Kegan Paul, London, 1963)
Johnson, S.C. *A History of Emigration from the United Kingdom to North America 1763-1912* (F. Cass, London, 1966)
Jones, Gareth Stedman *Outcast London* (Clarendon Press, Oxford, 1971)
Katz, Michael *The People of Hamilton, Canada West* (Harvard University Press, Cambridge, Mass., 1975)
Kett, Joseph F. *Rites of Passage* (Basic Books, New York, 1977)
Langsam, Miriam Z. *Children's West* (The State Historical Society of Wisconsin, Madison, 1964)

Latzer, Beth Good *Myrtleville: A Canadian Farm Family 1837-1967* (South Illinois University Press, Carbondale, 1976)

Macdonald, Norman *Canada, Immigration and Colonisation 1841-1903* (Macmillan, Toronto, 1966)

Meacham, Standish *A Life Apart* (Thames and Hudson, London, 1977)

Owen, David *English Philanthropy 1660-1960* (Belknap Press, Cambridge, Mass., 1964)

Perkin, Harold J. *The Origins of Modern English Society, 1780-1880* (Routledge and Kegan Paul, London, 1969)

Pinchbeck, Ivy and Margaret Hewitt *Children in English Society* (Routledge and Kegan Paul, London, 1969 and 1973)

Porter, John *The Vertical Mosaic* (University of Toronto Press, Toronto, 1965)

Prentice, Alison *The School Promoters* (McClelland and Stewart, Toronto, 1977)

Reaman, Elmore *A History of Agriculture in Ontario* (Saunders, Toronto, 1970)

Reed, Daphne (ed.) *The Great War and Canadian Society* (New Hogtown Press, Toronto, 1978)

Richmond, Anthony H. *Post-war Immigrants in Canada* (University of Toronto Press, Toronto, 1967)

Roberts, Robert *The Classic Slum* (Manchester University Press, Manchester, 1971)

Rubinstein, David *School Attendance in London 1870-1904* (University of Hull publications, Hull, 1969)

Schob, David E. *Hired Hands and Plowboys : Farm Labor in the Midwest, 1815-60* (University of Illinois Press, Urbana, 1975)

Scholes, Alexander G. *Education for Empire Settlement* (Longmans, London, 1932)

Shepperson, W.S. *British Emigration to North America* (Basil Blackwell, Oxford, 1957)

Simey, M.B. *Charitable Effort in Liverpool in the Nineteenth Century* (Liverpool University Press, Liverpool, 1951)

Spelt, Jacob *Urban Development in South-central Ontario* (McClelland and Stewart, Toronto, 1972)

Splane, Richard B. *Social Welfare in Ontario, 1791-1893* (University of Toronto Press, Toronto, 1965)

Sutherland, Neil *Children in English-Canadian Society* (University of Toronto Press, Toronto, 1976)

Thomas, Leslie *This Time Next Week* (Constable, London, 1964)

Thompson, Paul *The Edwardians* (Indiana University Press, Bloomington, 1975)

Timlin, Mabel *Does Canada Need More People?* (Oxford University Press, Toronto, 1951)

Trumble, David *When I was a Boy* (J.M. Dent, Toronto, 1976)

Vicinus, Martha *The Industrial Muse* (Croom Helm, London, 1974) *Suffer and be Still: Women in the Victorian Age* (Indiana University Press, Bloomington, 1972)

Wagner, Gillian, *Barnardo* (Weidenfeld and Nicolson, London, 1979)

Williams, A.E. *Barnardo of Stepney* (George Allen and Unwin, London, 1966)

Winch, Donald *Classical Political Economy and Colonies* (G. Bell, London, 1965)

Woodroofe, Kathleen *From Charity to Social Work* (Routledge and Kegan Paul, London, 1962)

Young, Michael and Peter Willmott *Family and Kinship in East London* (Routledge and Kegan Paul, London, 1957)

(b) Theses

Barber, Marilyn Jean 'The Assimilation of Immigrants in the Canadian Prairie Provinces, 1896-1918; Canadian Perception and Canadian Policies' (unpublished PhD thesis, University of London, 1975)

Davey, Ian E. 'Educational Reform and the Working Class: School Attendance in Hamilton, Ontario, 1851-1891' (unpublished PhD thesis, University of Toronto, 1975)

Hall, David John 'The Political Career of Clifford Sifton, 1896-1905' (unpublished PhD thesis, University of Toronto, 1973)

Houston, Susan E. 'The Impetus to Reform: Urban Crime, Poverty and Ignorance in Ontario, 1850-1875' (unpublished PhD thesis, University of Toronto, 1974)

Magnuson, Norris Alden 'Salvation in the Slums: Evangelical Social Work, 1865-1920' (unpublished PhD thesis, University of Minnesota, 1968)

Ross, Alexander Michael 'The care and education of pauper children in England and Wales, 1834 to 1896' (unpublished PhD thesis, University of London, 1955)

Young, W.R. 'The Countryside on the defensive: agricultural Ontario's views of rural depopulation, 1900-1914' (unpublished MA thesis, University of British Columbia, 1971)

(c) Articles

Abell, Helen C. 'The adaptation of the way of life of the rural family in Canada to technological, economic and social changes', *The Family in the Evolution of Agriculture* (Vanier Institute of the Family, Ottawa, 1968)

Anderson, Michael 'Family and class in nineteenth century cities', *Journal of Family History*, vol. 2, no. 2 (1977), pp. 139-49

Ball, Rosemary R. 'A Perfect Farmer's Wife: Women in 19th-Century Rural Ontario', *Canada, an Historical Magazine*, vol. 3, no. 2 (1975), pp. 2-21

Beales, Ross W. 'In search of the historical child: miniature adulthood and youth in colonial New England', *American Quarterly*, vol. 27, no. 3 (1975), pp. 379-98

Bennett, John 'The care of the poor', *The English Catholics, 1850-1950* (Burns Oates, London, 1950), pp. 559-84

Bliss, Michael 'Pure Books on Avoided Subjects: Pre-Freudian Sexual Ideas in Canada', *Canadian Historical Association Annual Report* (1970), pp. 89-108

Bogue, Allan 'The progress of the cattle industry in Ontario during the 1880's', *Agricultural History*, vol. 21, no. 3 (1947), pp. 163-8

Davey, Ian E. 'The rhythm of work and the rhythm of school', in Neil McDonald and Alf Chaiton (eds.) *Egerton Ryerson and his Times* (Macmillan, Toronto, 1978), pp. 221-53

Davidoff, Leonore 'Mastered for Life: servant and wife in Victorian and Edwardian England', *Journal of Social History*, vol. 7, no. 4 (1974), pp. 406-22

Englehardt, H. Tristram 'The disease of masturbation: values and the concept of disease', *Bulletin of the History of Medicine*, vol. 48, no. 2 (1974), pp. 234-48

Erickson, Charlotte 'Agrarian myths of English immigrants', in Oscar F. Ander (ed.) *In the Trek of the Immigrants* (Augustana College Library, Rock Island, Illinois, 1964), pp. 59-80

Gaffield, Chad and David Levine 'Dependency and adolescence on the Canadian frontier: Orillia Ontario in the mid-nineteenth century', *History of Education Quarterly*, vol. 18 (1978), pp. 35-47

Gagan, David and Herbert Mays 'Historical demography and Canadian social history: families and land in Peel County, Ontario', *Canadian Historical Review*, vol. 54, no. 1 (1973), pp. 27-47

Gagan, David 'Indivisibility of land: a microanalysis of the system of inheritance in nineteenth-century Ontario', *Journal of Economic History*, vol. 36, no. 1 (1976), pp. 126-41

'Land, population and social change: the "Critical Years" in rural Canada West', *Canadian Historical Review*, vol. 59, no. 3 (1978), pp. 293-318

Graham, Clara 'Journey to Yesterday', in Edward L. Affleck (ed.), *Kootenay Yesterdays* (Alexander Nicolls, Vancouver, 1976), pp. 1-86

'Homestead Adventure: an Ayrshire man's letters home', *Saskatchewan History*, vol. 15 (1962), pp. 30-6

Jones, Gareth Stedman 'Working-class culture and working-class politics in London, 1870-1900; notes on the remaking of a working class', *Journal of Social History*, vol. 7, no. 4 (1974), pp. 460-508

Katz, Michael B. and Ian E. Davey 'Youth and early industrialisation in a Canadian city', in John Demos and Saraine Spence Boocock *Turning Points: Historical and Sociological Essays on the Family* (University of Chicago Press, Chicago, 1978), pp. 81-119

Kitteringham, Jennie 'Country work girls in nineteenth-century England', in Raphael Samuel *Village Life and Labour* (Routledge and Kegan Paul, London, 1975), pp. 73-138

Lawr, D.A. 'The development of Ontario farming, 1870-1914; patterns of growth and change', *Ontario History*, vol. 64, no. 4 (1972), pp. 239-51

MacDonald, Robert H. 'The frightful consequences of onanism: notes on the history of a delusion', *Journal of the History of Ideas*, vol. 28, no. 3 (1967), pp. 423-31

McInnis, R.M. 'Childbearing and land availability: some evidence from individual household data', in Ronald D. Lees (ed.) *Population Patterns in the Past* (Academic Press, New York, 1979)

Neuman, R.P. 'Masturbation, madness and the modern concepts of childhood and adolescence', *Journal of Social History*, vol. 8, no. 3 (1975), pp. 1-27

Oren, Laura 'The welfare of women in labouring families: England, 1860-1950', *Feminist Studies*, vol. 1 (1973), pp. 107-21

Plumb, J.H. 'The great change in children', *Horizon*, vol. 13, no. 1 (1971), pp. 6-12

'The new world of children in eighteenth century England', *Past and Present*, no. 67 (1975), pp. 64-95

Reeds, Lloyd G. 'Agricultural regions of southern Ontario 1880 and

1951', *Economic Geography*, vol. 35 (1959), pp. 219-27

'The environment', in Louis Gentilcore *Ontario* (University of Toronto Press, Toronto, 1972), pp. 1-22

Shortt, S.E.D. 'Social change and political crisis in rural Ontario', in Donald Swainson (ed.) *Oliver Mowat's Ontario* (Macmillan, Toronto, 1972), pp. 211-35

Stannard, David E. 'Death and the Puritan child', *American Quarterly*, vol. 26, no. 5 (1974), pp. 456-72

Thistlewaite, Frank 'Migration from Europe overseas in the nineteenth and twentieth centuries', in H. Moller (ed.) *Population Movements in Modern European History* (Macmillan, New York, 1964)

Thompson, John Herd 'Bringing in the Sheaves: the harvest excursionists, 1890-1929', *Canadian Historical Review* vol. 59, no. 4 (1978), pp. 467-89

Tilly, Louise A, Joan Scott and Miriam Cohen 'Women's work and European fertility patterns', *Journal of Interdisciplinary History*, vol. 6 (1976), pp. 447-76

Timlin, Mabel F. 'Canada's immigration policy 1896-1910', *Canadian Journal of Economics and Political Science*, vol. 26, no. 4 (1960), pp. 517-32

Trachtenberg, Alan 'The camera and Dr. Barnardo', *Aperture*, vol. 19, no. 4 (1975), pp. 68-77

Turner, Wesley '80 stout and healthy girls', *Canada, an Historical Magazine*, vol. 3, no. 2 (1975), pp. 36-49

'Miss Rye's children', *Ontario History*, vol. 68, no. 3 (1976), pp. 169-203

Watson, J.W. 'Rural depopulation in south western Ontario', *Annals of the Association of American Geographers*, vol. 37 (1947), pp. 145-54

INDEX

admission to homes: and kin
network 64-6; disrupting kin
contact 70; reasons for 62;
separation of siblings 66
Adoption Act of 1920 151
adult locations: men 130; women
126
adult occupations: coding
categories 131, 138; men –
agriculture 132-3, casual labour
133, comparison with European
immigrants 137-8, comparison
with non-emigrant Britons 139,
comparison with other British
immigrants 136, factory work
134-5, seasonal labour 133,
statistics 131; sources for study
124-6; women 126-30 – domestic
service 127, factory work 128,
nursing 129, secretary 129,
teaching 128
after-sailing notices 71-2
agricultural idealism 45-7, 123-4,
143
Almonte, Ontario 134
Anderson, Michael 24n6, 25n24,
26n28
Anne of Green Gables 99
apprenticeship: abuse of terms 93;
agricultural productivity of
placement locations 88-9; and
schooling 109; contrast with
family ties 91, 95-6, 117; job
choice on completion of –
men 131, women 127; movement
between stages 88, 91-2; preferred
to adoption 84; stages in 85
Australia 28, 30, 152

Barnardo sample, citation convention
161
Barnardo, Thomas John 35-6; and
philanthropic abduction 67-9;
conservative policies 34
Barnardo's Homes: admission
policies 71; apprenticeship
indentures 85-6, 91; Canadian
locations 48; case records 159;
emigration notification 71;

premarital pregnancy, policy 117
barter stage: locations 89; terms 85
bed-wetting 103-4
before-sailing notices 71-2
Bell, F.N. Harrison 153
Birt, Louisa: admission policies 71;
apprenticeship indentures 91;
beginning of work 32; Canadian
locations 48; premarital pregnancy,
policy 117, *see also* Liverpool
Sheltering Homes
blind-alley jobs, Britain 22
boarding out: Britain 31-2; Canada
85 – locations 87, 89
Boards of Guardians: Chorlton 146;
critical of child emigration 145-6,
152; Kensington 28; Liverpool 30;
Marylebone 28; Poplar 29; proce-
dures for child emigration 34;
Southampton 152; Wolverhampton
30
Boer War, effect on social policy 142
Bondfield, Margaret 153
Booth, Charles 14, 16
Booth, William 45
Bosanquet, Helen Denby 142
Brace, Charles Loring 46
Brantford, Ontario 134
Bray, Reginald 19, 21, 63, 142
British emigrants: adjustment to
Canada 29-30, 136; compared
with child emigrants 136-8
Bulpitt, Charles 152
business college, accessibility for
child emigrants 129

Canada Land Inventory 89-90
Canadian Council on Child Welfare
153
Cape of Good Hope 28
caretakers, in family economy
17-19, 23
case records: biases of record-keepers
160; codebook construction 159;
contents 153; origins 158;
sampling procedures 159-60
Charity Organisation Society 34
childhood: definition of 14, 16, 21,
23, 146; demand for in Canada
86-8; evangelical views of 37; in
Britain 17-22; malleability 38
Children's Friend Society 28
Christian 35, 99
Church of England Waifs and Strays
Society: beginning of Canadian

work 38; Canadian locations 48
citation convention, sample 161
Close, Elinor 145
codebook construction 159-61
conflict: in clerical households 102;
    with homes 92-6; with masters
    92-4, 108, 132; with mistresses
    102, 104, 108
contributors, and family economy
    20-3
Copping, Arthur 143
Cossar School 144
cost, of emigration 30
cottage homes 37
Cox, J. Benson 152
Cranfield, Walter 143
Cruikshank, George 31
Custody of Children Act (1891)
    68-9

Dakeyne Lads' Club 144
Dauphin, Manitoba 87
Davin, Anna 26n31
demand for child labour, Canada 88
dispensationalist thought and child
    emigration 36
distributing homes, locations 47, 49
Dixon, William 29
domestic industry: children's role
    in 16, 18, 19
domestic service: Britain 65; Canada
    127
Dominions Royal Commission of
    1912 143
Dominion Trades and Labor Con-
    gress 54-5
Doyle, Andrew 32, 51

economic crisis: Britain – 1848 28,
    1867 29, 1883 33, 1908 148
emigration: and kin management
    72; as safety valve 33; as trans-
    portation 70; benefits for home
    girls 130; cost 30; statistics 17, 31,
    33-4, 40, 151
Empire Settlement Act of 1922
    151-2
enuresis 103-4
European immigrants, compared
    with child immigrants 137-8
evangelicals: attitudes toward dis-
    tressed families 63, 66; dispen-
    sationalists 36; expectations for
    child emigrants as adults 123-4,

127; importance of the family
    37; premillenarians 35-6; views
    of children 37

factory work: of former home
    boys 134-5; of former home
    girls 128
Fairbridge, Kingsley 151
family *see* kin
family economy: and inheritance
    84; Britain 15-21; Canada 83
Fegan, J.W.C. 35-6
Fegan Home: and farm school 46;
    Canadian locations 48
Findlay, Helen 107
Fliedner, Pastor of Kaiserwerth 45
'Foggartism' 151
'friends' 99

Galt, Alexander 33
Gooderham, William 56
Gossage, Harry 68
Green, George Everitt 107
Greenwood, Walter 22

Haggard, Rider 45, 144, 147
Haliburton, Ontario 87
Hardie, George D. 152
health: Britain, physical 14, 23;
    Canada – effect on social and
    economic adjustment 113-14,
    improves 111, linked to class
    background 114, medical certi-
    ficates for entry 53, 150,
    mental illness increases 113,
    statistics 112; coding categories
    121n35
Hertz, Olga 146
Hespeler, Ontario 144
hired boys, Canada 85
hired girls, Canada 85
homesickness 75
household, differs from family
    91-6, 99-108
housework: Britain 18; Canada 83

illegitimacy, thought hereditary 114,
    116 *see also* pregnancy premarital
ill treatment: coding categories
    119n18; examples of 107; inci-
    dence of 105; law concerning
    105; regulation of 106
Immigration Branch 56, 106, 123,
    149-50, 153

immigration policy, Canada 30,
147-9
Imperial Conferences 143
imperialism, and child saving 143
incontinence 103-4
indentures, advantages for immigrant children 84, *see also*
apprenticeship
industrial schools, emigrants from
145
infants, in family economy 16
inheritance: and the family economy
84; Ontario 83
inspection: of girls' placements
115; of pauper children 34,
55-6, 106, 149-50
Irish: emigrant girls to Australia
28; migrants in Britain 28
Irish Local Government Board 144
isolation, in Canadian placements
101, 103, 118, 132

Jury, Alfred 55-6

Kelso, J.J. 57, 150
Kett, Joseph 21
kin: affective ties, Britain 16; contact with after emigration 72-6;
economic ties, Britain 15-16, 22;
management by admission to the
homes 70; management by
emigration 72; return to Britain
to visit 75; reunions in Canada
76; siblings in Canada 74;
solidarity 62; stress of not
knowing 77
Kinloch-Cooke, Charles 151

legislation to protect child immigrants
57, 115
Liverpool Sheltering Homes: admission policies 71; apprenticeship
indentures 91; beginning of 32;
Canadian locations 48, *see also*
Birt, Louisa
Local Government Board: and
Andrew Doyle 32; children cared
for, statistics 28; encourages child
emigration 31, 144-5; pressed to
re-open child emigration 33;
procedures for child emigration
34; suspends child emigration
32, 34
locations: of adult men 130; of

adult women 126; of apprenticeship placements 50, 88; of distributing homes 48-9
London Children's Aid Society 48
London, Ontario 134
Lower Gagetown, New Brunswick
144

Macnamara, T.J. 144
Macpherson, Annie: admission
policies 71; and Andrew Doyle
32, 51; and case records 158;
and Charles Loring Brace 46;
and German Protestants 45;
apprenticeship indentures 86,
91; background 35-6; Canadian
locations 48; concept of 'friends'
100; premarital pregnancy, policy
on 117
Manchester 146
Manning, Cardinal 38
marriage: age at, Britain 23; Canada,
of home girls 129-30; patterns
among parents of child emigrants
63-4
Masterman, Charles 142
masters: conflict with 92-4, 108, 132;
expectations of child emigrants
100
Masters and Servants Act, Ontario 92
masturbation 104
Merry, Rachel Macpherson 35
Middlemore, J.T. 32
Milner, Lord 151
mistresses: conflict with 102, 104,
108; expectations of child
emigrants 100
Montgomery, Lucy Maude 99
mortality, children, Britain 14
Mundella Committee 69
murder 108
Muskoka 87

National Children's Homes 33;
apprenticeship indentures 85-6,
91; Canadian locations 48;
farm school 46, *see also* Stephen-
son, Thomas Bowman
National Council of Women 56, 149
New Brunswick 28
New South Wales 28
New York Children's Aid Society 46
Nipissing 87
Nugent, Father 39

nursing, as an occupation for home
girls 129

occupations *see* adult occupations
O'Donoghue, D.J. 55
Oliver, Frank 135, 148
opposition to child emigration:
and 1924 suicides 152; Bondfield
Commission 153; British Labour
Party 152; British press 147;
Boards of Guardians 146;
Canadian Council on Child Welfare
153; Cruikshank, George 31;
doctors 52-3; Dominion Trades
and Labor Congress 54-5;
Grainger, Allerdale 42n24; rural
communities 53, 149; sheriffs,
rural 52-3; Social Service Council
of Canada 153; urban reformers
56-7
'Our Gutter Children' 31, 42n19
Owen, Alfred 124

parents: control over children's
choice of work 19, 22; control
over children's earnings 21-2, *see
also* kin
Paris, Ontario 134
Paterson, Alexander 19, 21
Peel County, Ontario 84
philanthropic abduction: incidence
67; legal prosecutions 68
placement policies 47
Plant, G.F. 153
play, Britain 18
Poor Law Act (1834) 28
Poor Law Amendment Act (1858)
28
poverty cycle 15
pregnancy: detection 121n47;
premarital – circumstances
surrounding 116, homes provided
for 117, incidence 115-17
premillenarian theology 35
Prentice, Alison 140n11
Prevention of Cruelty to Children
Act (1889) 69, (1894) 69

Quarrier, William 35-6
Quarrier's Homes: admission policies
71; apprenticeship indentures 91;
Canadian location 48; farm
school 45; premarital pregnancy,
policy 117

Ragged Schools 28-9
Rauhe Haus 37
reformatories, emigrants from 144
Roberts, Robert 21
Roman Catholics: apprenticeship
indentures 85, 91; beginning of
Canadian work 39; Canadian
locations 48; financial incentives
to emigration 39
Rowntree, Benjamin Seebohm 15-16,
142
Royal Colonial Institute 143
Rudolf, Edward de Montjoie 38, 136
runaways 102; Homes' counsel 92;
in harvest season 93
rural Canada, images of 50, 52
rural-urban migration 50, 54, 126-7,
130-2, 134
Rye, Maria Susan: and Andrew Doyle
32, 51; and Charles Loring Brace
46; and emigration policy 33;
background 30; premarital pregnancy, policy 117

safety valve, emigration as 33
Salvation Army 45, 117
sample: citation convention 161; how
constructed 159-60
Saskatchewan 87
school: Britain – and wage work
19-20, attendance 17, 20, 23;
Canada – accessibility of high
school for child emigrants 128,
and apprenticeship terms 109,
attendance rates 108-10,
resistance to attendance 111,
slow progress in 110, treatment
of child emigrants in 110
secretary, as occupation for home
girls 129
sexual assault: legal prosecutions
115; vulnerability to 114-15
Shaftesbury, Lord 11, 30, 37
Shaw, Leonard 35
Sherbrooke, Quebec 38
siblings: in Canada 74-5; separation
of by admission to homes 66
Sifton, Clifford 56, 147
Smart, G. Bogue 106, 123, 149-50
Smith, Goldwin 56
Smith, Samuel: and philanthropic
abduction 67; emigration as
safety valve 33
Smyly Mission 144

Social Service Council of Canada
153
South Australia 28
State Children's Association 144
Stephenson, Thomas Bowman 33;
and philanthropic abduction 67;
beginning of Canadian work 38,
see also National Children's
Homes
step-parents 63
Strathcona, Lord 147
street arabs 37; as adults 133
suicide 108; of 1924 152
Swan River, Australia 28
Swan River, Manitoba 87

teaching, as occupation for home
girls 128-9
temperament, of child emigrants
101, 103
'time' obligation, Canada 83

toddlers, in family economy 16
Trades and Labor Congress 54-6
Tye, Martha Ann 68-9

wage stage: bargaining in 94;
children reject 94-6; locations
89; terms 86
Walker, J. Bruce 148
Waugh, Benjamin 38
White, William 107
Wichern, Johann-Heinrich of
Hamburg 45
widows: and child care 17, 63;
and household management 18;
in domestic service 65; relief
practices for 65, *see also* kin
Windsor, Nova Scotia 144
Woodsworth, James Shaver 136
workhouses, children in, statistics
28
World War One 21, 150